A Special Issue of
Cognition & Emotion

Child Anxiety Theory and Treatment

Edited by

Andy P. Field
University of Sussex, Falmer, UK

Sam Cartwright-Hatton
University of Manchester, Manchester, UK

Shirley Reynolds
University of East Anglia, Norwich, UK

and

Cathy Creswell
University of Reading, Reading, UK

Routledge
Taylor & Francis Group
LONDON AND NEW YORK

First published 2008 by Psychology Press

Published 2018 by Routledge
2 Park Square, Milton Park, Abingdon, Oxon OX14 4RN
52 Vanderbilt Avenue, New York, NY 10017

First issued in paperback 2018

Routledge is an imprint of the Taylor & Francis Group, an informa business

British Library Cataloguing in Publication Data
A catalogue record for this book is available from the British Library

Cover design by Hybert Design
Typeset in the UK by Datapage International, India

ISSN 0269-9931
ISBN 13: 978-1-138-88322-2 (pbk)
ISBN 13: 978-1-84169-851-9 (hbk)

Contents*

(*continued overleaf*)

* This book is also a special issue of the journal Cognition & Emotion, and forms issue 3 of
Volume 22 (2008). The page numbers are taken from the journal and so begin with p. 385

COGNITION AND EMOTION
2008, 22 (3), 385–394

Future directions for child anxiety theory and treatment

Andy P. Field

University of Sussex, Brighton, East Sussex, UK

Sam Cartwright-Hatton

University of Manchester, Manchester, UK

Shirley Reynolds

University of East Anglia, Norwich, East Anglia, UK

Cathy Creswell

University of Reading, Reading, Berkshire, UK

The aim of this introductory paper, and of this special issue of *Cognition and Emotion*, is to stimulate debate about theoretical issues that will inform child anxiety research in the coming years. Papers included in this special issue have arisen from an Economic and Social Research Council (ESRC, UK) funded seminar series, which we called Child Anxiety Theory and Treatment (CATTS). We begin with an overview of the CATTS project before discussing (1) the application of adult models of anxiety to children, and (2) the role of parents in child anxiety. We explore the utility of adult models of anxiety for child populations before discussing the problems that are associated with employing them uncritically in this context. The study of anxiety in children provides the opportunity to observe the trajectory of anxiety and to identify variables that causally influence its development. Parental influences are of particular interest and new and imaginative strategies are required to isolate the complex network of causal relationships therein. We conclude by suggesting that research into the causes and developmental course of anxiety in children should be developed further. We also propose that, although much is known about the role of parents in the development of anxiety, it would be useful for research in this area to move towards an examination of the specific processes involved. We hope that these

Correspondence should be addressed to: Andy P. Field, Department of Psychology, University of Sussex, Falmer, Brighton, East Sussex BN1 9QH, UK. E-mail: andyf@sussex.ac.uk

We are grateful to the Economic and Social Research Council (ESRC) for awarding us research seminar grant RES-451-25-4103 (Child Anxiety: Developments in Theory and Treatment). Without this funding this article and special issue would not have been possible.

For more information on the CATTS project please see http://www.statisticshell.com/research/catts.htm.

views represent a constructive agenda for people in the field to consider when planning future research.

THE PAST

Even the most conservative estimates (Ford, Goodman, & Meltzer, 2003) suggest that at least 3% of British children are experiencing a serious anxiety disorder (and associated impairment) at any one time. Many more children will experience subclinical anxiety. Childhood anxiety is also a major risk factor for adult mental-health problems: adult anxiety disorders are very regularly preceded by their childhood counterpart (Kim-Cohen et al., 2003). Anxious children also often go on to develop depression (Kovacs, Gatsonis, Paulauskas, & Richards, 1989), may be at an increased risk of substance misuse (Kushner, Sher, & Beitman, 1990) and often show poor academic and social functioning (Pine, 1997).

Despite the known impact of childhood anxiety, the development of theories and interventions for anxiety in younger populations (under 12 years) has lagged behind developments in the adult field. This lack of advancement in theory and treatment of child anxiety has arisen in part because child anxiety researchers and clinicians often work in isolated groups and the opportunities for regular face-to-face meetings that will foster multi-site collaborative projects are rare. In 2005, with funding from the Economic and Social Research Council (ESRC) in the UK, we set up a research network. This was called the Child Anxiety Theory and Treatment Seminars (CATTS). One of our aims was to bring together a group of isolated researchers, clinicians and their teams working in Europe and beyond. The funding was for a two-year series of research seminars Over the course of six one-day meetings, researchers from the UK, the Netherlands, Switzerland, the USA, Australia, Portugal, Spain, and Denmark met to discuss their work and to identify priorities for child anxiety theory and treatments. This special issue, and a sister special issue to be published in *Behavioural and Cognitive Psychotherapy*, are the culmination of these two years of meetings and, we hope, present the cutting edge of research into child anxiety theory and treatment. Consistent with the mission statements of the two journals, this special issue is concerned primarily with the "theory", whereas the sister special issue will be focused more on the "treatment".

Over the course of CATTS, two main themes for research into child anxiety emerged: (1) the applicability of adult models of anxiety to children; and (2) the role of parents and the family in the development of anxiety in children. We are not suggesting that these are the only areas in which more research is needed, but they are certainly two important topics that emerged repeatedly in the seminar series and they are reflected in the content of this special issue. All of the articles featured in this special issue reflect one or both of those themes. This article aims to set out our views on these two issues in relation to the articles in this special issue and also to make suggestions for the direction of future research, which we hope will stimulate other researchers in the field.

ARE ADULT MODELS OF ANXIETY APPROPRIATE FOR CHILDREN?

The utility of adult models

There have been numerous extremely successful cognitive models of adult anxiety; for example, models of social anxiety (Clark & Wells, 1995), obsessive-compulsive disorder (Salkovskis, Forrester, & Richards, 1998), and panic disorder (Clark, 1986). All of these models have, unquestionably, had an enormous impact on both theories of the maintenance cycles of these disorders and in developing highly successful intervention strategies. Nevertheless, these models were never intended to be viewed as anything other than pure maintenance models, and consciously make no attempt to explain how the maintaining cognitions and behaviours might arise. Clark and Wells' model of social anxiety, for example, acknowledges that adults with social anxiety hold assumptions and schemas about the social world, but does not attempt to explain how a child develops these assumptions and schemas. Similarly, it has been enormously beneficial therapeutically to formalise the catastrophic misinterpretation of bodily sensations in panic disorder, but we are still left with the tantalising puzzle of how a child develops this tendency to misinterpret their bodily sensations in such a catastrophic way. This focus on what maintains anxiety once it has developed is understandable because clinical interventions can be improved by targeting those maintenance factors. In the short term, this has enabled the rapid development of very successful cognitive behavioural interventions in adults based on these, and other, models (e.g., Westbrook & Kirk, 2005). However, there are good reasons to want to unravel the developmental antecedents of the various cognitive and behavioural components of these models. First, a better understanding of the causal factors in anxiety will lead to a better understanding of how to reverse these causes. For example, recent research has shown that information-processing biases can be trained and that once trained these biases have a causal effect on anxiety (e.g., Mathews & MacLeod, 2002); this has in turn led to interventions that reduce anxiety by training benign information-processing biases in place of ones that maintain anxiety (Mathews, Ridgeway, Cook, & Yiend, 2007; Murphy,

Hirsch, Mathews, Smith, & Clark, 2007). Second, the *prevention* of anxiety will be considerably better informed by an increased knowledge base about the causal variables involved and how they develop during childhood. Finally, therapies for child anxiety are currently very limited. Cognitive behavioural interventions appear to be effective in less than 60% of anxious children and for younger children, the picture is bleaker still: there is precious little evidence that CBT, as it is currently practiced, is effective at all (Cartwright-Hatton, Roberts, Chitsabesan, Fothergill, & Harrington, 2004). Part of the problem is the assumption that maintenance models (and the interventions based upon them) are downwards compatible. Many of the cognitive processes implied in adult models (for example, meta-cognitive beliefs in generalised anxiety disorder, the observer perspective in social anxiety, catastrophising) all require fairly sophisticated mental processes and representations that may not yet have developed in younger children. At a more general level, all interventions targeting these processes necessarily require the sophisticated manipulation of complex verbal material. Further-more, maintenance models commonly imply that likely causal factors (e.g., family processes) are no longer present (e.g., Beck, 1979), which may not be true for younger populations where, for example, parental reinforcement of maladaptive cognitions and behaviours may be present and ongoing (e.g., Barrett, Rapee, Dadds, & Ryan, 1996). It is little wonder that success rates for younger children are relatively poor.

The problems in applying adult models to children

There are several issues that arise out of this general point. The first is that, as a bare minimum, we need to know whether the cognitive and emotional processes found in anxious adults are also found in anxious children. Carter, Williams, and Silverman's study is a good example of a rigorous validation in a young sample (8–13 years) of a model of anxiety (test anxiety in this case) based originally on older samples. However, not all research on the downward compatibility of adult models reaches such unequivocal conclu-sions. Muris and Field review the growing body of research addressing this issue. One conclusion from their review is that, because of conflicting evidence, it is not at all clear that anxious children do show the same cognitive processes as anxious adults. One reason for the inconsistency in the evidence is likely to be that paradigms used to examine these processes in adults may not be appropriate for children. (We are reminded of Donaldson's, 1984, pioneering work, which showed that the age at which children displayed cognitive abilities depended on the methodologies used to test these abilities). One of the big challenges for child anxiety researchers in the future will be to develop age-appropriate tools for examining cognition and emotion in child samples. Many of our articles are noteworthy for their methodologies. Creswell et al., by looking at eye gaze, tackle the difficult problem of assessing attentional biases in age groups for which language or reaction-time tasks could not be used. Their results are generally consistent with research on adults with social phobia, which has shown that social anxiety is associated with avoidance of fearful expressions. Perez-Olivas, Stevenson, and Hadwin and Gifford, Reynolds, Bell, and Wilson both implemented tasks previously used successfully in children and both found evidence for attentional and interpretational biases respectively. Finally, In-Albon, Klein, Rinck, Beckerb, and Schneider have developed a new age-appropriate methodology aimed at testing interpretation biases in separation anxiety of social phobia. These continued attempts to explore and validate child-appropriate tasks are vital for the future of the field.

The causes and development of anxiety in children

Establishing that anxious children share the psychological processes of anxious adults is just the beginning, because although this knowledge will greatly improve child interventions, to reverse or prevent these processes we must understand their causes and their developmental trajectory. Notwithstanding genetic factors that contribute to cognitive and emotional processing in children, if we assume that some learning is involved, then the interesting question is how and when a child develops thought processes that lead to anxiety. Many of the articles in this special issue have attempted to answer the "how" question. Field and Lawson, for example, report a study that builds on an established experimental methodology that has shown how verbal threat information has a causal impact on the different response systems of the fear emotion in children. Field and Lawson show that beliefs created by verbal threat information bias future judgements about the contingencies between a stimulus and a negative outcome. This research in non-clinical samples demonstrates the usefulness of addressing clinical questions in normally developing children. Experiments such as these, in which causal variables are manipulated, provide invaluable information about the causal mechanisms underlying the development of anxiety. Similarly, Creswell et al., by looking at very young age groups (i.e., before a child has the cognitive capacity to have the though processes of anxious adults), have a powerful procedure for unpicking the causal precipitants of anxiety. In addition, several articles in this special issue look at the causal role of parenting (Bögels, Bamelis, & Bruggen; Gifford et al.; Perez-Olivas et al.), and these articles will be discussed in due course. These studies paint an encouraging picture of anxiety research in which researchers go beyond measuring correlates of child anxiety, and instead attempt to unpick the underlying mechanisms through which anxiety develops. Long may this trend continue.

Not so encouraging is research (or the lack of it) into the developmental trajectory of cognitions and behaviours that precede anxiety; it is noteworthy that, in this issue, only Perez-Olivas et al. attempt to examine age-related change in cognitive processes. They found that children with high levels of separation anxiety took less time to detect the presence of an angry face, but only in children aged over 10. Developmental analyses such as these are seldom done, but are absolutely vital if we are to understand how to prevent or reverse cognitions that contribute to anxiety. However, the need to study the developmental trajectory brings with it theoretical issues that as yet have not been considered. For example, should we consider the development of anxious cognitions as a step function (rather like Piaget's stages), a continuous function (and in which case, a linear growth model, or quadratic, or maybe something else?), or as a catastrophe process (van der Maas & Molenaar, 1992) in which anxious cognitions "come and go" as the cognitive resources necessary to sustain them wax and wane before they solidify? The answers could lie in empirical tests of the different conceptualisations, by fitting step functions, various growth models, and catastrophe models (Alexander, Herbert, Deshon, & Hanges, 1992): Perez-Olivas et al. test both a linear function and a stage transition. To do this though, child anxiety researchers need to rise to the challenge of collecting data that can show up these transitions either through large sample research across broad age ranges, or through research that follows up cohorts of children as they develop. There also needs to be a sea change in the consideration of a child's social and cognitive development when thinking about how cognitions about anxiety will develop. It is the exception rather than the rule that researchers measure "normal" cognitive abilities (such as Theory of Mind) that might be expected to affect anxious cognitions. Future research will benefit immensely from giving greater thought to the developmental trajectory of cognitive and behavioural precursors of anxiety, and to how this developmental trajectory interacts with that of cognitive and social processes not specific to anxiety.

PARENTING AND CHILD ANXIETY

The second theme to emerge from CATTS was the increasing emphasis on the family in research into both the development of anxiety and its treatment. Half of this special issue is dedicated to articles that explore the role of parents in their child's anxiety. To date there has been a growing body of research showing that anxiety runs in families (Turner, Beidel, & Costello, 1987) and that the way in which parents behave towards their children is associated with anxiety (see Wood, McLeod, Sigman, Hwang, & Chu, 2003, for a review). For example, in a recent meta-analysis, parental rejection, control, warmth, aversiveness, and autonomy granting all significantly moderated child anxiety (McLeod, Wood, & Weisz, 2007). This impressive body work shows the importance of family factors in the developing child. However, as McLeod et al. (2007) pointed out, their analysis showed that parenting styles explained only about 4% of the variance in child anxiety, and that there was considerable variability in study findings and inconsistency in which parenting styles predicted anxiety. There could be several explanations for these inconsistencies, such as methodological factors, the fact that the transmission of anxiety is often treated as a "one-way street" (see below) or that parenting styles interact with other experiences (a parenting style might predict anxiety only in the context of some other variable). Perez-Olivas et al., explore this mediation hypothesis by looking at the interaction of parenting styles and attentional biases, and this is an excellent development. However, the expected significant link between maternal over involvement and a child's separation anxiety was not found, and therefore only partial support was found that vigilance for threat mediated the association between maternal over involvement and separation anxiety in children. Field and Cartwright-Hatton (2007) have argued another explanation for the inconsistency in data linking parenting styles and child anxiety: they suggest that parenting styles themselves are not the critical variable but epiphenomena of more specific anxiety-related behaviours in which parents engage. For example, they argue that anxious parents will provide both anxiety-specific verbal information and observational learning opportunities for their child, both of which have been shown to have a causal role in the development of child anxiety (Field, Lawson, & Banerjee, in press; Murray, Cooper, Creswell, Schofield, & Sack, 2007). As such, we believe that future efforts could usefully be focused on unpicking the specific components of the intergenerational transmission of anxiety. Gifford et al., for example, examine the specific relationship between mothers' and children's threat interpretations. Although, mothers of anxious children had significantly higher self-reported anxiety than mothers of non-clinical children, and anxious children had higher threat interpretation scores than non-anxious controls, the association between mothers' and children's threat interpretations was not significant. However, mothers' interpretation bias was significantly positively correlated with child anxiety and child interpretation bias was significantly associated with maternal anxiety. Parental anxiety probably does not lead to a blanket transfer of anxiety processes, but instead affects the learning experiences that a parent provides to their child. The effect of these experiences on the child will interact with the other experiences that they have (at school, or from siblings and other family members), their learning history (Field, 2006), and the child's temperament. As such, a parent is likely to transmit only a subset of their specific anxiety-related thoughts and behaviours. Gifford et al.'s study is a useful step towards trying to look at the transfer of specific anxiety cognitions (see also Creswell, O'Connor, & Brewin, 2006), because once the transfer of these specific components of anxiety can be identified, it will be possible to look at the learning processes that underpin them. For example, we can start to understand what learning experiences anxious parents provide, and what effect these specific effects have rather than looking at very broadly defined variables such as "parental anxiety" and "parenting style".

The other fact that is abundantly clear from the literature on parenting is that the focus has been too strongly on mothers. However, the typical nuclear family will be composed of a father and mother, one or both of whom could be anxious. The power of learning experiences provided by one parent will be a function of whether learning experiences from the other parent are consistent or inconsistent. We might expect children of two anxious parents to have more consistent anxiogenic learning experiences (verbal information and vicarious learning) than a child who has only one anxious parent. Bögels et al.'s study shows that anxious fathers make an important contribution to the intergenerational transmission of anxiety. Studies such as this in which both mothers and fathers are involved are vital if we are to understand how family dynamics contribute to child anxiety. However, even including both parents is probably not enough. As Muris and Field point out, parent and child interactions are dynamic processes and Tiwari et al.'s review develops this theme. A strong implication from their review is that parents do not passively transmit facets of their anxiety onto their child but are in a dynamic system with their children in which their child's behaviour has an impact on their own. This issue is going to be extremely hard to unpick empirically, but we believe that it is something towards which we should strive.

We believe that fully understanding the dynamic relationships between parents and children, and isolating the specific causal learning experiences through which parents transmit fears to their children is an incredible undertaking, but is a challenge worth rising to. First, the success of therapeutic interventions for children that do not address the family dynamic will be attenuated (parents are likely to undo the therapist's good work). Second, given the difficulties that are faced by therapists attempting to work individually with younger anxious children, working with families is likely to be fruitful (Cartwright-Hatton, McNally, & White, 2005a; Cartwright-Hatton, McNally, White, & Verduyn, 2005b). Despite early promise, these therapies are still in the very early stages of development. Until we know substantially more about the role of families in the development of anxiety, therapists will be unable to refine these interventions further. Finally, there is a growing recognition that in working with parents, their own cognition and cognitive biases need to be addressed (e.g., Creswell &

Cartwright-Hatton, 2007). By breaking the intergenerational transmission down into more specific processes, clinicians will be better informed about which processes to address in therapy, and how these might be targeted.

CONCLUSIONS

It is a very exciting time for child anxiety research. After many years of adult-dominated theories and interventions, there is a growing momentum and desire to understand how anxiety develops in children. In our sister special issue, due in *Behavioural and Cognitive Psychotherapy* in October 2008, we will talk more directly to the issue of treatment but in this article we have tried to highlight the theoretical issues that we believe have arisen from CATTS. In combination, these special issues showcase state-of-the-art research that, in one way or another, raises important issues to consider when moving child anxiety research forward. We do not believe for a second that the issues we have discussed here are the only ones, or that our views on where research should go are exhaustive, or universally accepted. The road ahead will not be easy, and it will undoubtedly be a roller-coaster ride, but it certainly will not be dull and with so many questions still to be answered it could just be the ride of our lives.

REFERENCES

Alexander, R. A., Herbert, G. R., Deshon, R. P., & Hanges, P. J. (1992). An examination of least-squares regression modeling of catastrophe-theory. *Psychological Bulletin, 111*(2), 366–374.

Barrett, P. M., Rapee, R. M., Dadds, M. M., & Ryan, S. M. (1996). Family enhancement of cognitive style in anxious and aggressive children. *Journal of Abnormal Child Psychology, 24*(2), 187–203.

Beck, A. T. (1979). *Cognitive therapy and the emotional disorders.* New York: International Universities Press.

Cartwright-Hatton, S., McNally, D., & White, C. (2005a). A new cognitive behavioural parenting intervention for families of young anxious children: A pilot study. *Behavioural and Cognitive Psychotherapy, 33*(2), 243–247.

Cartwright-Hatton, S., McNally, D., White, C., & Verduyn, C. (2005b). Parenting skills training: An effective intervention for internalising symptoms in younger children? *Journal of Child and Adolescent Psychiatric Nursing, 18*(2), 45–52.

Cartwright-Hatton, S., Roberts, C., Chitsabesan, P., Fothergill, C., & Harrington, R. (2004). Systematic review of the efficacy of cognitive behaviour therapies for childhood and adolescent anxiety disorders. *British Journal of Clinical Psychology, 43*, 421–436.

Clark, D. A. (1986). A cognitive approach to panic. *Behaviour Research and Therapy, 24*, 461–470.

Clark, D. M., & Wells, A. (1995). A cognitive model of social phobia. In R. Heimberg, M. Liebowitz, D. A. Hope, & F. R. Schneier (Eds.), *Social phobia: Diagnosis, assessment and treatment.* New York: Guilford Press.

Creswell, C., & Cartwright-Hatton, S. (2007). Family treatment of child anxiety: Outcomes, limitations and future directions. *Child and Family Clinical Psychology Review*, *10*(3), 232–252.

Creswell, C., O'Connor, T. G., & Brewin, C. R. (2006). A longitudinal investigation of maternal and child "anxious cognitions". *Cognitive Therapy and Research*, *30*(2), 135–147.

Donaldson, M. (1984). *Children's minds*. London: Fontana.

Field, A. P. (2006). Is conditioning a useful framework for understanding the development and treatment of phobias? *Clinical Psychology Review*, *26*(7), 857–875.

Field, A. P., & Cartwright-Hatton, S. (2007). *Parental anxiety: Cognitive-behavioural processes in the intergenerational transmission of fear to children*. Manuscript submitted for publication.

Field, A. P., Lawson, J., & Banerjee, R. (in press). The verbal information pathway to fear in children: The longitudinal effects on fear cognitions and the immediate effects on avoidance behavior. *Journal of Abnormal Psychology*.

Ford, T., Goodman, R., & Meltzer, H. (2003). The British child and adolescent mental health survey 1999: The prevalence of DSM-IV disorders. *Journal of the American Academy of Child and Adolescent Psychiatry*, *42*(10), 1203–1211.

Kim-Cohen, J., Caspi, A., Moffitt, T. E., Harrington, H., Milne, B. J., & Poulton, R. (2003). Prior juvenile diagnoses in adults with mental disorder—Developmental follow-back of a prospective-longitudinal cohort. *Archives of General Psychiatry*, *60*(7), 709–717.

Kovacs, M., Gatsonis, C., Paulauskas, S. L., & Richards, C. (1989). Depressive-disorders in childhood. 4. A longitudinal-study of co-morbidity with and risk for anxiety disorders. *Archives of General Psychiatry*, *46*(9), 776–782.

Kushner, M. G., Sher, K. J., & Beitman, B. D. (1990). The relation between alcohol-problems and the anxiety disorders. *American Journal of Psychiatry*, *147*(6), 685–695.

Mathews, A., & MacLeod, C. (2002). Induced processing biases have causal effects on anxiety. *Cognition and Emotion*, *16*(3), 331–354.

Mathews, A., Ridgeway, V., Cook, E., & Yiend, J. (2007). Inducing a benign interpretational bias reduces trait anxiety. *Journal of Behavior Therapy and Experimental Psychiatry*, *38*(2), 225–236.

McLeod, B. D., Wood, J. J., & Weisz, J. R. (2007). Examining the association between parenting and childhood anxiety: A meta-analysis. *Clinical Psychology Review*, *27*, 155–172.

Murphy, R., Hirsch, C. R., Mathews, A., Smith, K., & Clark, D. M. (2007). Facilitating a benign interpretation bias in a high socially anxious population. *Behaviour Research and Therapy*, *45*(7), 1517–1529.

Murray, L., Cooper, P., Creswell, C., Schofield, E., & Sack, C. (2007). The effects of maternal social phobia on mother–infant interactions and infant social responsiveness. *Journal of Child Psychology and Psychiatry*, *48*(1), 45–52.

Pine, D. S. (1997). Childhood anxiety disorders. *Current Opinion in Pediatrics*, *9*, 329–339.

Salkovskis, P. M., Forrester, E., & Richards, C. (1998). Cognitive-behavioural approach to understanding obsessional thinking. *British Journal of Psychiatry*, *173*, 53–63.

Turner, S. M., Beidel, D. C., & Costello, A. (1987). Psychopathology in the offspring of anxiety disorder patients. *Journal of Consulting and Clinical Psychology*, *55*(2), 229–235.

van der Maas, H. L. J., & Molenaar, P. C. M. (1992). Stagewise cognitive-development: An application of catastrophe theory. *Psychological Review*, *99*(3), 395–417.

Westbrook, D., & Kirk, J. (2005). The clinical effectiveness of cognitive behaviour therapy: Outcome for a large sample of adults treated in routine practice. *Behaviour Research and Therapy*, *43*(10), 1243–1261.

Wood, J. J., McLeod, B. D., Sigman, M., Hwang, W. C., & Chu, B. C. (2003). Parenting and childhood anxiety: Theory, empirical findings, and future directions. *Journal of Child Psychology and Psychiatry and Allied Disciplines*, *44*(1), 134–151.

COGNITION AND EMOTION
2008, 22 (3), 395–421

Distorted cognition and pathological anxiety in children and adolescents

Peter Muris

Erasmus University Rotterdam, Rotterdam, The Netherlands

Andy P. Field

University of Sussex, Brighton, East Sussex, UK

The present article provides a review on the role of distorted cognition in the pathogenesis of childhood anxiety problems. A comprehensive model of information processing that can be employed for discussing various types of anxiety-related cognitive distortions is presented. Evidence for the occurrence of these cognitive distortions in anxious children and adolescents is summarised. Then, the origins of cognitive distortions in anxious children and adolescents are addressed with reference to genetic-based vulnerability, environmental influence, and gene–environment interactions. Finally, the article provides a critical discussion of the developmental aspects of cognitive distortions, their precise role in the aetiology and maintenance of childhood anxiety disorders, and their relevance for the treatment of this type of psychopathology. Throughout the article many leads are given that may guide future research in this area.

Anxiety is generally viewed as an adaptive emotion because it is very useful to become anxious under threatening circumstances. The cognitive (e.g., thoughts such as "I am in danger!"), physiological (e.g., accelerated respiration, increased heart rate), and behavioural manifestations (fight or flight) of the anxiety emotion (Lang, 1985) are all focused on facing and coping with the threat, thereby increasing one's chances of survival (Craske, 2003). Anxiety is a normal phenomenon occurring during the development of children, and although childhood fears can be quite intense, most of them will disappear just as quickly as they have appeared (Gullone, 2000). However, in some children, fear and anxiety will persist and become so intense that they start to interfere with their daily functioning. Anxiety may

Correspondence should be addressed to: Peter Muris, Institute of Psychology, Erasmus University Rotterdam, Burgemeester Oudlaan 50, Suite T13–37, PO Box 1738, NL-3000 DR Rotterdam, The Netherlands. E-mail: muris@fsw.eur.nl

AF was supported by ESRC grant RES-062-23-0406 during the writing of this manuscript.

DOI: 10.1080/02699930701843450

hinder the child during its contact with other children and adults, or may cause the child to underachieve in school and other domains of life. In these cases, fear and anxiety can be qualified as "abnormal" and may even take the form of an anxiety disorder (American Psychiatric Association, 2000). Epidemiological research by Costello, Mustillo, Erkanli, Keeler, and Angold (2003) has shown that 9.9% of all youths have suffered from a clinically significant anxiety problem before the age of 16, which means that anxiety disorders belong to the most prevalent types of psychopathology during childhood.

Since the 1980s, various theorists have emphasised the role of cognition in emotional problems such as anxiety disorders (e.g., Beck, Emery, & Greenberg, 1985; Eysenck, 1992; Harvey, Watkins, Mansell, & Shafran, 2004; Williams, Watts, MacLeod, & Mathews, 1997). Most of these authors agree on the notion that cognition and emotion are intimately related, without strictly claiming that a causal status exists between the two concepts. For example, even Beck et al. (1985) who assume that (dysfunctional) cognition lies at the core of emotional disorders, have noted that: "The primary pathology or dysfunction during a depression or an anxiety disorder is in the cognitive apparatus. However, that is quite different from the notion that the cognition causes these syndromes—a notion that is just as illogical as an assertion that hallucinations cause schizophrenia" (p. 85).

Kendall's (1985) cognitive theory provides a good framework for discussing distorted cognition in the context of childhood anxiety problems. According to this theory, pathological manifestations of the anxiety emotion result from the chronic over-activity of schemas organised around themes of vulnerability and danger. These overactive schemas are assumed to focus processing resources chronically on threat-relevant information and manifest themselves in so-called cognitive distortions. These distortions pertain to cognitive processes that are biased and erroneous, and therefore yield dysfunctional and maladaptive thoughts and behaviours.

Information processing models represent a fruitful way to conceptualise the aberrant cognitive processes that typify anxiety disorders (see Williams et al., 1997). Briefly, such models describe the sequence of steps through which information is processed and modified as it progresses through the cognitive system (Massaro & Cowan, 1993). For example, the well-known model of Crick and Dodge (1994) proposed several subsequent information-processing stages ranging from encoding (i.e., selecting information for further processing) and interpretation (i.e., attaching meaning to the information that is decoded) to response search and selection (i.e., retrieving and choosing an appropriate response) and eventually enactment (i.e., the production of the selected response). One advantage of such a step-wise approach is that researchers can identify cognitive distortions in each of the stages, thereby providing a comprehensive framework for understanding the effects of aberrant cognition in psychopathological conditions such as anxiety disorders. Another amenity is that this type of model not only considers conscious cognitive processes that occur during the later stages of information processing, but also has an eye for more automatic and non-conscious processes that take place during earlier stages. This too has methodological implications: while conscious cognition is usually open to self-report, experimental performance-based measures are commonly employed for uncovering automatic, unconscious processes (Harvey et al., 2004; Williams et al., 1997).

More than a decade ago, Daleiden and Vasey (1997) applied Crick and Dodge's (1994) model to describe various cognitive distortions that may occur during the information-processing sequence of anxious youths. Since then, this research field has evolved considerably (e.g., Bijttebier, Vasey, & Braet, 2003) and so the time is ripe to make an inventory of the findings that have accumulated in this important domain. The current article provides a review on distorted cognition in childhood anxiety problems. First, a comprehensive model of information processing will be presented that can be employed in discussing various types of anxiety-related cognitive distortions. Then, evidence for the occurrence of these cognitive distortions in anxious children and adolescents will be summarised and evaluated. We will proceed with current notions on the origins of cognitive distortions in anxious children and adolescents. Finally, the article will close with a critical discussion of the developmental aspects of cognitive distortions, their precise role in the aetiology and maintenance of childhood anxiety disorders, and their relevance for the treatment of this type of psychopathology.

BIASED INFORMATION PROCESSING IN ANXIOUS YOUTHS

Figure 1 displays a model combining Kendall's (1985) cognitive theory of childhood anxiety and the information processing perspective (Crick & Dodge, 1994; see Daleiden & Vasey, 1997). As can be seen in the right column of the figure, children are confronted with all kinds of situations that require an appropriate response. To achieve this goal, the stimuli that comprise each situation are quickly scanned and encoded, thereby attending to relevant cues while ignoring irrelevant stimuli. During the next stage of interpretation, the encoded stimuli are evaluated and meaning is attached to them. If the situation is interpreted as dangerous and threatening, the anxiety emotion will be elicited, which manifests itself in physiological, subjective, and behavioural symptoms.

As mentioned earlier, Kendall (1985) assumed that anxious youths have overactive schemas involving the themes of vulnerability and danger. When confronted with potential threat, novelty, or ambiguity, these maladaptive

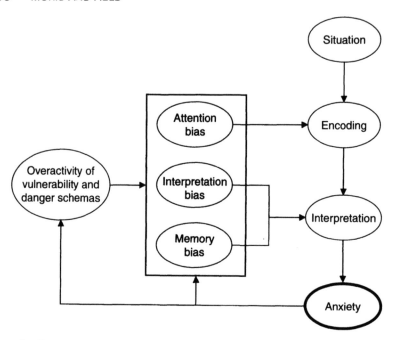

Figure 1. Theoretical model showing the influence of cognitive distortions on the processing of threat-related information, which is hypothesised to play a role in the maintenance and/or exacerbation of childhood anxiety.

schemas strongly guide the processing of information and chronically focus resources on threat-relevant information. The enduring focus on threat manifests itself in various types of cognitive biases. For example, during the encoding stage, anxious youths tend to shift their attention towards threatening stimuli (i.e., attention bias). Further, during the interpretation stage, anxious youths display enhanced memory for information about danger (i.e., memory bias) as well as a tendency to attach a threatening meaning to ambiguous stimuli (i.e., interpretation bias), which means that situations are readily evaluated as dangerous. Obviously, this biased information processing readily elicits feelings of fear and anxiety, which in turn enhances the occurrence of cognitive biases and may further strengthen the maladaptive vulnerability and danger schemas.

It is important to note that within each stage of information processing, two basic modes of processing can be distinguished, namely automatic and controlled (Shiffrin & Schneider, 1977). Automatic processing is unintentional, fast, and occurs outside of awareness, while controlled processing is deliberate, slower, and available to conscious awareness. This has repercussions for the assessment of the cognitive biases that are associated with each of the information-processing stages: automatic processes are usually measured by means of reaction-time paradigms, whereas controlled processes can be readily assessed with self-report-based tasks (Harvey et al., 2004). In the literature, questionnaires can be found that explicitly ask children and adolescents to what extent they display anxiety-related automatic negative thought (e.g., Children's Automatic Thoughts Scale; Schniering & Rapee, 2002) and cognitive errors such as catastrophising (e.g., Children's Negative Cognitive Error Questionnaire; Leitenberg, Yost, & Carroll-Wilson, 1986). However, as the present paper adopts an information-processing perspective, we will mainly focus on cognitive biases that specifically occur during the encoding and interpretation stages of processing (Figure 1), which are typically assessed by means of experimental paradigms.

COGNITIVE DISTORTIONS IN CHILDHOOD ANXIETY

Attention bias

One example of a cognitive distortion is attention bias, which refers to anxious people's tendency to display hyperattention towards potentially threatening material (MacLeod, Mathews, & Tata, 1986; Mathews & MacLeod, 1985; see Mogg & Bradley, 1998). This phenomenon takes place during the encoding stage, and as such is considered to have a distorting effect on further information processing (Harvey et al., 2004; see Figure 1). A frequently employed experimental technique for demonstrating attention bias is the modified Stroop task. In this task, people are required to name the colour in which words are printed while ignoring the meaning of these words. A consistent finding in Stroop studies is that anxiety disordered or phobic participants are slower in their colour naming of fear-relevant words relative to that of neutral words. This would be due to the fact that phobics automatically direct their attention to the content of the threatening words and this interferes with their main task of colour naming (e.g., Watts, McKenna, Sharrock, & Trezise, 1986). Several studies have demonstrated the Stroop effect in the context of childhood fear and anxiety. For example, Martin, Horder, and Jones (1992) employed the Stroop task to test spider-fearful and non-fearful children. The results of their study showed that spider-fearful children exhibited retarded colour-naming times when confronted with spider-related words (e.g., "creepy", "hairy"), but not when confronted with neutral words (e.g., "table", "cars"). Research has also yielded some evidence for the presence of attention bias as indexed by the modified Stroop task in clinically referred youths. That is, children and adolescents with generalised anxiety disorder (GAD) showed significantly slower colour-naming latencies in response to negative-laden emotional information (Taghavi, Dalgleish, Moradi, Neshat-Doost, & Yule, 2003), whereas youths with posttraumatic stress disorder (PTSD) showed greater interference when colour naming trauma-related words (Moradi, Taghavi, Neshat-Doost, Yule, & Dalgleish, 1999).

Another experimental paradigm that can be employed to measure attention bias towards threat is the dot-probe task. During this task, two competing stimuli (words or pictures) are briefly presented on a computer screen: one stimulus is threat-relevant, whereas the other is emotionally neutral. Following the disappearance of the stimuli, a small probe appears on the location previously occupied by one of the stimuli. The latency to identify this probe provides an index of the extent to which a child's attention was directed towards the stimulus that has just disappeared. Thus, faster latencies to detect a probe following threatening stimuli relative to neutral stimuli would indicate an attention bias towards threat, whereas the opposite pattern would reflect a tendency to direct attention away from the threat (see Vasey & MacLeod, 2001). A number of studies have used the dot-probe paradigm for assessing attention bias in relation to fear and anxiety in youths. For example, Vasey, Daleiden, Williams, and Brown (1995) administered the dot-probe detection task to a group of 9- to 14-year-old children with anxiety disorders and a group of age-matched non-anxious control children. The results of this study demonstrated that anxiety-disordered children, relative to controls, were faster to react to a probe if it was preceded by a threatening rather than a neutral word. This finding is in keeping with the hypothesis that anxious youths allocate significantly more processing resources towards threat-related material. Other studies have reported similar effects in non-clinical children and adolescents with high anxiety levels (e.g., Vasey, El-Hag, & Daleiden 1996) and clinically referred youths diagnosed with GAD and PTSD (Dalgleish, Moradi, Taghavi, Neshat-Doost, & Yule, 2001; Taghavi, Neshat-Doost, Moradi, Yule, & Dalgleish, 1999).

When reviewing the empirical evidence that has emerged on anxiety-related attention bias in children and adolescents, it can be concluded that, in general, there is a dearth of research in this domain. Furthermore, it should be acknowledged that several studies have failed to document an attention-related processing bias in youth populations, in particular when using the modified Stroop paradigm (e.g., Kindt, Bierman, & Brosschot, 1997; Kindt & Brosschot, 1999; Morren, Kindt, Van den Hout, & Van Kasteren, 2003). Nevertheless, available evidence seems to indicate that this cognitive distortion is present in high-anxious and anxiety-disordered youths, just like in anxious adults (see Bar-Haim, Lamy, Pergamin, Bakermans-Kranenburg, & van IJzendoorn, 2007, for a meta-analytic review). A strong aspect of the research on attentional bias is its reliance on experimental paradigms, as it is clear that performance-based measures like the Stroop and the dot-probe task are less sensitive to reporter bias effects (Bijttebier et al., 2003). At the same time, experimental indices of attentional bias may suffer from methodological problems, and this may be particularly true when they are employed in young people (Vasey, Dalgleish, & Silverman, 2003). There is surprisingly little evidence for the psychometric properties of these measures. As an example of this point, a recent study by Dalgleish and colleagues (2003) employed both the modified Stroop task and dot-probe paradigm to examine attentional bias in clinically anxious children and adolescents. Notably, no correlation emerged between the attentional bias scores as indexed by both tasks, which indicates that they "seem unlikely to be tapping identical underlying cognitive processes" (Dalgleish et al., 2003; p. 19) and hence tap different types of cognitive distortion. Alternatively, this finding may seriously question the validity of at least one of the attentional bias measures, and it is clear that more research on this issue is urgently needed.

Interpretation biases

Interpretation bias, which refers to the tendency to disproportionately impose threat upon ambiguous situations, occurs during the interpretation stage of information processing (Figure 1). This type of bias has been documented in various studies with youths. In an investigation by Barrett, Rapee, Dadds, and Ryan (1996), anxiety-disordered youths, youths with oppositional defiant disorder, and normal controls (all aged between 7 and 14 years) were presented with brief stories of ambiguous situations and asked about what was happening in each situation. Then, youths were given two possible neutral outcomes and two possible threatening outcomes and asked which outcome was most likely to occur. Results showed that both anxious and oppositional youths more frequently interpreted ambiguous situations as threatening than normal controls. Interestingly, anxious youths more often chose avoidant outcomes, whereas oppositional youths more frequently chose aggressive outcomes. A different experimental approach was employed by Hadwin, Frost, French, and Richards (1997) who measured general anxiety levels in 7- to 9-year-old children, and then confronted them with ambiguous homophones that either had a neutral or a threatening interpretation (e.g., dye versus die). The results showed that anxiety levels were positively associated with threatening interpretations of homophones. Thus, higher anxiety levels were accompanied by a higher frequency of threatening interpretations. Altogether, these and other studies (e.g., Bögels & Zigterman, 2000; Chorpita, Albano, & Barlow, 1996; Dineen & Hadwin, 2004; Taghavi, Moradi, Neshat-Doost, Yule, & Dalgleish, 2000) have demonstrated that interpretation bias is a cognitive distortion that occurs in high-anxious and anxiety-disordered children and adolescents.

A variation of interpretation bias is the "Reduced Evidence for Danger" (RED) bias (e.g., Muris, Rapee, Meesters, Schouten, & Geers, 2003b). In short, this cognitive distortion illustrates how quickly anxious youths make threatening interpretations when confronted with ambiguity. RED bias is typically demonstrated in interview studies in which children are exposed to ambiguous vignettes. Briefly, children are told that some of these vignettes are scary, i.e., these vignettes will have a bad end, whereas other vignettes are not scary, i.e., these vignettes will have a happy end. Children are instructed to find out as quickly as possible whether the pertinent vignette will be scary or not scary. Vignettes are presented sentence by sentence, and after each sentence children are asked whether they think that the vignettes will be scary or not scary. Muris, Merckelbach, and Damsma (2000c) employed this method to expose 8- to 13-year-old non-clinical children, high and low on social anxiety, to vignettes describing social situations. The results of their study demonstrated that children with high levels of social anxiety displayed lower thresholds for threat perception (i.e., needed to hear fewer sentences before deciding that a story was going to be threatening) as compared to children with low levels of social anxiety. Of course this finding indicates the presence of a RED bias and shows that anxious youths are very sensitive to threat cues and only need very little information before perceiving a situation as dangerous (see also Muris et al., 2000a; Muris, Luermans, Merckelbach, & Mayer, 2000b).

Anxious children and adolescents may also employ heuristics that distort their perception of reality, and hence result in an increased inclination to perceive danger and threat, thereby strongly guiding the interpretation of events. One good example is covariation bias, which refers to the tendency to overestimate the association between feared stimuli and negative outcomes (Tomarken, Mineka, & Cook, 1989). The experimental demonstration of this cognitive distortion is straightforward. Fearful and normal participants are shown a series of slides consisting of fear-relevant (e.g., spiders) and neutral (e.g., flowers) pictures. Slide offset is followed by an aversive shock (i.e., negative outcome), a tone, or nothing, in such a way that fear-relevant and neutral pictures are equally often paired with each of the outcomes. After the series of slides, participants are asked to estimate the contingencies between slides and various outcomes. Under these experimental conditions, it is found that phobic people systematically overestimate the contingency between phobic stimuli and negative outcomes. Due to ethical considerations, it is not acceptable to conduct such an experiment with young people. However, Muris, Huijding, Mayer, Den Breejen, and Makkelie (2007a) recently developed an alternative experimental approach to study this type of cognitive bias in youths. By means of a thought experiment (in which youths had to imagine that they participated in a typical covariation bias experiment as described above) and a computer game (in which participants presumably won or lost candy while looking at various types of pictures), the researchers were able to demonstrate that high-fearful youths estimated more negative and less positive outcomes in relation to spider pictures than their low-fearful counterparts. Another example involves probability bias, which pertains to the phenomenon that anxious individuals estimate future negative events as more likely to occur, and in particular to themselves (Butler & Mathews, 1987). Although the evidence for probability bias in children and adolescents is mixed (e.g., Dalgleish et al., 1997), there are many studies showing that this cognitive bias also occurs in youths. For example, Rheingold, Herbert, and Franklin (2003) asked a group of adolescents with a social anxiety disorder and a control group to complete the Probability/Cost Questionnaire for Children, which measures the likelihood and costs of negative social and non-social events. The results indicated that socially anxious adolescents clearly overestimated the probability and costs of negative social events as compared to non-anxious adolescents.

Youths' evaluations of threat are not only determined by external information (i.e., exposure to potential threat cues) but also by internal information, such as the experience of anxiety-related bodily sensations. An example of a cognitive bias that distorts the processing of internal information is emotional reasoning, which can be defined as the cognitive process of inferring danger on the basis of a physical anxiety response (Arntz, Rauner, & Van den Hout, 1995; Beck et al., 1985). Muris, Merckelbach, and Van Spauwen (2003a) were the first to examine whether emotional reasoning also occurs in (anxious) children. Non-clinical children first completed self-report questionnaires of anxiety and were then asked to rate the danger of scripts in which information about objective danger versus objective safety, and anxiety responses versus non-anxiety responses was systematically manipulated. Some evidence was obtained for an emotional reasoning effect. That is, children's danger ratings were not only determined by objective danger information, but also, in the case of objective safety scripts, by anxiety response information. Further analyses revealed that this emotional reasoning effect was present in high- and low-anxious children, although children with high anxiety levels displayed a significantly stronger tendency to use anxiety-response information for the ratings of the objective safety scenarios.

It is reasonable to conclude from this evidence that anxious children and adolescents display various cognitive biases that affect the interpretation of external and internal cues as potentially dangerous and threatening. Two remarks should be made with regard to this conclusion. First of all, so far the research on interpretation bias in children and adolescents has primarily focused on the more controlled cognitive processes, and this yields the impression that this type of cognitive distortion merely occurs at the more conceptual, conscious level. It should be borne in mind, however, that in the adult literature, experimental tasks (e.g., recognition memory task, visual blink measure) have been employed that tap automatic manifestations of interpretation bias (e.g., Harvey et al., 2004), which of course still need to be tested in anxious youths. Second, although there is evidence indicating that covariation and probability bias are quite specific for the anxiety problems from which youths are suffering (Muris et al., 2007a; Rheingold et al., 2003), several studies have indicated that other types of interpretation bias are not exclusively linked to anxiety in a certain domain. For instance, Bögels, Snieder, and Kindt (2003) examined whether children with high symptom levels of social phobia, separation anxiety disorder, and generalised anxiety disorder were characterised by a specific set of dysfunctional interpretations that were consistent with the cognitive model of their specific fear. The results of this study indicated that children high on separation anxiety displayed a relatively strong interpretation bias for separation-related scenarios. However, children with high symptom levels of other anxiety disorders did not show such content specificity in their interpretations. This disappointing finding can be explained in terms of comorbidity (i.e., substantial overlap among childhood anxiety disorders) and assessment (i.e., vignette paradigm might not be suitable to differentiate between anxiety disorders) issues, or may simply indicate that this type of cognitive bias is largely determined by general vulnerability (e.g., neuroticism or trait anxiety) rather than specific anxiety states. Of course, a more thorough analysis of the specificity of interpretation biases is clearly warranted.

Memory bias

Memory bias refers to a tendency to selectively recall memories congruent with an emotional state. In anxiety this would imply recall of memories congruent with the cause of one's anxiety, which ultimately results in a biased interpretation of ambiguous situations (see Figure 1). Despite ubiquitous evidence for memory biases in depressed adults (see Williams, 2001), the evidence in anxious adults is sketchy. An extensive review of the literature concluded that there is good evidence for explicit memory biases in panic disorder, some tentative evidence for similar biases in PTSD and obsessive-compulsive disorder (OCD) but not social phobia and GAD (Coles & Heimberg, 2002). Given the paucity of evidence for memory biases in anxious adults, it comes as no surprise that there are only a few studies which have examined this type of cognitive distortion in children and adolescents. One exception is a study by Moradi, Taghavi, Neshat-Doost, Yule, and Dalgleish (2000) in which 9- to 17-year-olds with PTSD and a group of non-clinical control youths were asked to memorise sets of negative (e.g., horror), positive (e.g., pleasant), and neutral (animal) words (e.g., lizard). After a 90-second distraction task, participants were given a free-recall task followed by a recognition test in which they had to detect words of the original sets from an extended list of 120 words. During free recall, PTSD and control youths did not differ with regard to the recall of negative words, but the control participants recalled significantly more neutral and positive words. Hence one might conclude that youths with PTSD showed an inclination for recalling relatively more negative words relative to positive and neutral words as compared with control youths. There were no significant group differences during the recognition test. As such, this study provided rather weak evidence for a memory bias in anxious children. In a similar study by the same research group (Dalgleish et al., 2003), 7- to 18-year-old clinically referred youths with PTSD or GAD showed no differences to controls in a free-recall test using the same methodology as previously described. Watts and Weems (2006) recently examined the relationship between self-reported and parent-reported anxiety and memory bias in 9- to 17-year-olds. In this study, memory bias was computed as the ratio of threat words remembered compared to distracter threat words minus the ratio of neutral words remembered to distracter words. This bias score correlated significantly with child- and parent-reported anxiety scores, although the magnitude of the correlations was rather modest ($r = .23$ and $r = .26$, respectively).

This brief overview of research on anxiety-related memory bias in children and adolescents makes it obvious that clear evidence for this type of cognitive distortion in youths is currently lacking. The picture of memory bias in children and adolescents is further complicated by dissociations in memory effects in different memory systems. For example, Daleiden (1998) asked 11- to 14-year-olds either high and low on trait anxiety to remember negative, positive, and neutral words. Then children were tested by means of a word fragment completion task (e.g., _OV_D as cue for the word LOVED) to measure perceptual memory processing, and a semantic cue task (e.g., ADORED as cue for the word LOVED) to index conceptual memory processing (Daleiden, 1998). Results indicated that high-anxious youths recalled more negative words relative to neutral words than their low-anxious counterparts on the conceptual memory task, but there were no group differences on the perceptual memory task. These findings seem to suggest that memory bias occurs only in tasks that require processing of the meaning of stimuli.

The little evidence that exists tentatively suggests that there may be biases for recalling threat memories in anxious children and adolescents. However, notwithstanding the need for more research to verify this basic finding, several issues remain unresolved. First, the boundary conditions of these biases need to be clarified: are these distortions specific to certain encoding or recall conditions, what are the effects of context, and—given a vast literature on mood congruency effects in memory recall and the overlap between anxiety and depression—what is the interaction between depressed mood and anxious mood in memory recall? A further issue, to which we will turn now, is from where biased memories (and other cognitive distortions) come.

ORIGINS OF COGNITIVE DISTORTIONS

Although there is supportive evidence indicating that various types of cognitive distortions occur in anxious children and adolescents, one of the key questions remains how these distortions develop. This section reviews the evidence for the impact of genetic-based vulnerability and environmental influences on cognitive distortions in children and adolescents. One important lacuna in the research literature that we will review is longitudinal research about the time course of these cognitive distortions. For example, although there is some evidence of age affecting covariation biases (Muris et al., 2007a) and memory biases (Watts & Weems, 2006) when looking at different categorical age ranges, large-scale studies are needed that look at whether these distortions get stronger over time when age is considered continuously. Furthermore, the relationship between age and cognitive distortions should not be assumed to be linear necessarily, and large-scale longitudinal research will allow conclusions to be drawn about the nature of the age–cognitive distortion relationship. One of the great problems of such research is developing age-insensitive measures of these distortions.

Genetically-based vulnerability

The first explanation of cognitive distortions in anxiety is that there are genetically-based individual difference variables, which increase youths' proneness to cognitive distortions. For example, Eysenck (1992) assumed that individuals high on the personality dimension of neuroticism are particularly vulnerable to biased information processing, which manifests itself in hypervigilance to threat. It has been proposed that individual differences in neuroticism are mainly due to heredity (Eysenck, 1967; Gray, 1987), and there are empirical data from twin studies that confirm this notion. For example, a large-scale study by Lake, Eaves, Maes, Heath, and Martin (2000) demonstrated that the majority of the family resemblance for neuroticism was explained by genetic factors. Other studies have obtained similar results, and on the basis of these findings it can be concluded that neuroticism "appears to be approximately 50 percent heritable in humans" (Craske, 2003; p. 46). This conclusion is further substantiated by research in children and adolescents showing that neuroticism-related personality traits such as trait anxiety and manifest anxiety have a clear-cut genetic basis (e.g., Legrand, McGue, & Iacono, 1999; Topolsky et al., 1997; see Eley & Gregory, 2004, for a review).

In the context of childhood anxiety, many researchers have focused on the obvious behavioural manifestation of neuroticism, which has been labelled as "behavioural inhibition" (Craske, 1997). Behavioural inhibition is the tendency of some children to interrupt ongoing behaviour and to react with vocal restraint and withdrawal when confronted with unfamiliar people or settings (Kagan, 1994). Approximately 10 to 15% of the children clearly exhibit the signs of this temperamental characteristic (e.g., Kagan, Reznick, Clarke, Snidman, & Garcia-Coll, 1984). Like its presumed underlying personality trait (i.e., neuroticism), behavioural inhibition has been shown to be largely genetically based (Robinson, Kagan, Reznick, & Corley, 1992), and there is increasing evidence showing that this well-observed tempera- ment factor plays a role in the development of childhood anxiety problems over longer time periods (e.g., Biederman et al., 1993).

Despite the widely accepted notion that neuroticism or associated constructs such as behavioural inhibition play an important role in the origins of anxiety-related cognitive distortions, it has to be concluded that straightforward evidence for this claim is rather meagre. That is, although there is some cross-sectional evidence showing that neuroticism is positively associated with cognitive distortions such as attentional bias (e.g., Hadwin et al., 1997) and interpretation bias (e.g., Muris, Meesters, & Rompelberg, 2007b), prospective research showing that high neuroticism is associated with the actual development of cognitive distortions (and in its wake anxiety pathology) is currently lacking in the literature. Another issue that remains to be addressed is to further establish the physiological underpinnings of neuroticism, as this may help us to understand where anxiety-related cognitive distortions come from. Biological personality theories assume that neuroticism is primarily based on the hyperexcitability of subcortical brain circuits (e.g., Eysenck, 1967). A recent model by Pine (2007) nicely conceptualises the role of information processing abnormalities in brain– anxiety associations. Briefly, Pine delineates a framework in which brain circuitry involved in the shaping of threat responses (amygdala–hippocam- pus, striatum, prefrontal cortex) is disregulated, which manifests itself in distorted information processing and in its wake anxiety pathology. Recently, evidence for the tenability of these ideas is starting to emerge. For example, Pérez-Edgar et al. (2007) carried out functional magnetic resonance imaging (fMRI) to demonstrate that behaviourally inhibited youths display pertur- bations in amygdala function that seem to be associated with selective processing of threat-related information (cf. McClure et al., in press).

On a final note, while there is a general trend to conceptualise the genetic origins of anxiety-related cognitive distortions in terms of vulnerability, there is increasing attention being paid to regulative temperament factors that may help children and adolescents to protect themselves against such information-processing biases. Effortful control refers to partly innate self-regulative processes and can best be defined as "the ability to inhibit a dominant response to perform a subdominant response" (Rothbart & Bates, 1998). This definition suggests that effortful control pertains to "controlling" one's cognitive processes (e.g., attention) and behaviour if this is required. Research on the influence of effortful control on information processing is just beginning to emerge (Lonigan, Vasey, Phillips, & Hazen, 2004; Muris et al., 2007c; see also Derryberry & Reed, 2002), and, indeed, the results have provided some support for the idea that a protective factor like effortful control buffers youths' susceptibility to cognitive distortions.

Environmental factors

Behavioural-genetic research has shown that around 37% of the variance in child anxiety is attributable to the non-shared environment and 18% to shared environments (Eley et al., 2003). As such, learning has a huge role to play in how childhood anxiety develops. Although direct traumatic experiences have been shown to affect anxiety in children (Dollinger, Odonnell, & Staley, 1984; Yule, Udwin, & Murdoch, 1990), these studies have not looked at whether such traumatic experiences influence cognitive distortions (although, of course, it is likely that they do). However, research into less-direct pathways to anxiety has provided some fruitful answers to whether cognitive distortions can be acquired.

In adults, some innovative experiments have shown that cognitive biases can be acquired in non-anxious individuals (see Mathews & MacLeod, 2005, for a review). For example, Mathews and colleagues (Mathews & Mackintosh, 2000; Mathews & MacLeod, 2002) have described an experimental paradigm to demonstrate that interpretation bias can be learned by training. Participants were exposed to verbal descriptions of ambiguous events and positive or negative resolutions to these events were either provided in the text or were actively generated by participants through a fragment-completion task. In this way, the researchers succeeded in installing an interpretation bias that persisted beyond the training trials. More important, state anxiety actually increased as a direct result of acquiring the interpretation bias through the active generation of negative (but not positive) resolutions for the ambiguous scenarios. A parallel stream of research has shown that attention biases can also be learnt. MacLeod, Rutherford, Campbell, Ebsworthy, and Holker (2002) used a modified dot-probe task as a training tool by presenting pairs of threat or neutral words, but with the probe consistently appearing behind the threat word for some participants, while for others the probe always appeared after the neutral word. Results showed that participants who were trained with probes to threat words did show faster latencies to detect probes in a normal dot-probe task when they appeared on the same location as threat words. In other words, these participants had acquired an attention bias to threat, and, interestingly, this induced bias also led to increased negative mood during a subsequent stress task.

The implications of this body of work to fear development are clear: attention and interpretation biases to threat can be learned by non-anxious individuals, and the acquisition of such biases is likely to increase anxiety. Although no studies have been conducted in youth populations, it is easy to conceive that normal children and adolescents can also acquire persistent attention and interpretation biases that drive anxious responding. It is worth noting that the adult participants in the studies by Mathews, MacLeod and co-workers brought to the experiments years of learning inconsistent with biases to threat, and so the results of these studies are really remarkable because they were not training a bias from scratch, but rather realigning attention and interpretation systems that were the product of years of learning. Probably, youths acquire such biases more easily because they have less prior learning experiences with potentially threatening stimuli and situations. It remains unclear how the acquisition of attention and interpretation biases exactly takes place, but it can be assumed that when surrounded by anxious parents, siblings or friends, a child's attention is frequently drawn to threatening stimuli through verbal instruction, whereas danger interpretations are more readily made when observing others interpreting ambiguous material in a negative way (vicarious learning).

The idea that fear is acquired through verbal information and vicarious learning is not new (Rachman, 1977). Over the past 30 years, a lot of retrospective research has shown that phobic children and adolescents will attribute their fear to both of these pathways (King, Gullone, & Ollendick, 1998; Merckelbach, de Jong, Muris, & van den Hout, 1996; Ollendick & King, 1991). Only recently have researchers begun to look prospectively at the effect that indirect learning has on normal youths. In a series of studies, Field and colleagues (Field, 2006a; Field, Argyris, & Knowles, 2001; Field, Hamilton, Knowles, & Plews, 2003; Field & Lawson, 2003; Field, Lawson, & Banerjee, in press; Field & Schorah, 2007; Lawson, Banerjee, & Field, 2007) have shown that verbal information is sufficient to create persistent fear beliefs of unknown animals (i.e., toy monsters, Australian marsupials) and social situations in non-clinical children. More relevant to the present context, Field (2006a, 2006b) has demonstrated that it is possible to induce a fear-related attention biases to novel animals (as measured with a dot-probe task) by giving children negative information about these stimuli. This finding is consistent with the above described work showing that attention biases can be trained (MacLeod et al., 2002); however, it did not require a long training phase on the dot-probe paradigm but merely a short burst of verbal threat information. In a similar vein, Field and Lawson (2008 this issue) have looked at fear-related causal learning and covariation bias in children following verbal threat information. Subsequent to verbal information, children were exposed to 80 trials in which pictures of animals were followed by either a bad outcome (i.e., a scared face) or a good outcome (i.e., a smiling face). Field and Lawson found that threat information about an animal did not lead to an overestimation of the contingency between that animal and "bad" outcomes; it led to an accurate estimate. In contrast, no information about an animal led to an underestimation of bad outcomes. In other words, children normally underestimated the number of negative outcomes that they had seen. However, negative information caused them to accurately assess the contingency that they had experienced. As such, there is a growing body of research showing that verbal information can lead to cognitive distortions similar to those found in anxious children. Further, although an experimental paradigm has been developed to examine the anxiety-promoting effects of vicarious learning (Askew & Field, 2007), so far no study has investigated its direct impact on cognitive distortions. Further research needs to address this issue as well as the role of negative information and vicarious learning on other types of cognitive distortions (e.g., memory bias).

Verbal information, vicarious learning, and direct conditioning offer potential causal pathways through which cognitive distortions can be formed. It is likely that in a child's formative years, the majority of these experiences will be provided by their parents. Furthermore, various other parental and family factors are at work, which may bolster children's vulnerability and danger schemas, and hence promote the occurrence of cognitive distortions. Examples of such variables are an insecure attachment relationship, controlling rearing styles, and a threatening family climate (Bögels & Brechman-Toussaint, 2006). In addition, parents may suffer from anxiety problems themselves and hence also display cognitive biases, which are then transferred to their children (see Hadwin, Garner, & Perez-Olivas, 2006). In keeping with this idea, children of separation-anxious parents were found to be more likely to have over-cautious perceptions of risk (Capps, Sigman, Sena, & Henker, 1996), children of panic-disorder patients made more anxious interpretations of ambiguous scenarios than children of a control group (Schneider, Unnewehr, Florin, & Margraf, 2002), and in non-clinical populations, maternal and child threat-related cognitions were found to be correlated (Creswell & O'Connor, 2006; Creswell, O'Connor, & Brewin, 2006). Thus, work is starting to accumulate to suggest that anxious parents pass on specific cognitive distortions to their children. Finally, parenting practices do appear to moderate the effect that verbal threat information has on creating fear beliefs in children (Field, Ball, Kawycz, & Moore, 2007). Although part of this transmission could be explained by genetics, the findings do suggest that learning is also important and especially the learning opportunities that parents provide to their children (see Field & Cartwright-Hatton, 2007, for a review).

To sum up, learning undoubtedly plays an important causal role in the development of cognitive distortions in children. However, at present, there is a distinct lack of research into: (1) whether verbal information, vicarious learning and direct traumatic incidents create specific cognitive distortions in children; (2) the mechanism through which these pathways achieve this change in the cognitive processing of threat material; and (3) the role of parents in providing anxiogenic learning environments through which children acquire distorted cognitive processes.

Gene–environment interactions

Genetics and learning do not operate independently (see, for example, Rutter, 2007; Rutter, Moffitt, & Caspi, 2006). For example, above we have identified parenting environments as a learning factor, but exposure to these environments will be affected by genes (i.e., gene–environment correlations). There are three types of gene–environment correlation (rGE): the parenting environments that a given parent provides depends on their genes (i.e., passive rGE); also a child's genes determine the environments to which they expose themselves (i.e., active rGE); and finally, a child's genes influence their behaviours, which in turn influence how others (including parents) behave towards them (i.e., evocative rGE). One important implication is that the learning environment to which youths are exposed will depend in part on their genetic make-up: a child with a genetically based tendency to interpret ambiguity in a threatening way, for example, may act in ways that evoke threat interpretations of ambiguous situations from their parents leading to a self-perpetuating cycle of learning. Extrapolating from Rutter (2007), part of the genetic influence on cognitive distortions will derive from rGE influencing individual differences in a child's exposure to environments that facilitate or protect against cognitive distortions. Also, the development of cognitive distortions from learning will be mediated genetically. For example, Field (2006a) has shown that attentional biases created through verbal threat information in children are mediated by the child's trait anxiety: as trait anxiety increased so did the acquired attentional bias to an animal about which threatening information has been given. The future of research into how cognitive distortions develop in children depends on further examining these interactions, but also on identifying ways in which a child's behaviour influences the environment around them to facilitate cognitive distortions.

Discussion

In conclusion, then, the past 10 years have seen a marked rise in research on anxiety-related information processing abnormalities in children and adolescents (Vasey & MacLeod, 2001). These studies have generally yielded promising results, which are in keeping with the idea that anxious youths display biases and distortions in various stages of the processing of anxiety-related information (Daleiden & Vasey, 1997). More precisely, there is some evidence indicating that anxious children and adolescents display attentional bias for threat during the encoding stage, whereas there is clear support for the presence of various types of interpretation biases occurring during the more conceptual stages of information processing. Admittedly, few studies have been able to demonstrate memory bias in youths with anxiety problems, but at the same time it should be noted that research in adult populations has also revealed less-consistent findings with regard to this type of cognitive distortion (Harvey et al., 2004).

Admittedly, there are quite a number of studies that have appeared in the literature that have failed to document differences in the processing of threat-related information between (clinically) anxious and non-anxious youths (e.g., Kindt et al., 1997; Morren et al., 2003; see also Alfano, Beidel, & Turner, 2002). This seems to point at methodological and developmental issues that play a role in respectively the assessment and phenomenology of cognitive biases in youths. More precisely, it may well be the case that certain experimental paradigms are less suitable for younger participants (Muris, 2003). Otherwise, it is also possible that certain distortions require a minimum level of cognitive maturation before they consistently emerge in (anxious) youths (see Alfano et al., 2002, for a detailed discussion). Some evidence for this idea has been obtained in a recent study by Muris, Mayer, Vermeulen, and Hiemstra (2007b), who investigated to what extent children's anxiety-related interpretations of physical symptoms and emotional reasoning are influenced by the level of cognitive development. Results clearly indicated that children's performance on conservation tasks and a Theory-of-Mind test were significant predictors of anxious interpretations and emotional reasoning scores, which suggests that these phenomena are influenced by cognitive development. On the other hand, other researchers have pointed out that certain cognitive distortions (e.g., attention bias) begin as normal developmental phenomena over which children gradually gain control as they become older. A failure to control or inhibit such biases would be indicative of children and adolescents with anxiety problems (Kindt & Brosschot, 1999; Kindt et al., 1997; Kindt, van den Hout, de Jong, & Hoekzema, 2000). As mentioned earlier, an important challenge for future research seems to be to evaluate such developmental issues of cognitive distortions.

There are a number of other issues concerning information-processing abnormalities in youths that require some further comment and that may also indicate some pathways for future work in this research area. First, according to Daleiden and Vasey's (1997) perspective on information processing in childhood anxiety, it seems plausible that distortions at an early stage of processing (e.g., encoding) increase the likelihood of biases at subsequent stages of processing (e.g., interpretation). Although there is no direct test of this proposition, Dalgleish et al. (2003) found quite differential patterns on tests measuring attentional, memory, and probability bias in clinically anxious youths, suggesting that distortion at one stage is not necessarily related to bias at another stage. On the one hand, this may be due to the psychometric qualities (i.e., reliability, validity) of the tests that are employed to measure various types of information-processing abnormalities. On the other hand, it is also possible that regulative mechanisms neutralise early cognitive distortions, so that processing at a subsequent stage is again quite normal.

Second, according to cognitive theory, various anxiety disorders can be typified by a specific content of cognition (Beck et al., 1985). For example, it can be assumed that socially-anxious children and adolescents display distortions in the processing of other information than youths with PTSD. So far, research has yielded little support for this content-specificity of cognitive distortions in anxious young people (see Bögels et al., 2003; Dalgleish et al., 2003). This is due to the fact that most studies in this domain mainly focused on the cognitive distortions of only one specific childhood anxiety disorder. In addition, it should be borne in mind that, unlike anxiety pathology in adults, anxiety disorders in youths may be less fully crystallised (Muris, 2007). There is evidence from prospective research demonstrating that although anxiety in general is fairly stable as children become older, the exact manifestation of the problem may vary from one point in time to another (e.g., Essau, Conradt, & Peterman, 2002; Keller et al., 1992). Thus, it may well be that more cognitive distortions in youths, and especially in younger children, are more of a general nature rather than specifically linked to a specific anxiety disorder.

Third, it is well-established that girls display higher levels of fear and anxiety than boys (e.g., Ollendick, King, & Muris, 2002). For example, Lewinsohn, Gotlib, Lewinsohn, Seeley, and Allen (1998), who examined gender differences in the prevalence of anxiety disorders in a large community sample of adolescents, concluded that girls more frequently met the diagnostic criteria for current and lifetime diagnosis of phobic and other anxiety disorders than boys. Interestingly, the results of this study indicated that this gender difference emerged early in life: at age 6, girls already suffered from twice as many anxiety disorders than did boys. Similar gender differences have been consistently reported for youths' fear and anxiety levels as measured with standardised rating scales (see Muris, 2007). If information-processing biases are indeed an important mechanism operating in anxiety problems in youths, one would expect girls to be more susceptible to such distortions. Unfortunately, research so far has largely neglected this issue (i.e., most studies simply control for gender effects in their design or statistical analyses), and this obviously is an interesting avenue for future investigations (Craske, 2003).

Fourth, although it is generally assumed that information-processing abnormalities play a role in the maintenance and even exacerbation of anxiety problems in youths, almost all the research on this topic has been cross-sectional in nature and so no conclusions can be drawn on the cause–effect relation between biased cognition and anxiety. One exception is a study by Muris, Jacques, and Mayer (2004) who examined the temporal stability and development of cognitive distortions and anxiety symptoms in non-clinical children aged 9 to 13 years. Children completed a self-report measure of anxiety symptoms, and were then interviewed individually using an ambiguous story paradigm from which a number of threat perception indices (i.e., interpretation bias, RED-bias) were derived. The assessment was repeated some 4 weeks later, so that it became possible to study prospective relationships for threat perception abnormalities and anxiety symptoms. The results indicated that, on both occasions, anxiety-disorder symptoms were significantly associated with threat-perception abnormalities. Furthermore, threat-perception abnormalities were moderately stable over the 4-week period. Finally, and most importantly, no evidence was obtained for a direct prospective link between threat perception and anxiety-disorder symptoms. Although it should be kept in mind that the time period of this study was fairly short, the findings at least suggest that cognitive distortions do not act as aetiological factors for childhood anxiety problems, but rather should be viewed as epiphenomena of high anxiety levels, which nevertheless may play a role in the continuation of such symptoms. Clearly, more research is necessary to examine the precise role of cognitive distortions on the development of youths' anxiety symptoms over longer time periods.

Fifth, very little research has explored how cognitive biases develop. Although there has been a growing literature (reviewed here) suggesting that parents can transmit specific cognitive biases (Creswell et al., 2006), and that verbal threat information can create attentional bias and that trait anxiety mediates the formation of these biases (Field, 2006a, 2006b), we still know very little about how cognitive distortions develop in non-anxious children. This knowledge is the key to understanding how to change these biases, and how to prevent them.

Finally, future studies could address the relevance of cognitive distortions for the treatment of childhood anxiety problems. If these biases are involved in the maintenance and/or exacerbation of anxiety symptoms among youths, it seems logical to assume that an undermining of such cognitive distortions should result in marked reductions of anxiety. The procedures that have been used to train attention bias (MacLeod et al., 2002) may be reversed into attention retraining programmes that may be helpful in correcting this cognitive distortion, thereby reducing anxiety symptoms. In a similar vein, more conceptually based cognitive distortions such as interpretation bias and RED bias may be removed by means of cognitive techniques. More precisely, children can be taught to recognise threat-perception abnormalities and to consciously try to combat them by using more adaptive self-talk (e.g., Barrett, 2001; Ollendick & King, 1998). Finally, if it is indeed true that the family environment is important for the formation of cognitive distortions in youths, it may also be important to reduce the vicarious and informational learning experiences that cause and maintain these biases. Obviously, this type of research would not only be important to further improve our arsenal of treatments for anxiety disordered youths, but at the same time might refine our understanding of the origins of the intimate relationship between cognitive distortions and anxiety in youths.

REFERENCES

Alfano, C. A., Beidel, D. C., & Turner, S. M. (2002). Cognition in childhood anxiety: Conceptual, methodological, and developmental issues. *Clinical Psychology Review, 22,* 1209–1238.

American Psychiatric Association. (2000). *Diagnostic and statistical manual of mental disorders, fourth edition–text revision (DSM-IV-TR).* Washington, DC: American Psychiatric Association.

Arntz, A., Rauner, M., & van den Hout, M. (1995). "If I feel anxious, there must be danger": Ex-consequentia reasoning in inferring danger in anxiety disorders. *Behaviour Research and Therapy, 33,* 917–925.

Askew, C., & Field, A. P. (2007). Vicarious learning and the development of fears in childhood. *Behaviour Research and Therapy, 45,* 2616–2627.

Bar-Haim, Y., Lamy, D., Pergamin, L., Bakermans-Kranenburg, M. J., & van IJzendoorn, M. H. (2007). Threat-related attentional bias in anxious and nonanxious individuals: A meta-analytic study. *Psychological Bulletin, 133,* 1–24.

Barrett, P. M. (2001). Current issues in the treatment of childhood anxiety. In M. W. Vasey & M. R. Dadds (Eds.), *The developmental psychopathology of anxiety* (pp. 304–324). New York: Oxford University Press.

Barrett, P. M., Rapee, R. M., Dadds, M. R., & Ryan, S. M. (1996). Family enhancement of cognitive style in anxious and aggressive children. *Journal of Abnormal Child Psychology, 24,* 187–203.

Beck, A. T., Emery, G., & Greenberg, R. L. (1985). *Anxiety disorders and phobias: A cognitive perspective.* New York: Basic Books.

Biederman, J., Rosenbaum, J. F., Bolduc-Murphy, E. A., Faraone, S. V., Chaloff, J., Hirshfeld, D. R., et al. (1993). A 3-year follow-up of children with and without behavioral inhibition. *Journal of the American Academy of Child and Adolescent Psychiatry, 32,* 814–821.

Bijttebier, P., Vasey, M. W., & Braet, C. (2003). The information-processing paradigm: A valuable framework for clinical child and adolescent psychology. *Journal of Clinical Child and Adolescent Psychology, 32,* 2–9.

Bögels, S. M., & Brechman-Toussaint, M. L. (2006). Family issues in child anxiety: Attachment, family functioning, parental rearing and beliefs. *Clinical Psychology Review, 26,* 834–856.

Bögels, S. M., Snieder, N., & Kindt, M. (2003). Specificity of dysfunctional thinking in children with symptoms of social anxiety, separation anxiety, and generalised anxiety. *Behaviour Change, 20,* 160–169.

Bögels, S. M., & Zigterman, D. (2000). Dysfunctional cognitions in children with social phobia, separation anxiety disorder, and generalized anxiety disorder. *Journal of Abnormal Child Psychology, 28,* 205–211.

Butler, G., & Mathews, A. (1987). Anticipatory anxiety and risk perception. *Cognitive Therapy and Research, 11,* 551–565.

Capps, L., Sigman, M., Sena, R., & Henker, B. (1996). Fear, anxiety and perceived control in children of agoraphobic parents. *Journal of Child Psychology and Psychiatry, 37,* 445–452.

Chorpita, B. F., Albano, A. M., & Barlow, D. H. (1996). Cognitive processing in children: Relationship to anxiety and family influences. *Journal of Clinical Child Psychology, 25,* 170–176.

Coles, M. E., & Heimberg, R. G. (2002). Memory biases in the anxiety disorders: Current status. *Clinical Psychology Review, 22,* 587–627.

Costello, E. J., Mustillo, S., Erkanli, A., Keeler, G., & Angold, A. (2003). Prevalence and development of psychiatric disorders in childhood and adolescence. *Archives of General Psychiatry, 60,* 837–844.

Craske, M. G. (1997). Fear and anxiety in children and adolescents. *Bulletin of the Menninger Clinic, 61*(Suppl. A), A4–A36.

Craske, M. G. (2003). *Origins of phobias and anxiety disorders. Why more women than men?.* Oxford, UK: Elsevier.

Creswell, C., & O'Connor, T. G. (2006). "Anxious cognitions" in children: An exploration of associations and mediators. *British Journal of Developmental Psychology, 24,* 761–766.

Creswell, C., O'Connor, T. G., & Brewin, C. R. (2006). A longitudinal investigation of maternal and child "anxious cognitions". *Cognitive Therapy and Research, 30,* 135–147.

Crick, N. R., & Dodge, K. A. (1994). A review and reformulation of social information-processing mechanisms in children's social adjustment. *Psychological Bulletin, 115,* 74–101.

Daleiden, E. L. (1998). Childhood anxiety and memory functioning: A comparison of systemic and processing accounts. *Journal of Experimental Child Psychology, 68*(3), 216–235.

Daleiden, E. L., & Vasey, M. W. (1997). An information-processing perspective on childhood anxiety. *Clinical Psychology Review, 17,* 407–429.

Dalgleish, T., Moradi, A. R., Taghavi, M. R., Neshat-Doost, H. T., & Yule, W. (2001). An experimental investigation of hypervigilance for threat in children and adolescents with post-traumatic stress disorder. *Psychological Medicine, 31,* 541–547.

Dalgleish, T., Taghavi, R., Neshat-Doost, H., Moradi, A., Canterbury, R., & Yule, W. (2003). Patterns of processing bias for emotional information across clinical disorders: A comparison of attention, memory, and prospective cognition in children and adolescents with depression, generalized anxiety, and posttraumatic stress disorder. *Journal of Clinical Child and Adolescent Psychology, 32,* 10–21.

Dalgleish, T., Taghavi, R., Neshat-Doost, H. N., Moradi, A., Yule, W., & Canterbury, R. (1997). Information processing in clinically depressed and anxious children and adolescents. *Journal of Child Psychology and Psychiatry, 38,* 535–541.

Derryberry, D., & Reed, M. A. (2002). Anxiety-related attentional biases and their regulation by attentional control. *Journal of Abnormal Psychology, 111,* 225–236.

Dineen, K. A., & Hadwin, J. A. (2004). Anxious and depressive symptoms and children's judgements of their own and others' interpretation of ambiguous social scenarios. *Journal of Anxiety Disorders, 18*, 499–513.

Dollinger, S. J., Odonnell, J. P., & Staley, A. A. (1984). Lightning-strike disaster: Effects on children's fears and worries. *Journal of Consulting and Clinical Psychology, 52*, 1028–1038.

Eley, T. C., Bolton, D., O'Connor, T. G., Perrin, S., Smith, P., & Plomin, R. (2003). A twin study of anxiety-related behaviours in preschool children. *Journal of Child Psychology and Psychiatry, 44*, 945–960.

Eley, T. C., & Gregory, A. M. (2004). Behavioral genetics. In T. L. Morris & J. S. March (Eds.), *Anxiety disorders in children and adolescents* (pp. 71–97). New York: Guilford Press.

Essau, C. A., Conradt, J., & Peterman, F. (2002). Course and outcome of anxiety disorders in adolescents. *Journal of Anxiety Disorders, 16*, 67–81.

Eysenck, H. J. (1967). *The biological basis of personality*. Springfield, IL: Thomas.

Eysenck, M. W. (1992). *Anxiety: The cognitive perspective*. Hove, UK: Lawrence Erlbaum Associates Ltd.

Field, A. P. (2006a). The behavioral inhibition system and the verbal information pathway to children's fears. *Journal of Abnormal Psychology, 115*(4), 742–752.

Field, A. P. (2006b). Watch out for the beast: Fear information and attentional bias in children. *Journal of Clinical Child and Adolescent Psychology, 35*, 431–439.

Field, A. P., Argyris, N. G., & Knowles, K. A. (2001). Who's afraid of the big bad wolf: A prospective paradigm to test Rachman's indirect pathways in children. *Behaviour Research and Therapy, 39*, 1259–1276.

Field, A. P., Ball, J. E., Kawycz, N. J., & Moore, H. (2007). Parent–child relationships and the verbal information pathway to fear in children: Two preliminary experiments. *Behavioural and Cognitive Psychotherapy, 35*, 473–486.

Field, A. P., & Cartwright-Hatton, S. (2007). *Parental anxiety: Cognitive-behavioural processes in the intergenerational transmission of fear to children*. Manuscript submitted for publication.

Field, A. P., Hamilton, S. J., Knowles, K. A., & Plews, E. L. (2003). Fear information and social phobic beliefs in children: A prospective paradigm and preliminary results. *Behaviour Research and Therapy, 41*, 113–123.

Field, A. P., & Lawson, J. (2003). Fear information and the development of fears during childhood: Effects on implicit fear responses and behavioural avoidance. *Behaviour Research and Therapy, 41*, 1277–1293.

Field, A. P., & Lawson, J. (2008). The verbal information pathway to fear and subsequent causal learning in children. *Cognition and Emotion, XX*, XXX–XXX.

Field, A. P., Lawson, J., & Banerjee, R. (in press). The verbal information pathway to fear in children: The longitudinal effects on fear cognitions and the immediate effects on avoidance behavior. *Journal of Abnormal Psychology*.

Field, A. P., & Schorah, H. (2007). The negative information pathway to fear and heart rate changes in children. *Journal of Child Psychology and Psychiatry, 48*(11), 1088–1093.

Gray, J. A. (1987). *The psychology of fear and stress*. Cambridge, UK: Cambridge University Press.

Gullone, E. (2000). The development of normal fear: A century of research. *Clinical Psychology Review, 20*, 429–451.

Hadwin, J., Frost, S., French, C. C., & Richards, A. (1997). Cognitive processing and trait anxiety in typically developing children: Evidence for interpretation bias. *Journal of Abnormal Psychology, 106*, 486–490.

Hadwin, J., Garner, M., & Perez-Olivas, G. (2006). The development of information processing biases in childhood anxiety: A review and exploration of its origins in parenting. *Clinical Psychology Review, 26*, 876–894.

Harvey, A., Watkins, E., Mansell, W., & Shafran, R. (2004). *Cognitive behavioural processes across psychological disorders: A transdiagnostic approach to research and treatment.* Oxford, UK: Oxford University Press.

Kagan, J. (1994). *Galen's prophecy: Temperament in human nature.* New York: Basic Books.

Kagan, J., Reznick, J. S., Clarke, C., Snidman, N., & Garcia-Coll, C. (1984). Behavioral inhibition to the unfamiliar. *Child Development, 55,* 2212–2225.

Keller, M. B., Lavori, P. W., Wunder, J., Beardslee, W. R., Schwartz, C. E., & Roth, J. (1992). Chronic course of anxiety disorders in children and adolescents. *Journal of the American Academy of Child and Adolescent Psychiatry, 31,* 595–599.

Kendall, P. C. (1985). Toward a cognitive-behavioral model of child psychopathology and a critique of related interventions. *Journal of Abnormal Child Psychology, 13,* 357–372.

Kindt, M., Bierman, D., & Brosschot, J. F. (1997). Cognitive bias in spider fear and control children: Assessment of emotional interference by a card format and a single-trial format of the Stroop task. *Journal of Experimental Child Psychology, 66,* 163–179.

Kindt, M., & Brosschot, J. F. (1999). Cognitive bias in spider-phobic children: Comparison of a pictorial and a linguistic spider Stroop. *Journal of Psychopathology and Behavioral Assessment, 21,* 207–220.

Kindt, M., van den Hout, M. A., de Jong, P. J., & Hoekzema, B. (2000). Cognitive bias for pictorial and linguistic threat cues in children. *Journal of Psychopathology and Behavioral Assessment, 22,* 201–219.

King, N. J., Gullone, E., & Ollendick, T. (1998). Etiology of childhood phobias: Current status of Rachman's three pathways theory. *Behaviour Research and Therapy, 36,* 297–309.

Lake, R. I., Eaves, L. J., Maes, H. H., Heath, A. C., & Martin, N. G. (2000). Further evidence against the environmental transmission of individual differences in neuroticism from a collaborative study of 45,850 twins and relatives on two continents. *Behavior Genetics, 30,* 223–233.

Lang, P. J. (1985). The cognitive psychophysiology of emotion: Fear and anxiety. In A. H. Tuma & J. Maser (Eds.), *Anxiety and the anxiety disorders.* Hillsdale, NJ: Lawrence Erlbaum Associates, Inc.

Lawson, J., Banerjee, R., & Field, A. P. (2007). The effects of verbal information on children's fear beliefs about social situations. *Behaviour Research and Therapy, 45,* 21–37.

Legrand, L. N., McGue, M., & Iacono, W. G. (1999). A twin study of state and trait anxiety in childhood and adolescence. *Journal of Child Psychology and Psychiatry, 40,* 953–958.

Leitenberg, H., Yost, L. W., & Carroll-Wilson, M. (1986). Negative cognitive errors in children: Questionnaire development, normative data, and comparisons between children with and without self-reported symptoms of depression, low self-esteem, and evaluation anxiety. *Journal of Consulting and Clinical Psychology, 54,* 528–536.

Lewinsohn, P. M., Gotlib, I. H., Lewinsohn, M., Seeley, J. R., & Allen, N. B. (1998). Gender differences in anxiety disorders and anxiety symptoms in adolescents. *Journal of Abnormal Psychology, 107,* 109–117.

Lonigan, C. J., Vasey, M. W., Phillips, B. M., & Hazen, R. A. (2004). Temperament, anxiety, and the processing of threat-relevant stimuli. *Journal of Clinical Child and Adolescent Psychology, 33,* 8–20.

MacLeod, C., Mathews, A., & Tata, P. (1986). Attentional bias in emotional disorders. *Journal of Abnormal Psychology, 95,* 15–20.

MacLeod, C., Rutherford, E., Campbell, L., Ebsworthy, G., & Holker, L. (2002). Selective attention and emotional vulnerability: Assessing the causal basis of their association through the experimental manipulation of attentional bias. *Journal of Abnormal Psychology, 111,* 107–123.

Martin, M., Horder, P., & Jones, G. V. (1992). Integral bias in naming of phobia-related words. *Cognition and Emotion, 6,* 479–486.

Massaro, D. W., & Cowan, N. (1993). Information processing models: Microscopes of the mind. *Annual Review of Psychology, 44*, 382–425.

Mathews, A., & Mackintosh, B. (2000). Induced emotional interpretation bias and anxiety. *Journal of Abnormal Psychology, 109*, 602–615.

Mathews, A., & MacLeod, C. (1985). Selective processing of threat cues in anxiety states. *Behaviour Research and Therapy, 23*, 563–569.

Mathews, A., & MacLeod, C. (2002). Induced processing biases have causal effects on anxiety. *Cognition and Emotion, 16*, 331–354.

Mathews, A., & MacLeod, C. (2005). Cognitive vulnerability to emotional disorders. *Annual Review of Clinical Psychology, 1*, 167–195.

McClure, E. B., Monk, C. S., Nelson, E. E., Parrish, J. M., Adler, A., Blair, R. J. R., et al. (in press). Abnormal attention modulation of fear circuit function in pediatric generalized anxiety disorder. *Archives of General Psychiatry*.

Merckelbach, H., de Jong, P. J., Muris, P., & van den Hout, M. A. (1996). The etiology of specific phobias: A review. *Clinical Psychology Review, 16*, 337–361.

Mogg, K., & Bradley, B. P. (1998). A cognitive-motivational analysis of anxiety. *Behaviour Research and Therapy, 36*, 809–848.

Moradi, A. R., Taghavi, M. R., Neshat-Doost, H. T., Yule, W., & Dalgleish, T. (1999). Performance of children and adolescents with PTSD on the Stroop colour-naming task. *Psychological Medicine, 29*, 415–419.

Moradi, A. R., Taghavi, M. R., Neshat-Doost, H. T., Yule, W., & Dalgleish, T. (2000). Memory bias for emotional information in children and adolescents with posttraumatic stress disorder: A preliminary study. *Journal of Anxiety Disorders, 14*, 521–534.

Morren, M., Kindt, M., van den Hout, M. A., & Van Kasteren, H. (2003). Anxiety and the processing of threat in children: Further examination of the cognitive inhibition hypothesis. *Behaviour Change, 20*, 131–142.

Muris, P. (2003). Information processing abnormalities in childhood anxiety. *Behaviour Change, 20*, 129–130.

Muris, P. (2007). *Normal and abnormal fear and anxiety in children and adolescents*. Oxford, UK: Elsevier.

Muris, P., Huijding, J., Mayer, B., Den Breejen, E., & Makkelie, M. (2007a). Spider fear and covariation bias in children and adolescents. *Behaviour Research and Therapy, 45*, 2604–2615.

Muris, P., Jacques, P., & Mayer, B. (2004). The stability of threat perception abnormalities and anxiety disorder symptoms in non-clinical children. *Child Psychiatry and Human Development, 34*, 251–265.

Muris, P., Kindt, M., Bögels, S., Merckelbach, H., Gadet, B., & Moulaert, V. (2000a). Anxiety and threat perception abnormalities in normal children. *Journal of Psychopathology and Behavioral Assessment, 22*, 183–199.

Muris, P., Luermans, J., Merckelbach, H., & Mayer, B. (2000b). "Danger is lurking everywhere". The relationship between anxiety and threat perception abnormalities in normal children. *Journal of Behavior Therapy and Experimental Psychiatry, 31*, 123–136.

Muris, P., Mayer, B., Vermeulen, L., & Hiemstra, H. (2007b). Theory-of-mind, cognitive development, and children's interpretation of anxiety-related physical symptoms. *Behaviour Research and Therapy, 45*, 2121–2132.

Muris, P., Meesters, C., & Rompelberg, L. (2007c). Attention control in middle childhood: Relations to psychopathological symptoms and threat perception distortions. *Behaviour Research and Therapy, 45*, 997–1010.

Muris, P., Merckelbach, H., & Damsma, E. (2000c). Threat perception bias in nonreferred socially anxious children. *Journal of Clinical Child Psychology, 29*, 348–359.

Muris, P., Merckelbach, H., & Van Spauwen, I. (2003a). The emotional reasoning heuristic in children. *Behaviour Research and Therapy, 41*, 261–272.

Muris, P., Rapee, R., Meesters, C., Schouten, E., & Geers, M. (2003b). Threat perception abnormalities in children: The role of anxiety disorders symptoms, chronic anxiety, and state anxiety. *Journal of Anxiety Disorders, 17*, 271–287.

Ollendick, T. H., & King, N. J. (1991). Origins of childhood fears—An evaluation of Rachman theory of fear acquisition. *Behaviour Research and Therapy, 29*, 117–123.

Ollendick, T. H., & King, N. J. (1998). Empirically supported treatments for children with phobic and anxiety disorders: Current status. *Journal of Clinical Child Psychology, 27*, 156–167.

Ollendick, T. H., King, N. J., & Muris, P. (2002). Fears and phobias in children: Phenomenology, epidemiology, and aetiology. *Child and Adolescent Mental Health, 7*, 98–106.

Pérez-Edgar, K., Roberson-Nay, R., Hardin, M. G., Poeth, K., Guyer, A. E., Nelson, E. E., et al. (2007). Attention alters neural responses to evocative faces in behaviorally inhibited adolescents. *NeuroImage, 64*, 97–106.

Pine, D. S. (2007). A neuroscience framework for pediatric anxiety disorders. *Journal of Child Psychology and Psychiatry, 48*, 863–871.

Rachman, S. (1977). Conditioning theory of fear-acquisition—Critical-examination. *Behaviour Research and Therapy, 15*, 375–387.

Rheingold, A. A., Herbert, J. D., & Franklin, M. E. (2003). Cognitive bias in adolescents with social anxiety disorder. *Cognitive Therapy and Research, 27*, 639–655.

Robinson, J. L., Kagan, J., Reznick, J. S., & Corley, R. (1992). The heritability of inhibited and uninhibited behavior: A twin study. *Developmental Psychology, 28*, 1030–1037.

Rothbart, M. K., & Bates, J. E. (1998). Temperament. In N. Eisenberg & W. Damon (Eds.), *Handbook of child psychology: Vol. 3. Social, emotional, and personality development* (pp. 105–176). New York: Wiley.

Rutter, M. (2007). Gene–environment interdependence. *Developmental Science, 10*, 12–18.

Rutter, M., Moffitt, T. E., & Caspi, A. (2006). Gene–environment interplay and psychopathology: Multiple varieties but real effects. *Journal of Child Psychology and Psychiatry, 47*, 226–261.

Schneider, S., Unnewehr, S., Florin, I., & Margraf, J. (2002). Priming panic interpretations in children of patients with panic disorder. *Journal of Anxiety Disorders, 16*, 605–624.

Schniering, C. A., & Rapee, R. M. (2002). Development and validation of a measure of children's automatic thoughts: The children's automatic thoughts scale. *Behaviour Research and Therapy, 40*, 1091–1109.

Shiffrin, R. M., & Schneider, W. (1977). Controlled and automatic human information processing: II. Perceptual learning, automatic attending, and a general theory. *Psychological Review, 84*, 127–190.

Taghavi, M. R., Dalgleish, T., Moradi, A. R., Neshat-Doost, H. T., & Yule, W. (2003). Selective processing of negative emotional information in children and adolescents with generalized anxiety disorder. *British Journal of Clinical Psychology, 42*, 221–230.

Taghavi, M. R., Moradi, A. R., Neshat-Doost, H. T., Yule, W., & Dalgleish, T. (2000). Interpretation of ambiguous emotional information in clinically anxious children and adolescents. *Cognition and Emotion, 14*, 809–822.

Taghavi, M. R., Neshat-Doost, H. T., Moradi, A. R., Yule, W., & Dalgleish, T. (1999). Biases in visual attention in children and adolescents with clinical anxiety and mixed anxiety-depression. *Journal of Abnormal Child Psychology, 27*, 215–223.

Tomarken, A. J., Mineka, S., & Cook, M. (1989). Fear-relevant selective associations and covariation bias. *Journal of Abnormal Psychology, 98*, 381–394.

Topolski, T. D., Hewitt, J. K., Eaves, L. J., Silberg, J. L., Meyer, J. M., Rutter, M., et al. (1997). Genetic and environmental influences on child reports of manifest anxiety and symptoms of separation anxiety and overanxious disorders: A community-based twin study. *Behavior Genetics, 27*, 15–28.

Vasey, M. W., Daleiden, E. L., Williams, L. L., & Brown, L. M. (1995). Biased attention in childhood anxiety disorders: A preliminary study. *Journal of Abnormal Child Psychology, 23,* 267–279.

Vasey, M. W., Dalgleish, T., & Silverman, W. K. (2003). Research on information-processing factors in child and adolescent psychopathology: A critical commentary. *Journal of Clinical Child and Adolescent Psychology, 32,* 81–93.

Vasey, M. W., El-Hag, N., & Daleiden, E. L. (1996). Anxiety and the processing of emotionally threatening stimuli: Distinctive patterns of selective attention among high- and low-test-anxious children. *Child Development, 67,* 1173–1185.

Vasey, M. W., & MacLeod, C. (2001). Information-processing factors in childhood anxiety: A review and developmental perspective. In M. W. Vasey & M. R. Dadds (Eds.), *The developmental psychopathology of anxiety* (pp. 253–277). New York: Oxford University Press.

Watts, F. N., McKenna, F. P., Sharrock, R., & Trezise, L. (1986). Colour naming of phobia-related words. *British Journal of Psychology, 77,* 97–108.

Watts, S. E., & Weems, C. F. (2006). Associations among selective attention, memory bias, cognitive errors and symptoms of anxiety in youth. *Journal of Abnormal Child Psychology, 34,* 841–852.

Williams, J. M. G. (2001). *Suicide and attempted suicide.* London: Penguin.

Williams, J. M. G., Watts, F. N., MacLeod, C., & Mathews, A. (1997). *Cognitive psychology and emotional disorders.* New York: Wiley.

Yule, W., Udwin, O., & Murdoch, K. (1990). The Jupiter sinking—Effects on children's fears, depression and anxiety. *Journal of Child Psychology and Psychiatry and Allied Disciplines, 31,* 1051–1061.

COGNITION AND EMOTION
2008, 22 (3), 422–436

Development and evaluation of a new paradigm for the assessment of anxiety-disorder-specific interpretation bias using picture stimuli

Tina In-Albon

University of Basel, Basel, Switzerland

Anke Klein, Mike Rinck, and Eni Becker

Radboud University, Nijmegen, The Netherlands

Silvia Schneider

University of Basel, Basel, Switzerland

An important factor in cognitive theories of anxiety disorders is the way in which information is processed. Findings support the existence of a biased information-processing style in anxious children. So far, cognitive biases in children with anxiety disorders are typically assessed as a general phenomenon. Thus, there is a lack of studies in children focusing on anxiety-disorder-specific interpretation bias. A new forced choice paradigm using anxiety-disorder-specific material was developed. Pictures illustrating separation and social situations were carefully generated and evaluated in a pre-study. In a school sample of 265 children the paradigm was investigated. The pictures were able to trigger emotional response and the paradigm demonstrated good internal consistency, and construct validity. Results clearly indicate evidence for content-specificity of the materials. Furthermore, preliminary results suggest a disorder-specific interpretation bias.

INTRODUCTION

Theoretical models of child anxiety disorders (e.g., Kendall, 1985) postulate cognitive factors as being central to the development and maintenance of anxiety. The interpretation bias is one of these factors, resulting in the favouring of emotionally negative interpretations of ambiguous information. Studies investigating children also support the hypothesis that anxious children or children at risk for anxiety disorders tend to favour threatening

Correspondence should be addressed to: Tina In-Albon, Klinische Kinder- und Jugendpsychologie, Institut für Psychologie, Universität Basel, Missionsstrasse 60/62, CH-4055 Basel, Switzerland. E-mail: tina.in-albon@unibas.ch

DOI: 10.1080/02699930701872293

over non-threatening interpretations in ambiguous situations (e.g., Barrett, Rapee, Dadds, & Ryan, 1996; Bögels & Zigterman, 2000; Chorpita, Albano, & Barlow, 1996; Schneider, Unnewehr, Florin, & Margraf, 2002).

In the adult literature, interpretation bias is usually investigated in a disorder-specific manner. These studies suggest that interpretation biases are content specific (e.g., Foa, Franklin, Perry, & Herbert, 1996; Voncken, Bögels, & de Vries, 2003). However, in childhood-anxiety research, most studies investigated groups of mixed anxiety disorders without differentiating between specific subtypes (e.g., Barrett et al., 1996; Bögels & Zigterman, 2000; Chorpita et al., 1996). For a better understanding of the specific anxiety disorders and the development of even more effective treatments than those currently available (In-Albon & Schneider, 2007), a comprehensive understanding of disorder-specific cognitive distortions is needed.

Only very few studies have investigated content specificity among anxiety disorders in children and in most of them the content specificity was only a side focus (Bögels, Snieder & Kindt, 2003; Dalgleish et al., 2003; Muris et al., 2000). Results from Dalgleish et al. (2003) support the hypothesis of a difference between anxious (PTSD and GAD) and depressed participants but not between GAD and PTSD participants. Muris and colleagues (2000) exposed non-clinical children to stories reflecting social anxiety, separation anxiety, and generalised anxiety. Results provided no evidence for a specific interpretation bias for different types of anxiety. Bögels et al. (2003) found partial support for a situation-specific bias. Children high on symptoms of separation anxiety and social anxiety displayed a more frequent negative interpretation bias in situations relevant to their fear than children high on symptoms of GAD. However, children high on separation anxiety and social anxiety could not be differentiated from each other. Summarising these results, it remains unclear whether there are cognitive biases specific to the different types of anxiety disorders. However, there are several weaknesses of these studies that need to be mentioned. Most important, the material used was often not developed for investigating disorder-specific interpretation bias (e.g., Bögels et al., 2003; Dalgleish et al., 2003; Muris et al., 2000). Another problem is that only a few studies systematically investigated the psychometric properties of the questionnaires or other measures of interpretation bias utilised in their studies (e.g., Muris, Jacques, & Mayer, 2004; Schneider, In-Albon, Rose, & Ehrenreich, 2006). However, a sufficient reliability and validity of the used materials is an essential condition for a proper and solid investigation of disorder-specific interpretation bias. Thus, the unclear findings may also be a consequence of the weak reliability and validity of the used material.

The present study had two aims: First, the development of a disorder-specific paradigm for the investigation of disorder-specific interpretation bias in children with separation anxiety disorder (SAD) or social phobia. Second, to test the reliability and validity of the paradigm in school children.

METHOD

Pre-study: Development of the pictures

Since interpretation bias in children with SAD and social phobia will be studied, it was decided to establish a language-free method due to the typically young age of these children (Cartwright-Hatton, McNicol, & Doubleday, 2006). A forced choice paradigm using pictures as stimuli was developed with a set of pictures consisting of separation situations and social situations. In a pre-study, a set of 86 standardised and disorder-specific colour photographs representing two disorders, SAD and social phobia, were developed and empirically validated with school children. Social-situation pictures represent social interactions between children and separa-tion-situation pictures represent arrival and departure situations between a mother and a child. Pictures consist of three different types of separation situations (departure, arrival, ambiguous departure/arrival) and social situations (popular, unpopular, ambiguous popular/unpopular). Girls and boys had separate sets of gender-specific pictures. Figure 1 presents an example of separation situation pictures. All pictures had a size of 600 × 450 pixels and were presented on a computer screen with a resolution of 1024 × 768 pixels.

For the validation of the pictures, 253 Swiss school children (134 girls and 119 boys, 6–14 years of age) were asked to indicate to what extent each

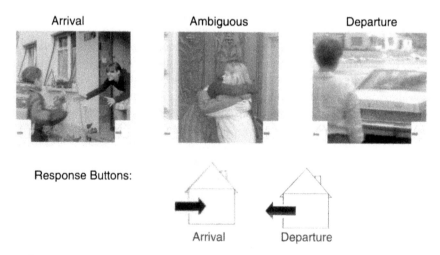

Figure 1.   Separation-related pictures (arrival, departure, ambiguous) and response buttons.

picture displayed an arrival/departure situation (for the separation-anxiety-related pictures) or a popular/unpopular child (for the social-phobia-related pictures), using a 9-point Likert scale ranging from "*definite arrival*" to "*definite departure*", or "*really popular*" to "*really unpopular*", respectively. Depending on the children's appraisal, each picture was assigned to one of the following stimulus categories: "definitive arrival", "definitive departure" or "ambiguous departure or arrival", and "definitive popular", "definitive unpopular" or "ambiguous popular or unpopular", respectively. On the basis of these appraisals, 6 non-ambiguous pictures, 8 ambiguous pictures, and 4 practice pictures of the separation situations and social situations were chosen for the forced choice paradigm.

Forced choice paradigm

A fixation cross in the centre of a white screen was presented for 500 ms. The child was shown one picture at a time and was asked to press one of two response buttons (departure or arrival and popular or unpopular, respectively) as quickly and as accurately as possible to indicate whether the picture represented a departure/arrival situation or a popular/unpopular child. Response buttons for arrival displayed a house with an arrow leading into the house; departure was indicated with an arrow leading out of the house. The symbol for popular displayed a group of figures all standing together, unpopular was represented by figures standing together except for one standing alone (see Figure 1). The presented picture remained on the screen until the child made the response. There were 4 practice trials. The experiment was created and run using the E-Prime 1.1.3 software package (Psychology Software Tool, Inc., Pittsburgh, USA).

The child was asked to classify 8 ambiguous pictures and 6 non-ambiguous pictures for each of the two categories (departure or arrival; popular or unpopular). The pictures within each category were presented in a random order to each child. The dependent variable was the frequency of chosen category. To be prepared for the task, children learned in a practice trial the location of the response buttons, which were positioned next to each other on the keyboard and had to be pressed with the index finger of the preferred hand.

To evaluate the paradigm and its feasibility, the paradigm was used in a first step with school children. Children were presented non-ambiguous and ambiguous pictures depicting social- and separation-related situations and were asked to choose either a response defined as positive (arrival, popular) or defined as negative (departure, unpopular) as quickly as possible.

Picture-rating task

After the forced choice paradigm, each child rated the set of 28 pictures with regard to their category (e.g., arrival/departure; popular/unpopular) without time pressure, in the same manner used during the pre-study. This was to control whether the children assigned the non-ambiguous pictures to the correct category (dependent variable: "category rating"). After the paradigm, the valence and arousal associated with the viewing of each picture was measured using the Self-Assessment Manikin (SAM; Bradley & Lang, 1994). The unlabelled dimensions were represented pictorially on a 9-point scale. Figure 2 shows the SAM figure with pleasure and arousal on the top and bottom rows, respectively. Children were instructed to make a mark for each dimension, either on or between the figures (dependent variable: "valence rating").

Measures

State anxiety.   Since there is evidence that high levels of state anxiety at baseline are associated with increased threat perception and lower threat threshold (MacLeod, 1990; Muris, Rapee, Meesters, Schouten, & Geers, 2003), children's level of state anxiety before and after the forced choice paradigm was assessed. The child was asked to indicate state anxiety on a 0- to 10-point Likert scale ranging from *"not anxious at all"* to *"very anxious"*.

Questionnaires.   To get a clinical description of the sample, general anxiety and depression were assessed as well as disorder-specific separation anxiety and social anxiety. Anxiety sensitivity was assessed due to its association with separation as well as social anxiety (e.g., Schneider & Hensdiek, 2003). Due to time limitations, short versions of widely used anxiety and depression self-report questionnaires were empirically developed and evaluated in a German-speaking sample (Scalbert, In-Albon, &

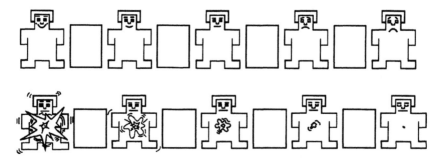

Figure 2.   Self-Assessment Manikin (SAM; Bradley & Lang, 1994). Figures assessing pleasure (top) and arousal (bottom).

Schneider, 2006, unpublished master thesis) and used instead of complete questionnaires.

The *Childhood Anxiety Sensitivity Index* (CASI; Silverman, Fleisig, Rabian, & Peterson, 1991; German translation by Schneider & Hensdiek, 1994) was administered in order to assess anxiety sensitivity. The CASI used in this study is a 10-item questionnaire assessing fear of anxiety symptoms in children on a 3-point Likert scale ranging from 1 *"never"* to 3 *"often"*. Internal consistency of the German short version was .72.

The *Revised Children's Manifest Anxiety Scale* (RCMAS; Reynolds & Richmond, 1978; Boehnke, Silbereisen, Reynolds, & Richmond, 1986) is a self-report measure to assess manifest anxiety. The RCMAS used in this study was a short version of 6 items in which the sum of the individual "yes" or "no" responses was calculated to yield a total anxiety score. The test–retest reliability of the RCMAS short version was 0.74 (Boehnke et al., 1986) and Cronbach's alpha for the German short version was .67. The *Children's Depression Inventory* (CDI; Kovacs, 1981; German Version DIKJ, Stiensmeier-Pelster, Schürmann, & Duda, 2000) is a self-report measure of depression for children and adolescents. The CDI used in this study included 10 items related to the cognitive, affective, and behavioural signs of depression. Each item had a range of three choices. Children were instructed to choose the choice that best characterised them over the past 2 weeks. The German short version of the CDI had an internal consistency of .76.

To assess separation anxiety 5 items were chosen from the separation subscale of the *Spence Children's Anxiety Scale* (SCAS; Spence, 1998; German version Essau, Muris, & Ederer, 2002). Each item is rated on a 4-point scale in terms of its frequency from 1 *"never"* to 4 *"always"*. Internal consistency of the SCAS subscale was .66. Social anxiety was assessed with 5 items of the *Social Anxiety Scale for Children* (SASC; La Greca, Dandes, Wick, Shaw, & Stone, 1988; German version Melfsen & Florin, 1997). The SASC is designed to assess anxiety in children in relation to social interactions. Remaining consistent with the scale used in the SCAS, children were asked to respond to various statements using a 4-point scale from 1 *"not at all true"* to 4 *"always true"*. Internal consistency of the SASC subscale was .59.

Pilot study

The paradigm was tested with 5 children (3 girls and 2 boys) with a mean age of 6.6 years ($SD = 0.55$, range 5–7 years). After the paradigm children were asked whether the task was easy or difficult, if they had fun or found it boring, and if the instructions and button-symbols were clear. Results confirmed feasibility and comprehensibility of the paradigm in these children.

Participants

A total of 265 children were recruited from different schools in Basel, Switzerland, and Nijmegen, The Netherlands. There was a minor, but significant age difference between the Basel and Nijmegen sample, $t(263) = 4.58$, $p < .01$. Gender and age distributions in the two groups and the combined sample are shown in Table 1.

Procedure

Children and their parents gave written consent to participate in this study, which informed them of the child's right to withdraw at any time. No child withdrew his or her participation. Children were tested individually or in pairs in a quiet room with the assistance of a graduate student. Before and after the paradigm, state anxiety was assessed. After the experiment, the children were asked to complete the picture rating task and the questionnaires. Duration of the paradigm was about 30 minutes.

RESULTS

Descriptives

An alpha level of .05 was used for all statistical tests. Table 2 presents the means and standard deviations on the RCMAS, CDI, CASI, SOC and SAD items as well as the internal consistency of each questionnaire of the current sample. As can be seen from Table 2, children in the present study displayed low means and little variation on all scales of anxiety and depression (SDs between 1.49 and 3.65). As expected, girls had higher anxiety and depression scores than boys. There was a significant age effect on the separation anxiety items, in that younger children reported higher levels of separation anxiety than older children, $F(1, 6) = 2.39$, $p = .03$. State anxiety assessed before the paradigm was low ($M = 0.97$, $SD = 1.79$; Range 1–10) and decreased further during the paradigm ($M = 0.78$).

TABLE 1
Gender and age distributions of the Basel, Nijmegen and the combined samples

	Basel	Nijmegen	Combined sample
N	103	162	265
Gender	52 girls, 51 boys	78 girls, 84 boys	130 girls, 135 boys
Age M (SD)	10.3 (1.98)	9.3 (1.57)	9.69 (1.8)
	Range 7–13 years	Range 7–12 years	Range 7–13 years

TABLE 2
Cronbach's α of questionnaires, means (standard deviations), and range of anxiety and depression measures of the total sample and for both sexes

	Cronbach's α	Total M (SD)	Range (min./max.)	Girls M (SD)	Boys M (SD)
RCMAS	.46	10.06 (1.49)	6–12 (6/12)	9.85 (1.66)	10.24 (1.27)
CASI	.74	15.77 (3.65)	8–27 (10/30)	16.20 (3.76)	15.27 (3.39)
SAD	.50	8.85 (2.51)	5–17 (5/20)	9.23 (2.52)	8.47 (2.46)
SOC	.54	9.96 (2.83)	5–20 (5/20)	10.47 (3.08)	9.45 (2.48)
CDI	.66	14.29 (2.91)	9–23 (0/30)	14.54 (2.92)	14.07 (2.89)

In a first step, we tested whether the sample from Basel and Nijmegen were comparable and could be treated as one sample. The dependent variables of these six analyses were: the chosen category for each picture type (social and separation pictures), ratings of the pictures, and valence ratings. Each of these analyses involved picture type as within-subject factor, sample site and gender as between-subject factors, and age as a covariate. Age was used as a covariate since there was a significant age difference between the Basel and the Nijmegen sample. The critical question was whether there was an interaction between sample site and picture type. This was neither the case for choices regarding social pictures ($p = .14$) nor separation pictures ($p = .18$). Concerning the picture ratings, there was a significant interaction for social pictures ($p = .01$), but not for separation pictures ($p = .11$), reflecting slightly more insecure ratings of the non-ambiguous social pictures in the Nijmegen sample. Concerning the valence ratings, there was no significant interaction for the social pictures ($p = .26$), but an interaction was found for separation pictures ($p < .01$), in that the Nijmegen sample rated the valence of the separation pictures as more unpleasant, however the means tended in the same direction ($M = 4.35$ vs. $M = 3.44$). In summary, both groups showed similar effects of the picture types and could therefore be treated as one sample.

Test of stimulus material. Before running main analyses (reliability, validity, disorder specificity), we tested whether children in the present study assigned the pictures to the same categories as the children of the pre-study.

Picture ratings. The children's ratings of the pictures' contents, their valence ratings, and the arousal associated with viewing the pictures, indicated that the children categorised the pictures in the hypothesised manner. Ratings of non-ambiguous pictures ranged from 1.33 (arrival) and 2.02 (popular) to 7.91 (departure) and 7.81 (unpopular). Ambiguous pictures ranged in between with a mean of 5.13 for ambiguous separation and 4.51 for ambiguous social pictures. Valence and arousal ratings indicate that the pictures elicited an emotional response. However, the unpleasantness of the departure/unpopular (negative) pictures was only mildly threatening ($Ms = 5.43$ and 6.25; $1 = very pleasant$, $9 = very unpleasant$).

Forced choices.   Similarly, under time pressure, children categorised the non-ambiguous pictures in the expected manner; 93.06% chose arrival when an arrival situation was displayed and 83.59% chose departure when viewing a departure picture (popular = 83.19%, unpopular = 85.61%). For the ambiguous separation pictures, children chose 53.84% arrival and for the ambiguous social pictures 54.5% popular.

Reliability

Cronbach's alpha for the category ratings, the valence ratings, and for the chosen categories of the ambiguous pictures are reported in Table 3. Results generally supported good internal consistencies. However, as expected, reliability of chosen category for ambiguous pictures showed the lowest Cronbach's alpha.

Construct validity

Correlations of valence ratings and category ratings, and correlations between questionnaire scores and valence ratings within the social or separation category are presented in Table 4. Correlations between the valence ratings and the category ratings indicated that the pictures categorised as arrival and popular were significantly associated with pleasantness, whereas the pictures categorised as departure and unpopular were significantly associated with unpleasantness. Pictures categorised as

TABLE 3
Internal consistency (Cronbach's α) for category ratings, valence ratings, and chosen responses of the separation and social ambiguous pictures

	Cronbach's α
Category rating	
Separation ambiguous picture	.59
Social ambiguous picture	.71
Valence rating	
Separation ambiguous picture	.79
Social ambiguous picture	.83
Chosen category	
Separation ambiguous picture	.44
Social ambiguous picture	.57

TABLE 4

Correlations between valence ratings and category ratings and between valence ratings and questionnaires

| | Valence ratings | | | | | |
| | Separation | | | Social | | |
Category rating	Arrival	Departure	Ambiguous	Popular	Unpopular	Ambiguous
Arrival	.35**	.09	.15*	–	–	–
Departure	-.26**	.16*	.02	–	–	–
Ambiguous separation	.01	.13*	.49**	–	–	–
Popular	–	–	–	.63**	.08	.11
Unpopular	–	–	–	-.23**	.19**	.14*
Ambiguous social	–	–	–	.09	.06	.42**
Questionnaire						
RCMAS	.10	.23**	.16**	.08	.21**	.12
CASI	.01	.30**	.22**	.05	.32**	.25**
SAD	.03	.14*	.15*	.08	.16*	.09
SOC	.04	.08	.08	.01	.15*	.09
CDI	.09	.23**	.12	.15*	.21**	.13*

Note: **$p < .01$; *$p < .05$.

ambiguous were rated as pleasant. Correlations between questionnaire scores and valence ratings displayed the expected pattern, in that higher levels of anxiety were accompanied with more unpleasantness when viewing negative (departure and unpopular) and ambiguous separation and social pictures. The same pattern was found for the correlations between arousal and anxiety level: as children's separation anxiety (SAD) and anxiety sensitivity (CASI) increased their tendency to be aroused when viewing departure pictures, $r(110) = -.28$, $p < .01$; $r(109) = -.25$, $p < .01$, and ambiguous separation pictures, $r(110) = -.28$, $p < .01$; $r(109) = -.22$, $p = .02$, increased also. Analyses were redone while controlling for gender, age, and state anxiety yielding the same results. Furthermore, when viewing ambiguous separation pictures, unpleasantness was associated with significantly more separation relevant threat (departure) interpretations, $r(259) = .16$, $p = .04$; controlled for gender and age, and when viewing ambiguous social pictures, unpleasantness was significantly correlated with social relevant threat (unpopular) interpretations, $r(259) = .26$, $p < .01$; controlled for gender and age.

In addition, correlations of valence ratings and chosen categories, as well as correlations of category rating and chosen categories were computed. The correlation of the valence of ambiguous separation pictures and arrival chosen for ambiguous separation pictures was significant, $r(259) = .16$, $p = .01$, as well as the correlation of the valence of ambiguous social pictures and popular chosen for ambiguous social pictures, $r(259) = .26$, $p < .01$, indicating that the unpleasantness of the pictures was associated with more threat interpretations. The correlation of category rating and chosen category was significant for ambiguous social pictures, $r(261) = .29$, $p < .01$, as well as for ambiguous separation pictures, $r(260) = .31$, $p < .01$, indicating that ratings and chosen categories are related, but do not measure the same construct.

Disorder specificity

Partial correlations (controlling for gender, age and state anxiety) between disorder-specific anxiety scores and chosen category indicated that as separation anxiety increased the tendency to chose arrival when viewing an ambiguous picture also increased, $r(252) = .15$, $p = .01$. The association between social anxiety and chosen category was significant, in that as children's social anxiety increased the tendency to chose unpopular when viewing an ambiguous social picture also increased, $r(252) = .13$, $p = .05$. In both cases the effects sizes were relatively small.

Additional analyses

There was a significant age effect, in that younger children categorised the ambiguous separation pictures as arrival significantly more often than older children, $F(1, 6) = 3.18$, $p = .01$. Conversely, older children categorised these pictures as departure significantly more often than younger children, $F(1, 6) = 3.59$, $p < .01$. No age effect was found for social ambiguous pictures. No differences were observed for error rates on the non-ambiguous pictures, indicating that younger children did not make more mistakes categorising the non-ambiguous pictures.

DISCUSSION

The present study had two aims: First, the development of a disorder-specific paradigm with picture stimuli. Second, to test the reliability and validity of the paradigm in school children. These aims were accomplished to the furthest extent possible.

Results of the evaluation of the pictures indicated that they trigger an emotional state. First, the ratings of the pictures confirmed that the children in the present study assigned the pictures to the same categories as the children of the pre-study. Second, valence and arousal ratings indicated that pictures defined as positive (arrival, popular) were more pleasant and relaxing than pictures defined as negative (departure, unpopular). The low arousal elicited by the pictures indicated that they are ethically appropriate.

Overall, results indicated that the pictures and the paradigm were reliable and valid. Analyses of the internal consistencies regarding the ambiguous pictures indicated good levels of internal consistency for the category ratings and the valence ratings, and, as expected, somewhat lower internal consistencies for the chosen categories.

The first step in establishing the construct validity was to correlate anxiety scores with valence and arousal. Correlations between anxiety scores and valence ratings displayed the expected pattern: Higher levels of anxiety were accompanied by more unpleasantness when viewing negative (departure and unpopular) and ambiguous separation and social pictures. The same pattern was found for the correlations between anxiety scores and arousal: Children high on separation anxiety (SAD) and anxiety sensitivity (CASI) were significantly more aroused when viewing departure pictures and when viewing ambiguous separation pictures. These results indicate that the pictures elicited the expected reaction. The association between rating and chosen category was low but significant, indicating that they are related, but do not measure the same construct. Therefore, it is useful to assess both the ratings without time pressure and the forced choice as a spontaneous measure.

In a next step, as yet another evidence for construct validity, while viewing ambiguous separation pictures, unpleasantness was associated with significantly more separation-relevant threat (departure) interpretations and, while viewing ambiguous social pictures, unpleasantness was significantly correlated with social-relevant threat (unpopular) interpretations.

Taken together, these results indicate that the material developed is disorder specific, which is an essential condition to assess a disorder-specific interpretation bias. Thus, disorder specificity could be investigated. The association between disorder-specific anxiety scores in relation to choices for ambiguous pictures indicated that as children's social anxiety increased so did the tendency to interpret ambiguous social pictures as more threatening. The relationship between separation anxiety and choices for ambiguous separation pictures indicated that as children's separation anxiety increased so did interpretations of ambiguous separation pictures as arrival. The socially anxious children results were as expected. However, the results of the separation anxious children went in the opposite direction, in that they did not choose more threatening interpretations of ambiguous pictures, but chose the arrival interpretation significantly more often, which was defined as a positive interpretation. Weems, Berman, Silverman, and Saavedra (2001) reported that age moderated the relation between types of cognitive errors (catastrophising, over generalising, personalising, and selective abstraction) and manifest anxiety. According to this, we conducted an additional analysis, to see whether the processing of ambiguous pictures was influenced by age, which was confirmed. Our finding that age moderated the interpretation of ambiguous situations may be due to cognitive development, in that younger children may "see" what they want to see and therefore show higher rates of positive interpretations, and chose more arrival when viewing ambiguous separation pictures. This interesting finding, indicating that young children may process threatening material differently to older children has to be further investigated. Independent of age, all children were accurate at identifying non-ambiguous separation and social pictures.

Another explanation for why separation anxious children may not have shown a threatening interpretation may be that, according to Mogg and Bradley (2004), one reason for lack of cognitive biases is low state anxiety. State anxiety in the current study, which was assessed before and after the paradigm, was low (< 1, Range 1–10) and had little variance ($SD < 1.85$). In addition, self-reported anxiety and mood levels were low and had, in comparison to other school samples studies, little variance (see also Table 2, Muris et al., 2000). Because of the small variance in the current study, correlations also had to be low. Therefore, any effect could be hidden due to a "deflated correlation".

Summarising the results of the present study, we found evidence for content specificity of the material, its reliability, validity, and ability to evoke emotional reactions. Furthermore, even in a school sample with small variance of anxiety we found first evidence for the association of disorder-specific threat interpretation in children showing higher social anxiety and a disorder-specific interpretation of ambiguous separation picture in children showing higher separation anxiety. In line with other studies (Bögels et al., 2003; Dalgleish et al., 2003), current results encourage further research for a disorder-specific interpretation bias in childhood anxiety disorders. Therefore as a next step, this paradigm needs to be investigated in clinically anxious children.

Limitations

Because of low anxiety scores and few variances in the current sample, the present study was not able to assess clinically relevant interpretation biases. Thus, a test with clinically anxious children is needed. We are currently recruiting children with clinical diagnoses of separation anxiety disorder, children with social phobia, children with other anxiety disorders, and healthy controls. Except for the CASI, the items chosen from the original questionnaires to form their abridged versions may not be completely adequate in assessing the desired construct, even though the choice of the individual items were based on empirical data.

In conclusion, the forced choice paradigm using disorder-specific pictures seems to be suitable for triggering emotional responses in children with no or limited reading abilities.

REFERENCES

Barrett, P. M., Rapee, R. M., Dadds, M. R., & Ryan, S. M. (1996). Family enhancement of cognitive style in anxious and aggressive children: Threat bias and the FEAR effect. *Journal of Abnormal Child Psychology, 24,* 187–203.

Boehnke, K., Silbereisen, R. K., Reynolds, C. R., & Richmond, B. O. (1986). What I think and feel—German experience with the revised form of the Children's Manifest Anxiety Scale. *Personality and Individual Differences, 7,* 553–560.

Bögels, S. M., Snieder, N., & Kindt, M. (2003). Specificity of dysfunctional thinking in children with symptoms of social anxiety, separation anxiety and generalized anxiety. *Behaviour Change, 20*(3), 160–169.

Bögels, S., & Zigterman, D. (2000). Dysfunctional cognitions in children with social phobia, separation anxiety disorder and generalized anxiety disorder. *Journal of Abnormal Child Psychology, 28*(2), 205–211.

Bradley, M. M., & Lang, P. J. (1994). Measuring emotion: The Self-Assessment Manikin and the Semantic Differential. *Journal of Behavior Therapy and Experimental Psychiatry, 25*(1), 49–59.

Cartwright-Hatton, S., McNicol, K., & Doubleday, E. (2006). Anxiety in a neglected population: Prevalence of anxiety disorders in pre-adolescent children. *Clinical Psychology Review, 26*(7), 817–833.

Chorpita, B. F., Albano, A. M., & Barlow, D. H. (1996). Cognitive processing in children: Relationship to anxiety and family influences. *Journal of Clinical Child Psychology, 25,* 170–176.

Dalgleish, T., Taghavi, R., Neshat-Doost, H., Moradi, A., Canterbury, R., & Yule, W. (2003). Patterns of processing bias for emotional information across clinical disorders: A comparison of attention, memory, and prospective cognition in children and adolescents with depression, generalized anxiety, and posttraumatic stress disorder. *Journal of Clinical Child and Adolescent Psychology, 32*(1), 10–21.

E-Prime 1.1.3. (2000). [Computer software]. Pittsburgh, PA: Psychology Software Tools.

Essau, C. A., Muris, P., & Ederer, E. M. (2002). Reliability and validity of the Spence Children's Anxiety Scale and the Screen for Child Anxiety Related Emotional Disorders in German children. *Journal of Behavior Therapy and Experimental Psychiatry, 33,* 1–18.

Foa, E. B., Franklin, M. E., Perry, K. J., & Herbert, J. D. (1996). Cognitive biases in generalized social phobia. *Journal of Abnormal Psychology, 105,* 433–439.

In-Albon, T., & Schneider, S. (2007). Psychotherapy of childhood anxiety disorders: A meta-analysis. *Psychotherapy and Psychosomatics, 76,* 15–24.

Kendall, P. C. (1985). Toward a cognitive-behavioral model of child psychopathology and a critique of related interventions. *Journal of Abnormal Child Psychology, 13,* 357–372.

Kovacs, M. (1981). Rating scales to assess depression in school-aged children. *Acta Paedopsychiatrica, 46,* 305–315.

La Greca, A. M., Dandes, S. K., Wick, P., Shaw, K., & Stone, W. L. (1988). Development of the social anxiety scale for children: Reliability and concurrent validity. *Journal of Clinical Child Psychology, 17,* 84–91.

MacLeod, C. (1990). Mood disorders and cognition. In M. W. Eysenck (Ed.), *Cognitive psychology: An international review* (pp. 9–56). Chichester, UK: Wiley.

Melfsen, S., & Florin, I. (1997). Die Social Anxiety Scale for Children Revised. Deutschsprachige Version (SASC-R-D). *Kindheit und Entwicklung, 6,* 224–229.

Mogg, K., & Bradley, B. P. (2004). A cognitive-motivational perspective on the processing of threat information and anxiety. In J. Yiend (Ed.), *Cognition, emotion, and psychopathology: Theoretical, empirical, and clinical approaches* (pp. 68–85). Cambridge, UK: Cambridge University Press.

Muris, P., Jacques, P., & Mayer, B. (2004). The stability of threat perception abnormalities and anxiety disorder symptoms in non-clinical children. *Child Psychiatry and Human Development, 34*(3), 251–265.

Muris, P., Kindt, M., Bögels, S. M., Merckelbach, H., Gadet, B., & Mouleart, V. (2000). Anxiety and threat perception abnormalities in normal children. *Journal of Psychopathology and Behavioral Assessment, 22,* 183–199.

Muris, P., Rapee, R., Meesters, C., Schouten, E., & Geers, M. (2003). Threat perception abnormalities in children: The role of anxiety disorders symptoms, chronic anxiety, and state anxiety. *Anxiety Disorders, 17,* 271–287.

Reynolds, C. R., & Richmond, B. O. (1978). What I think and feel: A revised measure of children's manifest anxiety. *Journal of Abnormal Child Psychology, 6,* 271–280.

Scalbert, M., In-Albon, T., & Schneider, S. (2006). *Psychometrische Gütekriterien des Trennungsangst-Inventars für Kinder [Psychometric properties of the Separation Anxiety Inventory]*. Unpublished Masters' Thesis, Universität Basel.

Schneider, S., & Hensdiek, M. (1994). *Children Anxiety Sensitivity Index (CASI) [Kinder Angstsensitivitätsindex (KASI)]*. Unpublished manuscript, Technische Universität Dresden, Deutschland.

Schneider, S., & Hensdiek, M. (2003). Panikanfälle und Angstsensitivität im Jugendalter. *Zeitschrift für Klinische Psychologie und Psychotherapie, 32,* 219–227.

Schneider, S., In-Albon, T., Rose, U., & Ehrenreich, J. T. (2006). Measurement of panic interpretation bias using the Anxiety Interpretation Questionnaire for children. *Journal of Cognitive Psychotherapy, 20*(1), 485–497.

Schneider, S., Unnewehr, S., Florin, I., & Margraf, J. (2002). Priming panic interpretations in children of patients with panic disorder. *Journal of Anxiety Disorders, 16,* 605–624.

Silverman, W. K., Fleisig, W., Rabian, B., & Peterson, R. A. (1991). Childhood Anxiety Sensitivity Index (CASI). *Journal of Clinical Child Psychology, 20,* 162–168.

Spence, S. H. (1998). A measure of anxiety symptoms among children. *Behaviour Research and Therapy, 36,* 545–566.

Stiensmeier-Pelster, J., Schürmann, M., & Duda, K. (2000). *Depressions-Inventar für Kinder und Jugendliche (DIKJ)*. Göttingen, Germany: Hogrefe.

Voncken, M. J., Bögels, S. M., & de Vries, K. (2003). Interpretation and judgmental biases in social phobia. *Behaviour Research and Therapy, 41,* 1481–1488.

Weems, C. F., Berman, S. L., Silverman, W. K., & Saavedra, L. M. (2001). Cognitive errors in youth with anxiety disorders: The linkages between negative cognitive errors and anxious symptoms. *Cognitive Therapy and Research, 25*(5), 559–575.

COGNITION AND EMOTION
2008, 22 (3), 437–458

Processing of faces and emotional expressions in infants at risk of social phobia

Cathy Creswell

University of Reading, UK

Matt Woolgar

Institute of Psychiatry, London, UK

Peter Cooper, Andreas Giannakakis, and Elizabeth Schofield

University of Reading, UK

Andrew W. Young

University of York, UK

Lynne Murray

University of Reading, UK

Individuals with social phobia display social information processing biases yet their aetiological significance is unclear. Infants of mothers with social phobia and control infants' responses were assessed at 10 days, 10 and 16 weeks, and 10 months to faces versus non-faces, variations in intensity of emotional expressions, and gaze direction. Infant temperament and maternal behaviours were also assessed. Both groups showed a preference for faces over non-faces at 10 days and 10 weeks, and full faces over profiles at 16 weeks; they also looked more to high vs. low intensity angry faces at 10 weeks, and fearful faces at 10 months; however, index infants' initial orientation and overall looking to high-intensity fear faces was relatively less

---

Correspondence should be addressed to: Cathy Creswell, Winnicott Research Unit, School of Psychology, University of Reading, Whiteknights, Reading, Berkshire RG6 6AH, UK. E-mail: c.creswell@reading.ac.uk

This work was supported by a programme grant from the Medical Research Council (UK) to LM and PC (ref G9324094).

We are grateful to Susan Campbell, Amber Davis, Melanie Edwards, Rachel Kelly, Paula Liberton, Chiara Navarra, Monika Parkinson, Joanna Pearson, Melanie Royal-Lawson, Caroline Sack, Barbara Sana, Hannah Seabrook, and Sheila Summers for assistance, variously, with recruitment and assessment of study participants, and coding of interaction data. We thank Nancy Snidman and Jerome Kagan for their support with assessment of infant behavioural inhibition. We thank Mark Johnson, John Morton and Francesca Simion for their invaluable advice on the design of this study.

DOI: 10.1080/02699930701872392

than controls at 10 weeks. This was not explained by infant temperament or maternal behaviours. The findings suggest that offspring of mothers with social phobia show processing biases to emotional expressions in infancy.

INTRODUCTION

Social phobia is a chronic, debilitating disorder, affecting 7 to 13% of individuals, and is characterised by intense fear of scrutiny and negative evaluation by others (Yonkers, Dyck, & Keller, 2001). Little is known about its aetiology (e.g., Rapee & Spence, 2004). Disturbances in social information processing, particularly of faces and emotional expressions, have been implicated in the maintenance of social phobia in both adults (e.g., Bögels & Mansell, 2004) and children (e.g., Hadwin et al., 2003; Stirling, Eley, & Clark, 2006); yet, whether they are of aetiological significance is unknown. The purpose of this study was to investigate early characteristics of processing of face and emotional expression in infants at risk of social phobia.

Processing of faces and emotional expressions in social anxiety

Studies of processing of faces and emotional expressions among individuals with social phobia can be considered in three categories of response to: (i) face vs. non-face stimuli; (ii) direct vs. averted gaze; and (iii) emotional expressions. In adults, studies of responses to face vs. non-face stimuli have shown that, in conditions of threat, socially anxious individuals direct attention away from faces, including those with positive expressions (Garner, Mogg, & Bradley, 2006; Mansell, Clark, Ehlers, & Chen, 1999), and, in clinic populations, this generalises to non-threat conditions (Chen, Ehlers, Clark, & Mansell, 2002). The avoidance of eye contact has been a frequently noted characteristic of the clinical profile of social phobia (Trower & Gilbert, 1989), and information-processing studies have shown that adults with social phobia spend less time scanning prominent facial features, such as the eyes, than non-anxious people (Horley, Williams, Gonsalvez, & Gordon, 2003).

More evidence exists regarding socially anxious adults' responses to emotional facial expressions. This suggests that affected individuals do not differ from non-socially anxious adults in their ability to correctly identify different types of emotion, whether in clinical (e.g., Merckelbach, Van Hout, Ven den Hout, & Mersch, 1989; Phillipot & Douillez, 2005) or non-clinical (Douillez & Phillipot, 2003) populations. However, studies show that socially anxious individuals exhibit distinctive attentional responses to emotional faces (e.g., Bögels & Mansell, 2004), identify angry faces at lower levels of emotional intensity (Joorman & Gotlib, 2006), and interpret ambiguous facial expressions as threatening (Yoon & Zinbarg, 2007). These studies suggest that, while social anxiety is not associated with differences in ability to recognise emotional expressions, it is associated with a heightened sensitivity to potentially threatening facial expressions at early stages in processing. Furthermore, there is growing support for the vigilance–avoidance hypothesis (e.g., Mogg, Bradley, de Bono, & Painter, 1997), which suggests that while socially anxious individuals initially direct attention towards relevant threat cues (hypervigilance), they then avoid them. It is not clear whether this reflects a general emotionality bias (e.g., Mansell et al., 1999), or else a more specific negativity bias (e.g., Winton, Clark, & Edelman, 1995).

Fewer studies have examined responses to face stimuli in socially anxious children, and only tentative conclusions can be drawn. First, in contrast to studies with adults, deficits in emotion discrimination *have* been reported among younger populations, in both clinic (Simonian, Beidel, Turner, Berkes, & Long, 2001) and non-clinic samples (Battaglia et al., 2004; Melfsen & Florin, 2002). Overall, studies suggest that socially anxious children have general difficulties in emotion discrimination, rather than their simply interpreting faces in an overly *negative* way.

Second, an association between social anxiety and attentional processes has been identified among younger populations. Specifically, child social anxiety symptoms (but not general anxiety) have been found to be associated with avoidance of both fearful and angry faces (Stirling et al., 2006).

The place of social information processing in the aetiology of social phobia

The extent to which the characteristic information-processing biases evident in adults and children with social phobia are implicated in the development of the disorder, or are a consequence of social anxiety, is unclear. Social phobia is known to aggregate in families (e.g., Lieb et al., 2000; Mancini, van Ameringen, Szatmari, Fugere, & Boyle, 1996), with a genetic contribution accounting for about 10% of heritability (Nelson et al., 2000). Some investigators have proposed that genetically-based individual differences in social skills, including poor abilities to discriminate facial expressions of emotion, lead to repeated experiences of social failure, which in turn lead to social anxiety (Rapee & Spence, 2004). Similarly, the "integral bias hypothesis" proposes that individual cognitive biases, such as the propensity to avoid certain social stimuli, are an integral part of (or a risk factor for) social anxiety, and, as such, should be detectable among at-risk infants (Richards, French, Nash, Hadwin, & Donnelly, 2007). The "inferred-bias hypothesis", by contrast, proposes that social anxiety itself may interfere with social information processing (McClure & Nowicki, 2001; Richards et al., 2007). This suggests that social information processing and skills deficits should increase with age and are unlikely to be apparent in early infancy. Finally, the "inhibition hypothesis", posits that a bias for threatening stimuli is normal in young children but, whereas non-anxious children learn to inhibit such responses, those with high anxiety are unable to do so (Kindt & van den Hout, 2001).

These hypotheses have been subjected to little investigation, and none in relation to the development of social anxiety. Nevertheless, infancy research has provided a wealth of data regarding the normative development of infants' responses to faces that could elucidate the merits of the competing hypotheses.

Face processing in infancy

Even young infants have specialised responses to the face (see Slater, 1998). Studies of face processing among infants can be considered in the same three categories as for adults.

Despite their poor visual acuity, even young infants show social perceptual abilities (Muir & Nadel, 1998), and fairly consistent evidence has emerged indicating that new-born infants can discriminate, and prefer, simple face-like vs., non-face-like stimuli (Easterbrook, Kisilevsky, Muir & Laplante, 1999; Johnson & Morton, 1991); and, by two months, this is well established (e.g., Maurer & Barrera, 1981). By 5 months, infants are more discriminating, and will only show a face preference if the stimuli are complex (Morton & Johnson, 1991).

With regard to responses to gaze, infants show particular interest in people's eyes from about 2 months (e.g., Maurer & Salapatek, 1976). Between 2 and 5 months, the ability to discriminate head and gaze direction shows rapid development (Caron, Caron, Roberts, & Brooks, 1997), including a growing preference for social partners who make eye contact (Hains & Muir, 1996).

Infants can discriminate between different types of facial expressions from an early age. Even newborns can detect changes in expression (e.g., Field, Woodson, Greenberg, & Cohen, 1982); and over the subsequent four months, infants become able to discriminate happy expressions from a range of negative ones (Nelson & Ludeman, 1986), with a preference shown for the former (Oster & Ewy, 1980). By 5 months, discrimination between different negative expressions is achieved (Schwartz, Izard, & Ansul, 1985). Notably, however, 7-month-olds look consistently more at fearful vs. happy faces (de Haan & Nelson, 1998; Kotsoni, de Haan, & Johnson, 2001).

Individual differences and psychopathology

Although individual differences in infant responses to face stimuli have been noted (e.g., Easterbrook, Kisilevsky, Hains, & Muir, 1999), few studies have addressed this issue systematically, and the extent to which they are a function of social experience, or more constitutional factors such as temperament, is unknown. Research with some clinical populations, including autism (Baron-Cohen, 1997) and Turner's syndrome (Skuse et al., 1997), suggests that some aspects of recognition of emotional expressions may well have a genetic basis. Nevertheless, social experience may also be important. Thus, Kuchuk, Vibbert, and Bornstein (1986) found an association between mothers' encouragement of attention to their face and 3-month-old infants' responses to faces. The role of interaction experience is also suggested by studies showing that infants look more to faces showing expressions differing from those to which they have previously been exposed (de Haan, Belsky, Reid, Volein, & Johnson, 2004; Field, Pickens, Fox, Gonzalez, & Nawrocki, 1998; Striano, Brennan, & Vanman, 2002). Notably, mothers with social phobia have been found to show specific parenting difficulties with their infants in social contexts. Thus, in the presence of a stranger, affected mothers encourage their infants' interaction with the stranger less, and display more anxious behaviour (Murray, Cooper, Creswell, Schofield, & Sack, 2007). Whether such parental responses influence infants' processing of social stimuli has not been established.

The current study aimed to elucidate the development of social information processing in infants of mothers with social phobia, compared to infants of unaffected, control, mothers, in order to determine whether, and at what point in development, equivalent responses to social stimuli that are characteristic of older children and adults with social phobia emerge. Specifically, we focused on infants' responses to (i) faces versus non-faces; (ii) forward-facing versus averted gaze; and (iii) emotional expressions of varying kinds and intensity. With regard to the latter, given that social anxiety is associated with an avoidance of extreme expressions, even when positive (Mansell et al., 1999), we examined infant responses to extreme emotional expressions in comparison to moderate expressions. In addition, based on the suggestion that early face processing differences may be a result of experiences with caregivers, we aimed to assess whether responses to faces develop as a function of (i) endogenous infant characteristics, i.e., temperament, and/or (ii) characteristics of mother–infant interactions. We assessed infant face processing at four time points. As we were interested in the extent to which face-processing characteristics represent endogenous characteristics, the first assessment was conducted when the infants were 10 days old. Numerous studies have established that neonates are able to discriminate between face-like and non-face-like images, yet at this age infants will have had little exposure to maternal expressions of social anxiety. The next assessment was conducted at 10 weeks of age. At this age face-to-face interactions are a primary source of infant social interactions. While social phobia does not seem to impair maternal social responsiveness to her child in this context, early signs of reduced social responsiveness begin to emerge at around this age in infants of socially phobic mothers that are predicted by concurrent maternal regulation of infant behaviour (Murray et al., 2007). We were therefore interested to assess the infants independently of maternal active involvement, within an experimental paradigm. The next assessment was conducted at 16 weeks, when infant visual abilities have developed rapidly and numerous processes relevant to the processing of faces (e.g., discrimination of gaze direction and emotional expressions) are established (e.g., Caron et al., 1997; Nelson & Ludeman, 1986). Finally, the infants were assessed at 10 months. This was of particular interest since, at this age, social-referencing abilities emerge, and children have the ability to identify their mother's responses to other people (e.g., Baldwin & Moses, 1996), and maternal social behaviours may therefore be particularly influential.

METHOD

Sample

Mothers attending antenatal clinics were screened with an 8-item version of the Social Interaction and Anxiety Scale and the Social Phobia Scale (SIAS and SPS; Mattick & Clarke, 1998) to detect social phobia. Items were included on the basis of their high factor loadings on these measures. A pilot of each screen identified cut-off scores for the top 10% of respondents. High scoring women were interviewed to confirm diagnosis using the Structured Clinical Interview for DSM-IV Axis I disorders (SCID-1; First, Spitzer, Gibbon, & Williams, 1995), administered by trained psychologists and mental-health clinicians. Those meeting criteria for a DSM-IV diagnosis of social phobia were recruited. Controls were selected randomly from the low-scoring women, who were also interviewed to confirm the absence of psychiatric disorder. A total of 96 women were recruited into the index group, and 94 as controls (see Murray et al., 2007, for full recruitment details). Numbers of infants with complete data at the different ages are given in Tables 1–3.

Procedure

Infants were assessed when aged 10 days in the home, in quiet conditions, and in university research rooms at 10 weeks, 16 weeks and 10 months of age. Response to faces vs. non-faces was assessed at the first three time points. Response to emotional expressions of varying intensity was assessed

TABLE 1
Infant looking times to faces and non-faces; Means (*SDs*)

	10 days		10 weeks		16 weeks	
	SP (*n=45*)	*Control* (*n=53*)	*SP* (*n=74*)	*Control* (*n=81*)	*SP* (*n=82*)	*Control* (*n=71*)
Faces	30.79 (39.20)	37.14 (44.79)	54.29 (51.24)	45.85 (38.43)	15.99 (14.34)	17.18 (14.08)
Non-faces	24.57 (31.49)	23.20 (29.64)	43.97 (38.22)	37.87 (40.35)	18.45 (12.64)	17.53 (13.30)

at all but the 10-day assessment; and response to gaze direction was assessed at 16 weeks and 10 months. Assessments of maternal behaviours and infant temperament (behavioural inhibition) were made at 10 and 16 weeks, respectively. For all infant looking procedures in the laboratory, infants sat facing a screen within a booth with low-lighting, on the experimenter's lap at 16 weeks and on their mother's lap at 10 months (to avoid effects of infant stranger fear at later visits). Stimuli were displayed on a projection screen at 90 cm distance from the infant. The infants' attention was first attracted to the screen by an image of a mobile doll. Infants were videotaped throughout, and their behaviour scored by two researchers who were blind to maternal diagnosis and stimulus condition.

Infant face-processing assessments

10-day assessment

Face vs. non-face. At 10 days, infants completed a preferential looking task using the procedure for assessments of neonates of Turati, Simion, Milani, and Umiltà (2002) and others. Infants were simultaneously presented with two head-shaped, head-sized, boards with black on white features, shown either as a face or else inverted—retaining symmetry (following Morton & Johnson, 1991; Johnson, Dziurawiec, Ellis, & Morton, 1991; see Figure 1). The head boards were mounted against a black background at an angle of 70° from the infant's viewing position. The infant was positioned on an experimenter's lap 50 cm from the board. A second experimenter, who was blind to stimulus position, viewed the infant through a spy-hole in the board and recorded infant gaze direction onto a DAT audio tape, using a button-box. Once the infant had looked away from both stimuli for a total of four seconds, the trial ended. There were two trials, with each stimulus being displayed to each side, and the order of presentation being counterbalanced across subjects.

TABLE 2

Emotional expression: Summed proportions of infant looking time to targets versus 50% emotional expression; Means (SDs)

Target/Side	10 weeks		16 weeks		10 months	
	SP (n=53)	Control (n=56)	SP (n=39)	Control (n=35)	SP (n=40)	Control (n=45)
Angry						
Low (0 & 25%)						
Right	0.73 (0.56)	0.84 (0.59)	0.92 (0.46)	1.07 (0.39)	0.89 (0.49)	0.82 (0.56)
Left	1.13 (0.59)	1.15 (0.60)	0.92 (0.46)	1.02 (0.45)	0.72 (0.55)	0.76 (0.64)
High (75 & 100%)						
Right	0.88 (0.60)	0.73 (0.51)	0.96 (0.45)	0.99 (0.41)	0.88 (0.49)	0.94 (0.48)
Left	1.21 (0.62)	1.30 (0.61)	1.04 (0.49)	0.95 (0.41)	0.79 (0.56)	0.73 (0.59)
Happy						
Low (0 & 25%)						
Right	0.95 (0.65)	0.89 (0.67)	0.87 (0.43)	1.06 (0.46)	1.03 (0.39)	0.98 (0.35)
Left	1.08 (0.66)	1.15 (0.69)	1.11 (0.50)	0.92 (0.41)	0.96 (0.36)	1.01 (0.39)
High (75 & 100%)						
Right	0.86 (0.69)	0.94 (0.64)	0.98 (0.52)	0.96 (0.51)	1.08 (0.32)	1.03 (0.27)
Left	1.14 (0.68)	1.17 (0.67)	1.11 (0.48)	1.04 (0.47)	0.99 (0.36)	1.00 (0.31)
Fearful						
Low (0 & 25%)						
Right	1.06 (0.72)	0.97 (0.67)	0.97 (0.47)	1.02 (0.58)	1.01 (0.41)	0.95 (0.32)
Left	1.12 (0.72)	1.02 (0.61)	1.01 (0.47)	1.11 (0.51)	0.96 (0.45)	1.06 (0.43)
High (75 & 100%)						
Right	0.92 (0.62)	1.01 (0.63)	1.00 (0.41)	1.06 (0.53)	1.10 (0.41)	1.07 (0.35)
Left	1.05 (0.64)	1.05 (0.60)	0.98 (0.42)	1.04 (0.58)	1.10 (0.42)	1.04 (0.42)

Note: Variability in *n* across trials due to infant fatigue or irritability (max *n* given).

TABLE 3
Gaze direction: Infant responses to full-face and profile

	16 weeks		10 months	
	SP (n =32)	Control (n =33)	SP (n =37)	Control (n =44)
Total looking time to full-faces	80.68 (22.08)	82.32 (19.34)	68.49 (24.37)	74.13 (18.31)
Total looking time to profile-faces	80.27 (26.10)	81.20 (18.77)	63.90 (22.80)	70.68 (18.47)
	SP (n =36)	Control (n =43)	SP (n =35)	Control (n =41)
Positive behaviours to full-faces	3.06 (3.62)	3.19 (3.46)	3.94 (3.47)	4.32 (3.27)
Positive behaviours to profile faces	1.86 (2.66)	2.28 (2.76)	3.97 (3.50)	3.85 (2.87)
Negative behaviours to full faces	5.26 (3.28)	6.58 (3.61)	4.06 (3.22)	4.44 (2.92)
Negative behaviours to profile faces	5.28 (3.38)	5.98 (3.41)	4.17 (3.29)	4.61 (3.37)

10-week assessment

Face vs. non-face. At this assessment the face and inverted array (equivalent to stimuli shown at 10 days) were presented alternately, each being shown twice, with order of presentation across subjects counterbalanced (1: face/inversion/inversion/face; 2: inversion/face/face/inversion), following the procedure of Morton and Johnson (1991). The experimenter, who was blind to condition, recorded infant fixations on the stimuli using a button-box. When the infant had looked away from the stimulus for 5 seconds, the attractor was shown again, before displaying the next trial. Infant responses were video recorded and duration of infant gaze was scored from the video using a button-box.

Emotional expression. To assess infants' responses to varying intensities of emotional expression, continua depicting different intensities of anger, happiness, and fear were taken from the FEEST (Young, Perrett, Calder, Sprengelmeyer, & Ekman, 2002). Each continuum consisted of a prototype expression face (considered to be 100% intensity for that expression) from the Ekman and Friesen (1976) series, and morphed images interpolated between the prototype expression and its corresponding neutral. So, for example, the neutral face of model MF in the Ekman and Friesen series was taken to represent 0% happiness, and then 25%, 50%, and 75% happy morphs were created by interpolating between MF's neutral (0% happy) and her prototype happy (100%) expressions. A different model was used for each continuum, and the stimuli are shown in Figure 2. The faces from the

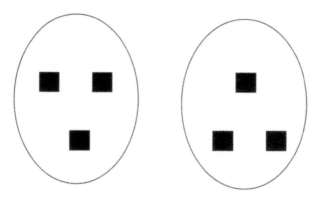

Figure 1.   Face–non-face stimuli (10 weeks).

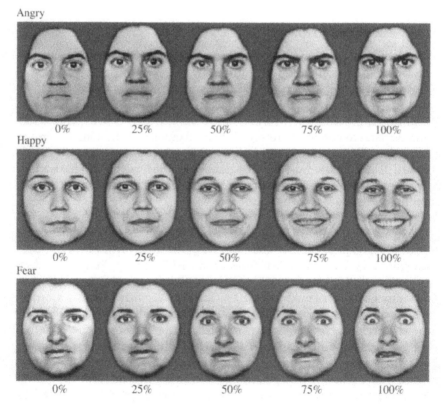

Figure 2.   Emotional faces of varying intensity.

Ekman and Friesen (1976) series used to create these continua were as follows: anger (neutral NR-1-03, anger NR-2-07), happiness (neutral MF-1-02, happy MF-1-06), fear (neutral MO-1-05, fear MO-1-23). Hairstyles and picture backgrounds were masked, so that all differences between stimuli were emotion-relevant.

Twenty-four face pairs were shown. Within each, one face was shown at 50% intensity and the other showed varying intensities of the same emotion, either happiness, anger or fear (8 pairs including each emotion type). In this way, the standard (50%) face could be of higher or lower emotional intensity than the comparison face. The order of emotion type was counterbalanced across participants and visits. Each face pair was presented for 10 seconds, and the same attractor was shown at the start of each trial.

16-week assessment

Face vs. non-face. At 16 weeks, looking to faces vs. non-faces was assessed using more complex, moving stimuli (see Morton & Johnson, 1991). Stimuli were either a head-sized, black on white moving schematic face or a moving scrambled array (with symmetrical elements; see Figure 3). In each case, the appearance of movement was achieved by the display of internal features being alternated each second from one static presentation to another. The procedure for the assessment of infant responses to faces vs. non-faces and to emotional faces was the same as at the 10-week visit. The order of presentation was counterbalanced with the order of presentation from the previous visit.

Gaze direction. Infants were shown video clips of two female models, smiling and addressing the infant for 50 seconds, and either facing the infant

Figure 3.   Face–non-face stimuli (16 weeks).

or with head and eyes averted (i.e., in profile).The full-face vs. profile clips were recorded simultaneously, using different camera angles. There were four trials, counterbalanced for each of the two models, and across gaze direction conditions and assessments.

10 months

Responses to emotional expressions and varying gaze direction were assessed following the same procedures used at the 16-week assessment.

Maternal behaviour

Maternal behaviour was assessed at 10 weeks. This was video recorded during a two-minute period when a female stranger entered the room where mother and infant were settled, approached, and attempted to engage the infant in play (see Murray et al., 2007, for full details). The mother's behaviour was scored by two researchers who were unaware of maternal diagnosis.

Infant behavioural inhibition

Behavioural inhibition was assessed at 16 weeks using the procedure devised by Kagan and colleagues (1994). Infants were exposed to a series of unfamiliar visual, auditory, and olfactory stimuli. Their behaviour was video recorded throughout. The assessment was administered and scored by two trained researchers who were blind to maternal group (see Cooper, Murray, Schofield, Sadiqui, & Wehl, 2008).

Measures

Infant responses to face vs. non-face stimuli, emotional expressions and gaze direction

Looking times. The duration of infant looking to each stimulus type within each trial was recorded using a button box by scorers trained to a high level of reliability on a sample of 36 videotapes (ICC = .97).

Infant behaviours. The extent to which infants displayed a range of positive and negative behaviours was coded for the gaze-direction procedure (unlike the other, static face, stimuli, presentations for this assessment afforded more active social participation). Positive behaviours were: leaning/reaching towards the screen, positive shaping of the mouth, tonguing, smiling and mother-referencing in a positive way. Negative behaviours were back arching/squirming, pouting, crying, yawning, frowning, touching of face/clothes/hand-wringing, grimacing, clenching fists and sucking fists/thumb. Intra-class correlations, based on ratings of 40 infants were .74 for positive behaviours and .83 for negative behaviours.

Infant behavioural inhibition

On the basis of the degree of movement and distress shown in response to each stimulus, infants were classified as being either behaviourally inhibited or not, following the criteria established by Kagan and colleagues. Intra-class correlations for the two scales, based on ratings for 20 infants were each .99. For the classification of infants as inhibited or non-inhibited kappa was 1.00.

Maternal behaviour

This was scored on the following 5-point scales: (i) engagement with the stranger (greeting, eye-contact, smiling, conversing); (ii) encouragement to the infant to interact with the stranger (e.g., making positive comments, encouraging facial expressions and gestures); and (iii) expressed anxiety (e.g., biting lip, tense posture, worried expression). A random sample of 20 videotapes were scored by two researchers and confirmed a high level of reliability (mean $ICC = .86$, range .78–.94).

Data analysis

In procedures in which two faces were presented simultaneously (face vs. non-face at 10 days; emotional faces at all visits) cases were excluded from analyses if the infant looked to one side (left/right) only throughout all trials. Associations between infant responses and gender were first explored; none were significant, so gender was not considered further. Comparisons between responses to face stimuli by infants of mothers in the social phobia and control groups were made using paired samples t-tests or repeated measures analysis of variance where variables were normally distributed. Otherwise, transformed data were used where this improved the distribution, or non-parametric tests were used. Where significant differences were found between groups we (i) assessed the pattern of looking responses in more detail to explore whether differential looking to high intensity faces were consistent with differences in initial (hypervigilance) and subsequent (avoidance) responses; and (ii) examined associations with infant temperament and maternal behaviour. For dichotomous data (BI classification), this was based on repeated measures analysis of variance; for continuous data, repeated measures analyses were used with maternal behaviours entered as covariates.

RESULTS

Throughout the results effect sizes are reported as r. Demographic characteristics of the sample have been described elsewhere (e.g., Murray et al., 2007); the two study groups were similar in terms of maternal age, ethnicity, socioeconomic status and marital status, and the distribution of infant gender. Means and SDs for infant behaviours in response to the face vs. non face, intensity of emotional expression, and full-face vs. profile stimuli are shown in Tables 1–3, respectively.

Face vs. non-face

A main effect for stimulus type (face/non-face) was found at the first two assessments, 10 days: $F(1, 96) = 3.95$, $p = .05$, $r = .20$; 10 weeks: $F(1, 153) = 5.47$, $p = .02$, $r = .19$, representing a general preference for faces over non-faces, but was this not significant at 16 weeks, $F(1, 151) = 1.82$, $p = .18$. The interaction between stimulus type and infant group was not significant at any assessment, 10 days: $F(1, 96) = 1.29$, $p = .26$; 10 weeks: $F(1, 153) = 0.28$, $p = .60$; 16 weeks: $F(1, 151) = 1.17$, $p = .28$.

Emotional expression

Due to the infants' young age, participant numbers across trials varied due to fatigue/distress or side bias, and therefore separate analyses were conducted to avoid significant data loss. Responses to emotional expressions were first assessed based on the proportion of time spent looking at the target versus the 50% expression. For this procedure, responses to the left and right side typically did not correlate sufficiently highly to combine them ($r = .06$ to .73), so these were analysed separately. No group differences were found in the proportion of time spent looking at the target expression for all emotion types, presented to either side, at all assessments (see Table 2). As we were particularly interested in infants' differential responses to varying intensity emotions, repeated measures analyses were conducted to compare responses to the 50% morphed expressions to high intensity (75 and 100%) versus low intensity (0 and 25%) expressions. At the 10-week assessment, a main effect of intensity of angry expressions was found when the target stimulus was presented on the left side, $F(1, 91) = 3.86$, $p = .05$, $r = .20$, reflecting a general tendency to look more to high-intensity faces. The effect was not significant when the target was presented on the right side, $F(1, 90) = 0.90$, $p = .35$, although the data followed the same pattern (see Table 2). The interaction with group was not significant for either side, Left: $F(1, 91) = 1.70$, $p = .20$; Right: $F(1, 90) = 2.66$, $p = .11$. For happy faces, there was no effect of emotional intensity, Left: $F(1, 102) = 0.02$, $p = .88$; Right: $F(1, 97) = 0.19$, $p = .66$, or interaction between intensity and group, Left:

$F(1, 102) = 0.34$, $p = .56$; Right: $F(1, 97) = 0.42$, $p = .52$. For fearful faces, no main effect of intensity was identified, Left: $F(1, 69) = 0.04$, $p = .85$; Right: $F(1, 74) = 1.73$, $p = .19$, however the Group × Intensity interaction was significant when the target stimulus was presented on the right, $F(1, 74) = 3.95$, $p = .05$, $r = .22$, reflecting a pattern of increased looking to high-intensity faces by controls, and reduced looking to high-intensity faces by index group infants (see Figure 4). The interaction was not significant when the target was presented on the left, $F(1, 69) = 0.28$, $p = .60$, although the pattern of results was the same. In order to explore whether differential looking to high-intensity faces represented differences in initial (hypervigilance) and subsequent (avoidance) responses, we compared groups on the following variables (i) which stimulus the infant looked to first (target/neutral); (ii) the length of the first look to target/control stimuli; and (iii) the total number of looks to target/control stimuli. Infants of non-anxious mothers' first looks were more frequently to the target stimulus (presented on the right) than infants of socially phobic mothers, $\chi^2(1) = 4.02$, $p = .04$, Odds Ratio = 2.59. There were not significant interactions, however, between maternal group and either the length of the first look to the target versus control stimuli, $F(1, 66) = 0.10$, $p = .76$, or the number of looks to target vs. control stimuli, $F(1, 66) = 1.36$, $p = .25$.

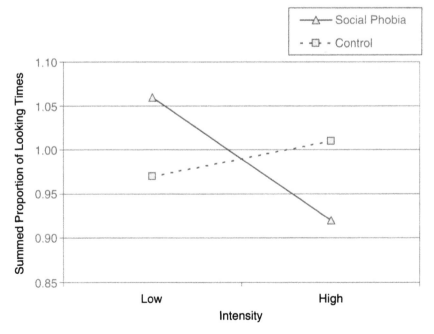

Figure 4. Interaction between participant group and level of emotional intensity of fearful expressions (presented on the right side).

At 16 weeks and 10 months, neither main effects nor interaction effects were significant for any emotion type (see Table 3), with the exception of a main effect for intensity of fearful faces at 10 months, when presented on the right, $F(1, 85) = 8.63$, $p = .004$; $r = .30$. Notably, the pattern of results for high- versus low-intensity fearful faces for the social phobia and control groups at this assessment was consistent with that at 10 weeks, with controls showing a heightened preference for high-intensity faces, which was absent among the social phobia group; specifically there was a significant effect of intensity for controls, who looked more at high-intensity fearful faces presented on the right, $t(47) = 2.99$, $p = .004$; $r = .24$, but not for the index group, $t(38) = 1.42$, $p = .16$.

Gaze direction

At 16 weeks, an overall preference for full faces compared to profile was not found based on infant looking time (Wilcoxon $Z = 0.06$, $p = .95$); however, infants did look longer at full faces compared to profiles at the 10-month assessment ($Z = 2.86$, $p = .004$, $r = .33$). The same pattern was found for the infants of socially phobic mothers (16 weeks: $Z = 0.26$, $p = .79$; 10 months: $Z = 2.45$, $p = .01$, $r = .40$) and infants of control mothers (16 weeks: $Z = 0.53$, $p = .60$; 10 months: $Z = 1.76$, $p = .08$, $r = .26$). There were no significant group differences (Social phobia vs. Control) at either time point on total looking times to full face (16 weeks: Mann–Whitney $U = 523.00$, $p = .95$; 10 months: $U = 623.00$, $p = .40$) or profile (16 weeks: $U = 495.00$, $p = .67$; 10 months: $U = 577.00$, $p = .18$).

When infant emotional responses were considered, at 16 weeks, infants were significantly more positive towards full vs. profile faces ($Z = 3.15$, $p = .002$, $r = .36$), although there was no difference in the frequency of negative behaviours ($Z = 0.33$, $p = .74$). The same pattern was found for infants of socially phobic mothers (positive behaviours: $Z = 2.62$, $p = .009$, $r = .45$; negative behaviours: $Z = 0.23$, $p = .82$) and control mothers (positive behaviours: $Z = 1.95$, $p = .05$, $r = .30$; negative behaviours: $Z = 0.64$, $p = .52$). The groups did not differ in the frequency of positive behaviours to full faces ($U = 692.00$, $p = .69$), profiles ($U = 730.50$, $p = .65$) or negative behaviours to full ($U = 579.00$, $p = .12$) or profile faces ($U = 668.50$, $p = .30$).

At 10 months, infants did not differ in either positive or negative behaviours to full faces compared to profile faces (positive: $Z = 0.91$, $p = .36$; negative: $Z = 0.56$, $p = .58$), and this was also the case for each group when considered separately (Social Phobia: positive behaviours, $Z = 0.16$, $p = .87$; negative behaviours, $Z = 0.40$, $p = .69$; Control: positive behaviours, $Z = 1.10$, $p = .27$; negative behaviours $Z = 0.40$, $p = .69$). The groups did not differ in the frequency of positive behaviours to full faces (Mann–Whitney

$U = 658.50$, $p = .54$), profiles ($U = 702.00$, $p = .87$) or negative behaviours to full ($U = 630.50$, $p = .36$) or profile faces ($U = 659.00$, $p = .54$).

Associations with infant temperament and maternal behaviours

Infants' responses to high- or low-intensity fearful faces, presented on the right side, at the 10-week assessment were not significantly associated with the infants' behavioural inhibition classification, $F(1, 100) = 0.19$, $p = .67$, or maternal behaviours, engagement with the stranger: $F(1, 104) = 0.43$, $p = .51$; encouragement: $F(1, 103) = 0.01$, $p = .91$; expressed anxiety: $F(1, 103) = 0.13$, $p = .72$.

DISCUSSION

Distinctive responses to faces and emotional expressions among individuals with social phobia have been frequently reported (e.g., Bögels & Mansell, 2004); however, their aetiological significance is unclear. We addressed this issue by assessing face processing among infants at risk of developing social phobia (i.e., offspring of socially phobic mothers) and a comparison group (i.e., offspring of mothers with no history of anxiety disorder). Specifically, we focused on infant responses to faces versus non-faces, emotional expressions of varying type and intensity, and variations in gaze direction. We also aimed to assess the contribution of infant temperament and maternal behaviours to infant face-processing differences.

The results were consistent with findings from normative infancy research (e.g., Hains & Muir, 1996; Morton & Johnson, 1991); thus, overall, infants showed a preference in terms of looking times for (i) faces over non-faces at 10 days and 10 weeks; and in terms of behavioural response for (ii) full faces over profile faces at 16 weeks. Furthermore, at 10 weeks, infants looked more to high- than low-intensity angry faces, and fearful faces at 10 months. The latter finding extends previous research, which has not been able to determine whether differential responses occur specifically to emotional expressions, or whether they relate to differences in stimulus complexity. In the current study, our methodology allowed investigation of the effect of intensity *within* emotion types (i.e., angry, happy, fearful), with faces being morphed so that only the extent of emotional expression changed. This provides more direct evidence that infants respond specifically to emotional characteristics of faces.

We found no effects of maternal social phobia assessments of faces versus non-faces or of gaze direction, at any age; however, differences between infants of socially phobic and control mothers were apparent in responses to intensity of emotional expression. Specifically, at 10 weeks, control infants initially oriented to and spent more time looking to high- than low-intensity fearful faces whereas infants of socially phobic mothers did the reverse. These results do not provide evidence for initial hypervigilance to potentially threat-related faces, but rather suggest relative avoidance in infants at risk of developing social phobia. While caution is required when considering these results, they do suggest that infants of mothers with social phobia may show characteristic processing biases to emotional expressions at an early age.

This pattern of results is consistent with findings with adults (e.g., Bögels & Mansell, 2004) and children (Stirling et al., 2006) in that social anxiety is associated with avoidance of fearful expressions. Unlike these studies, however, the current findings favour a specific response to fearful expressions, rather than a negativity (e.g., Winton et al., 1995) or general emotionality bias (e.g., Mansell et al., 1999).

While we found a similar pattern of results at 10 weeks and 10 months, it was not found at the 16-week assessment. The reasons for this are unclear; however, Morton and Johnson (1991) have suggested that, as children's representation of faces develops, increasingly complex stimuli are required; for example, by 5 months, a still, black and white representation of a face is uninteresting. Consistent with this suggestion, there was less variability in response to emotional faces generally at this age in our study; however we also failed to find the anticipated main effects of looking times to both faces versus non-faces (using moving stimuli) and gaze direction (full-face vs. profile) at 16 weeks. The fact that infants in our study altered their looking behaviour less at this age on the basis of a range of social information may reflect the general reduction in interest seen between 12 weeks (Sylvester-Bradley & Trevarthen, 1972) and the onset of social referencing skills from about 9–10 months (Baldwin & Moses, 1996).

We were interested to assess whether infants' responses were linked to endogenous infant characteristics, or early experiences with caregivers, and we chose infant behavioural inhibition and maternal behaviours with a stranger as markers of these constructs. Infant responses to high- versus low-intensity fearful faces were not accounted for by either measure, leaving open the possibility of more specific genetic bases for intergenerational transmission of social responses. It is important to note, of course, that the maternal behaviours assessed within a laboratory setting represent a small fraction of infant social experience, so this null finding does not necessarily rule out early environmental influences. Further, it will be interesting to continue to track responses to emotional expressions as these infants develop, as it is likely that the influence of social experience may become particularly salient after 10 months of age.

There are a number of reasons to remain cautious when considering our results. In particular, significant findings represented small–medium effect sizes, showing that maternal group appears to explain a relatively small proportion of the variance in children's social emotion processing. A large number of tests were required to evaluate the emotional expression data, due to significant numbers of young infants having incomplete trials because of fatigue, etc. Nevertheless, due to the novel line of investigation, we did not want to be overly conservative in an attempt to reduce Type 1 error, and our findings' general consistency with both infancy research and findings from children and adults with social phobia is encouraging. Second, for infant responses to emotional expressions, the side of presentation of the index face was important: responses to angry faces were pronounced for left-side presentations, while the interaction effects of group and intensity of fearful expressions were most pronounced for presentations on the right. Our results for angry faces are consistent with those of other studies with adults (Mogg & Bradley, 1999, 2002), suggesting that lateralised brain mechanisms may play a critical role in the processing of these face stimuli (Morris, Öhman, & Dolan, 1998); lateralisation results for fear faces, are not, however, so clear-cut, and further research on this issue is warranted.

With these limitations in mind, the current study provides tentative support for the integral bias hypothesis, which suggests that individual cognitive biases are an integral part of social anxiety and as such are detectable among at-risk infants (e.g., Richards et al., 2007). Specifically, infants of mothers with social phobia appear to show avoidance of high-intensity fearful faces. The longer term consequences of these early social information-processing characteristics are unclear, and whether this behaviour is a precursor of the development of later socially anxious behaviour remains to be investigated.

REFERENCES

Baldwin, D. A., & Moses, L. J. (1996). The ontogeny of social information gathering. *Child Development*, *67*, 1915–1939.

Baron-Cohen, S. (1997). *Mindblindness: An essay on autism and theory of mind*. Cambridge, MA: Massachusetts Institute of Technology.

Battaglia, M., Ogiari, A., Zanoni, A., Villa, F., Citterio, A., Binaghi, F., et al. (2004). Children's discrimination of expressions of emotions: Relationships with indices of social anxiety and shyness. *Journal of the American Academy of Child and Adolescent Psychiatry*, *43*, 358–365.

Bögels, S. M., & Mansell, W. (2004). Attention processes in the maintenance and treatment of social phobia: Hypervigilance, avoidance, and self-focused attention. *Clinical Psychology Review*, *24*, 827–856.

Caron, A. J., Caron, R., Roberts, J., & Brooks, R. (1997). Infant sensitivity to deviations in dynamic facial-vocal displays: The role of eye regard. *Developmental Psychology*, *33*, 802–813.

Chen, Y. P., Ehlers, A., Clark, D. M., & Mansell, W. (2002). Patients with generalised social phobia direct their attention away from faces. *Behaviour Research and Therapy*, *40*, 677–687.

Cooper, P. J., Murray, L. M., Schofield, E. M., Sadiqui, M., & Wehl, T. (2008). *Continuity and discontinuity in behavioural inhibition in the context of maternal social phobia.* Manuscript in preparation.

de Haan, M., Belsky, J., Reid, V., Volein, A., & Johnson, M. H. (2004). Maternal personality and infants' neural and visual responsivity to facial expressions of emotion. *Journal of Child Psychology and Psychiatry, 45,* 1209–1218.

de Haan, M., & Nelson, C. A. (1998). Discrimination and categorisation of facial expressions during infancy. In A. Slater (Ed.), *Perceptual development: Visual, auditory and speech perception in infancy* (pp. 287–309). Hove, UK: Psychology Press.

Douillez, C., & Phillipot, P. (2003). Biais dans l'evaluation volontaire de stimuli verbaux et non-verbaux: Effet de l'anxiete sociale. *Revue Francophone de Clinique Comportementale et Cognitive, 8,* 12–18.

Easterbrook, M. S., Kisilevsky, B. S., Hains, S. M. J., & Muir, D. (1999). Faceness or complexity: Evidence form newborn visual tracking of facelike stimuli. *Infant Behaviour and Development, 1,* 17–35.

Easterbrook, M. A., Kisilevsky, B. S., Muir, D. W., & Laplante, D. P. (1999). Newborns discriminate schematic faces from scrambled faces. *Canadian Journal of Experimental Psychology, 53,* 231–241.

Ekman, P., & Friesen, W. V. (1976). *Pictures of Facial Affect.* Palo Alto, CA: Consulting Psychologists Press.

Field, T., Pickens, J., Fox, N. A., Gonzalez, J., & Nawrocki, T. (1998). Facial expression and EED responses to happy and sad faces/voices by 3 month old infants of depressed mothers. *British Journal of Developmental Psychology, 16,* 485–494.

Field, T. M., Woodson, R., Greenberg, R., & Cohen, D. (1982). Discrimination and imitation of facial expression by neonates. *Science, 218,* 179–181.

First, M. B., Spitzer, R. L., Gibbon, M., & Williams, J. B. W. (1995). *Structured Clinical Interview for DSM-IV Axis I Diagnoses.* New York: Biometrics Research Department.

Garner, M. J., Mogg, K., & Bradley, B. (2006). Orienting and maintenance of attention to facial expressions in social anxiety. *Journal of Abnormal Psychology, 115*(4), 760–770.

Hadwin, J. A., Donnelly, N., French, C. C., Richards, A., Watts, A., & Daley, A. (2003). The influence of children's self-report trait anxiety and depression on visual search for emotional faces. *Journal of Child Psychology and Psychiatry, 44,* 432–444.

Hains, S. M. J., & Muir, D. W. (1996). Infant sensitivity to adult eye direction. *Child Development, 67,* 1940–1951.

Horley, K., Williams, L. M., Gonsalvez, C., & Gordon, W. (2003). Face to face: Visual scanpath evidence for abnormal processing of facial expressions in social phobia. *Psychiatry Research, 127,* 45–53.

Johnson, J., Dziurawiec, S., Ellis, H., & Morton, J. (1991). Newborns' preferential tracking of face-like stimuli and its subsequent decline. *Cognition, 40,* 1–19.

Johnson, M. H., & Morton, J. (1991). *Biology and cognitive development. The case for face recognition.* Cambridge, MA: Blackwell.

Joormann, J., & Gotlib, I. H. (2006). Is this happiness I see? Biases in the identification of emotional faces in depression and social phobia. *Journal of Abnormal Psychology, 115*(4), 705–714.

Kagan, J. (1994). *Galen's prophecy.* New York: Basic Books.

Kindt, M., & van den Hout, M. (2001). Selective attention and anxiety: A perspective on developmental issues and the causal status. *Journal of Psychopathology and Behavioural Assessment, 23,* 193–202.

Kotsoni, E., de Haan, M., & Johnson, M. H. (2001). Categorical perception of facial expressions by 7-month-old infants. *Perception, 30,* 1115–1125.

Kuchuk, A., Vibbert, M., & Bornstein, M. H. (1986). The perception of smiling and its experiential correlates in three-month-old infants. *Child Development, 57,* 1054–1061.

Lieb, R., Wittchen, H. U., Hofler, M., Fuetsch, M., Stein, M. B., & Merikangas, K. R. (2000). Parental psychopathology, parenting styles, and the risk of social phobia in offspring: A prospective-longitudinal community study. *Archives of General Psychiatry, 57,* 859–866.

Mancini, C., van Ameringen, M., Szatmari, P., Fugere, C., & Boyle, M. (1996). A high-risk pilot study of the children and adults with social phobia. *Journal of the American Academy of Child and Adolescent Psychiatry, 35,* 1511–1517.

Mansell, W., Clark, D. M., Ehlers, A., & Chen, Y. P. (1999). Social anxiety and attention away from emotional faces. *Cognition and Emotion, 13,* 673–690.

Mattick, R. P., & Clarke, C. (1998). Development and validation of measures of social phobia scrutiny fears and social interaction anxiety. *Behaviour Research and Therapy, 36,* 443–453.

Maurer, D., & Barrera, M. (1981). Infants' perception of natural and distorted arrangements of a schematic face. *Child Development, 52,* 196–202.

Maurer, D., & Salapatek, P. (1976). Developmental changes in the scanning of faces by young infants. *Child Development, 47,* 523–527.

McClure, E. B., & Nowicki, S. (2001). Associations between social anxiety and nonverbal processing skills in preadolescent boys and girls. *Journal of Nonverbal Behavior, 25,* 3–19.

Melfsen, S., & Florin, I. (2002). Do socially anxious children show deficits in classifying facial expressions of emotions? *Journal of Nonverbal Behavior, 26,* 109–126.

Merckelbach, H., Van Hout, W., Van den Hout, M. A., & Mersch, P. P. (1989). Psychophysiological and subjective reactions of social phobics and normals to facial stimuli. *Behaviour Research and Therapy, 27,* 289–294.

Mogg, K., & Bradley, B. (1999). Orienting of attention to threatening facial expressions presented under conditions of restricted awareness. *Cognition and Emotion, 13,* 713–740.

Mogg, K., & Bradley, B. (2002). Selective orienting of attention to masked threat faces in social anxiety. *Behaviour Research and Therapy, 40,* 1403–1414.

Mogg, K., Bradley, B., de Bono, J., & Painter, M. (1997). Time course of attentional bias for threat information in non-clinical anxiety. *Behaviour Research and Therapy, 37,* 595–604.

Morris, J. S., Öhman, A., & Dolan, R. J. (1998). Conscious and unconscious emotional learning in the human amygdala. *Nature, 393,* 467–470.

Morton, J., & Johnson, M. (1991). CONSPEC and CONLEARN: A two-process theory of infant face recognition. *Psychological Review, 98,* 164–181.

Muir, D. W., & Nadel, J. (1998). Infant social perception. In A. Slater (Ed.), *Perceptual development: Visual, auditory and speech perception in infancy* (pp. 247–286). Hove, UK: Psychology Press.

Murray, L., Cooper, P., Creswell, C., Schofield, E., & Sack, C. (2007). The effects of maternal social phobia on mother–infant interactions and infant social responsiveness. *Journal of Child Psychology and Psychiatry, 48,* 45–52.

Nelson, C. A., & Ludeman, P. M. (1986). *The discrimination of intensity changes of emotion by 4 and 7 month infants.* Paper presented at the Midwest Psychology Association, Chicago, IL.

Nelson, E. C., Grant, J. D., Buchollz, K. K., Glowinski, A., Madden, P. A. F., Reich, W., et al. (2000). Social phobia in a population-based female adolescent twin sample: Comorbidity and associated suicide related symptoms. *Psychological Medicine, 30,* 797–804.

Oster, H., & Ewy, R. (1980). *Discrimination of sad vs. happy faces by 4 month olds: When is a smile seen as a smile?* Unpublished manuscript, University of Pennsylvania.

Phillipot, P., & Douillez, C. (2005). Social phobics do not misinterpret facial expression of emotion. *Behaviour Research and Therapy, 43,* 639–652.

Rapee, R. M., & Spence, S. H. (2004). The etiology of social phobia: Empirical evidence and an initial model. *Clinical Psychology Review, 24,* 737–767.

Richards, A., French, C., Nash, G., Hadwin, J. A., & Donnelly, N. (2007). A comparison of selective attention and facial processing biases in typically developing children high and low in self-reported trait anxiety. *Development and Psychopathology, 19*(2), 481–495.

Schwartz, G. M., Izard, C. E., & Ansul, S. E. (1985). The 5 month old's ability to discriminate facial expressions of emotion. *Infant Behaviour and Development, 8*, 65–77.

Simonian, S. J., Beidel, D. C., Turner, S. M., Berkes, J. L., & Long, J. H. (2001). Recognition of facial affect by children and adolescents diagnosed with social phobia. *Child Psychiatry and Human Development, 32*, 137–145.

Skuse, D., James, R. S., Bishop, D. V., Coppin, B., Dalton, P., & Aamodt-Leeper, G. (1997). Evidence from Turner's syndrome of an imprinted X-linked locus affecting cognitive functioning. *Nature, 387*, 705–708.

Slater, A. (1998). The competent infant: Innate organisation and early learning in infant visual perception. In A. Slater (Ed.), *Perceptual development: Visual, auditory and speech perception in infancy* (pp. 105–130). Hove, UK: Psychology Press.

Stirling, L. J., Eley, T. C., & Clark, D. M. (2006). Preliminary evidence for an association between social anxiety symptoms and avoidance of negative faces in school-age children. *Journal of Clinical Child and Adolescent Psychology, 35*, 440–445.

Striano, T., Brennan, P. A., & Vanman, E. J. (2002). Maternal depressive symptoms and 6 month old infants' sensitivity to facial expressions. *Infancy, 3*, 115–126.

Sylvester-Bradley, B., & Trevarthen, C. B. (1978). Talk as an adaptation to the infant's communication. In N. Waterson & C. Snow (Eds.), *The development of communication: Social and pragmatic factors in language acquisition*. New York: Wiley.

Trower, P., & Gilbert, P. (1989). New theoretical conceptions of social anxiety and social phobia. *Clinical Psychology Review, 9*, 19–35.

Turati, C., Simion, F., Milani, I., & Umiltà, C. (2002). Newborns' preference for faces: What is crucial? *Developmental Psychology, 38*, 875–882.

Winton, E. C., Clark, D. M., & Edelman, R. J. (1995). Social anxiety, fear of negative evaluation and the detection of negative emotion in others. *Behaviour Research and Therapy, 33*, 193–196.

Yonkers, K. A., Dyck, I. R., & Keller, M. B. (2001). An eight-year longitudinal comparison of the clinical course of social phobia among men and women. *Psychiatric Services, 52*, 637–643.

Yoon, K. L., & Zinbarg, R. E. (2007). Threat is in the eye of the beholder: Social anxiety and the interpretation of ambiguous facial expressions. *Behaviour Research and Therapy, 45*, 839–847.

Young, A. W., Perrett, D. I., Calder, A. J., Sprengelmeyer, R., & Ekman, P. (2002). *Facial Expressions of Emotion: Stimuli and tests (FEEST)*. Bury St Edmunds, UK: Thames Valley Test Company.

COGNITION AND EMOTION
2008, 22 (3), 459–479

The verbal information pathway to fear and subsequent causal learning in children

Andy P. Field and Joanne Lawson

University of Sussex, Brighton, East Sussex, UK

Recent research has shown that verbal threat information creates long-term fear cognitions and can create cognitive biases and avoidance in children. However, the impact on future learning is untested. This experiment exposed a non-clinical sample of children (aged 7–9 years) to threat, positive or no information about three novel animals to see the impact on their subsequent causal learning. In this causal learning task, children saw a series of pictures of animals and had to predict on each trial whether there would be a good or bad outcome. They then saw a picture to indicate whether the outcome was good or bad. The probability of each outcome was either .2 or .8. At the end of a block of trials children were also asked to estimate how many trials they thought had concluded with a negative outcome. Results showed that verbal information directly affected the estimate of associative strength between animals and positive and negative outcomes in a causal learning task. These results support theories of fear acquisition that suppose that verbal information affects components of the fear emotion, and suggest possibilities for using information to protect children from acquiring animal fears.

Although genetic factors appear to explain around a third of the variance in childhood anxiety, shared and non-shared environments also have a role to play (Eley et al., 2003). Rachman (1977) suggested that in addition to direct conditioning experiences, indirect pathways of observational learning and threat information could lead to phobic responses. Although some believe that threat information is the most important of these pathways (Muris, Merckelbach, Gadet, & Moulaert, 2000; Ollendick & King, 1991), much of the supporting evidence is based on retrospective methodology using questionnaires on which adult phobics assign experiences to one of

Correspondence should be addressed to: Andy P. Field, Department of Psychology, University of Sussex, Falmer, Brighton, East Sussex, BN1 9QH, UK. E-mail: andyf@sussex.ac.uk

This research was supported by ESRC grant R000239591 to AF and Robin Banerjee.

We would like to thank the staff and pupils of Southover C. E. Primary School, Lewes, East Sussex and Uckfield Community Technology College, Uckfield, East Sussex for their co-operation.

Rachman's pathways. This methodology is problematic for a variety of well-documented reasons (see Field, Argyris, & Knowles, 2001; Ollendick & King, 1991), which has led researchers to think of ways in which the causal role of threat information on anxiety can be investigated. Field et al. (2001) developed a prospective experimental paradigm: 7- to 9-year-olds received either positive or threat information about previously un-encountered toy monsters. Children's fear beliefs towards the monster about which they had received threat information significantly increased and a subsequent study based on the same paradigm showed that these beliefs persisted for a week (Muris, Bodden, Merckelbach, Ollendick, & King, 2003). Field and Lawson (2003) and Field, Lawson, and Banerjee (in press) improved the paradigm to relate more closely to real animal fears. They used real animals, unheard of by children in the UK, as stimuli and employed the Implicit Association Task (IAT; Greenwald, McGhee, & Schwartz, 1998) as an indirect measure of emotional responses to the animals. Threat information significantly increased children's fear beliefs regardless of how they were measured; it also promoted behavioural avoidance of the animals. Field and Lawson's paradigm has been used to demonstrate that verbal information creates attentional biases to animals about which threat information has been given (Field, 2006a), that trait anxiety mediates these effects on avoidance and attentional biases (Field, 2006b), and that threat information can be used to manipulate social fear beliefs too (Field, Hamilton, Knowles, & Plews, 2003; Lawson, Banerjee, & Field, 2007).

Rachman did not formalise a mechanism through which fear information has its effect. However, Field (2006b,c) has noted that modern theories of fear development are intrinsically linked to the threat information pathway. For example, in Davey's (1997) conditioning model of phobias there are two roles for threat information: the first is creating expectancies about the likely outcome of an encounter with a conditioned stimulus (CS; expectancy evaluations); the second is revaluing a previously innocuous experience such that its mental representation comes to act as an aversive unconditioned stimulus (US). Expectancy evaluations are important in shaping the consequences of future experiences. Davey (1997) described a body of conditioning research showing that the core CS–US association driving acquired fear responses in humans is influenced by existing beliefs about the likely outcome of interacting with the CS. For example, a child believing that a dog will bite it and that is subsequently bitten will have a stronger dog-trauma association than a child for whom the bite conflicts with its prior assumptions (see Field, 2006c). As such, threat information, by creating negative expectancies, should increase the strength and speed of acquisition of a CS–US association if the CS subsequently predicts a negative outcome.

It would be unethical to expose children to traumatic conditioning episodes of the sort implied in Davey's model. However, this experiment seeks to test the basic idea that fear beliefs will facilitate associative learning using a fear relevant (but not fear-evoking) post-information task. Although USs are typically defined as biologically significant (in the anxiety literature this equates to anxiety evoking), this is a rather old-fashioned view of a US (see Field, 2006c). Studies of causal learning in humans have shown that predictive relations between neutral stimuli and neutral outcomes are easily learnt (see De Houwer & Beckers, 2002; Dickinson, 2001; Shanks, Holyoak, & Medin, 1996, for reviews). For example, humans can learn to predict whether pictures of butterflies (CS) will mutate (US) when exposed to radiation (Collins & Shanks, 2002; Lober & Shanks, 2000) or whether certain foods (CS) predict an allergic reaction US (Aitken, Larkin, & Dickinson, 2000; Le Pelly & McLaren, 2003). In both cases the apparent US does not evoke an unconditioned response; the outcome of these learning trials is not a US in the traditional sense. Nevertheless, this form of learning can be successfully characterised as associative learning in which the cause acts as a CS and the outcome is viewed as a US (see Dickinson, Shanks, & Evenden, 1984). More important, predictions (or conditioned responses) show characteristics of associative learning such as sensitivity to the statistical contingency between the CS and US (Perales & Shanks, 2003), blocking (Dickinson, 2001; Dickinson et al., 1984), learnt inhibition and learning under negative contingency (Chapman & Robbins, 1990; Dickinson, 2001), super-learning (Aitken et al., 2000; Dickinson, 2001), second-order conditioning (Jara, Vila, & Maldonado, 2006) and data from these studies fit predictions from well-established mathematical models of conditioning such as the Rescorla–Wagner (1972) and Mackintosh (1975) models (De Houwer & Beckers, 2002; Dickinson, 2001; Le Pelley & McLaren, 2003; Lober & Shanks, 2000). These sorts of tasks are appropriate for demonstrating covariation biases in anxious children (see Muris & Field, 2008 this issue, for a review): for example, the overestimation of negative outcomes to spiders varies as a function of spider anxiety in children and adolescents (Muris, Huijding, Mayer, den Breejen, & Makkelie, 2007).

As such, this experiment uses a fear-relevant causal learning task as an ethical way to establish the effect of threat information on subsequent associative learning. The prediction from Davey's model would be that threat information should lead children to overestimate the associative strength between an animal and a negative outcome and also cause a posteriori covariation bias similar to that found in anxious children.

METHOD

Design

There were 12 counterbalancing orders overall. Information was given about the three unfamiliar Australian marsupials in a counterbalanced order across groups, such that each animal was, in different groups, associated with threat, positive and no information: (1) cuscus (threat), quoll (positive), quokka (no information); (2) quokka (threat), cuscus (positive), quoll (no information); and (3) quoll (threat), quokka (positive), cuscus (no information). Therefore, across groups, all types of information were associated with all animals. Each of these three groups was subdivided into two groups according to whether the causal learning task compared learning rates for the no-information animal to either positively or negatively described animals. Each of these groups was further divided into two groups on the basis of whether the causal learning trials were congruent or incongruent with the initial verbal information given first. The design was a 2 (animal: valenced or no information) × 4 (trial block) × 2 (contingency: .8 or .2) × 2 (order: .8/.2 or .2/.8) × 2 (valenced animal used: threat vs. positive) with repeated measures on the first three variables.

The dependent variables were the self-reported fear beliefs and subsequent estimations of the contingency between different animals and positive or negative outcomes in the causal learning prediction task. The Fear Survey Schedule for Children–Revised (FSSC-R) subscale incorporating animal fears was measured as a covariate.

Participants

One hundred twenty-two children (61 boys, 61 girls) between the ages of 7 and 9 years ($M = 105.81$ months, $SD = 7.63$) participated. There were four main groups of children that varied on whether they heard positive (P) or threat (T) information, and within this whether the order of causal learning blocks was congruent–incongruent (C–I) or vice versa (I–C). The age and gender splits for each group were: TC–I ($M = 7.97$, $SE = 0.11$, 16 boys, 16 girls); TI–C ($M = 7.97$, $SE = 0.12$, 12 boys, 18 girls); PC–I ($M = 8.29$, $SE = 0.12$, 19 boys, 12 girls); and PI–C ($M = 8.31$, $SE = 0.12$, 14 boys, 15 girls). The gender ratio over these four groups was not significantly different, $\chi^2(3, N = 122) = 2.82$, $p = .42$. An information type (threat or negative) by causal learning block order (congruent–incongruent vs. incongruent–congruent) performed on age showed that children who received positive information were significantly older than those receiving negative information, $F(1, 118) = 8.19$, $p < .01$. There were no significant age differences for the causal learning block order or the interaction of information type and causal learning block order, $Fs(1, 118) < 0.01$, $ps > .90$. The children were all recruited from schools in West Sussex, UK. Informed consent was obtained from parents on an opt-out basis.

Materials

Animals.   Pictures of three Australian marsupials, the quoll, the cuscus and the quokka were used (see Field & Lawson, 2003; Field, 2006a,b). These were animals about which the children had no prior experience and so it was assumed that they would have no prior fear expectations.

Information.   The two sets of information (one threat, one positive) used by Field and Lawson (2003) and Field (2006a, 2006b) were used: the two vignettes are almost exactly matched for length and word frequency.

Fear Beliefs Questionnaire (FBQ).   The FBQ devised by Field and Lawson (2003) was used: this consists of 21 statements (7 repeated once for each animal) about the animals, each with a 5-point Likert response scale (0 = *"No, not at all"*; 1 = *"No, not really"*; 2 = *"Don't Know/Neither"*; 3 = *"Yes, probably"*; 4 = *"Yes, definitely"*). This results in a mean fear belief score for each animal ranging from 0 (no fear belief) to 4 (maximum fear belief). The internal consistencies in the current sample were high and consistent with values across several previous studies (see Field, 2006a): $\alpha = .96$ (cuscus subscale), .95 (quokka subscale) and .93 (quoll subscale).

Fear Survey Schedule for Children–Revised (FSSC-R).   The FSSC-R (Ollendick, 1983) is standardised measure of children's fearfulness, involving 89 items each with a 3-point response scale of *"none"*, *"some"*, or *"a lot"*. Ollendick (1983) reported excellent internal consistency for the FSSC-R across two American samples (αs = .94 and .95), with test–retest reliability of .82 after 1 week and .55 after 3 months. Patterns of intense fears emerging from the FSSC-R can also be used to differentiate groups of clinically anxious children (Last, Francis, & Strauss, 1989).

Causal learning task.   A computerised causal learning prediction task based on Collins and Shanks (2002) was used. In this adaptation, children were told that the experimenters had found 80 people who had met a quokka, quoll or cuscus. Some of them had had a good time when they met the animal; but for some of them something bad had happened. The child's task was to guess, from a picture of the animal, whether something good or bad happened to the person. On each trial, the child was shown one of two animals (depending on counterbalancing order either the positively or negatively described animal, and for all participants the no-information animal) and asked to make their prediction by clicking on either of two buttons labelled "Good" and "Bad". Once they had made their choice, a picture of a face (either happy or fearful) and a tick or a cross appeared to let the child know whether they had made a correct or an incorrect prediction.

The contingencies were set such that in one block of 40 randomly ordered trials ("congruent trials") there was a .8 contingency: that is, the outcome of meeting a positive or threat animal was congruent with the information (and a face of the same valence was displayed) in 80% of trials and an outcome incongruent with the earlier information occurred on the remaining 20% of trials. In these trials, the no-information animal had the opposite outcomes (i.e., in the threat animal group it would be followed by a positive outcome on 80% of trials and a negative outcome on 20% of trials). In a different block of 40 trials ("incongruent trials"), the reverse .2 contingency was experienced: that is, the outcome of meeting a positive or threat animal was incongruent with the information (and a face of the opposite valence was displayed) in 80% of trials and an outcome congruent with the earlier information occurred on the remaining 20% of trials. In these trials, the no-information animal had the opposite outcomes (i.e., in the threat animal group it would be followed by a negative outcome on 80% of trials and a positive outcome on 20% of trials). The program stored the child's prediction on each trial. Half of the children received the 40 congruent trials before the incongruent trials and vice versa for the remaining children. Table 1 shows the various conditions in the causal learning task.

After each block of 40 trials, the children were given an *a posteriori* covariation task in which the on-screen instructions read: "For each animal you have just seen, there were 20 people who met them. So, for each animal 20 people told us whether something good or bad happened when they met the animal. How many of the 20 people had a bad experience?" They moved a bar along an on-screen slider ranging from 0 to 20 to estimate how many of the 20 people had a bad experience with each animal. These instructions are very similar to those used by Muris et al. (2007).

Procedure

The procedure was computerised using custom written (by the first author) software in Visual Basic.net. The FBQ consisted of a screen showing a named picture of the animal under which a question appeared. Children responded to the question by clicking on one of 5 screen buttons with the labels described above. A button labelled "sure?" appeared and children had to click this button to confirm their response and move to the next question. The 21 questions of the FBQ appeared in random order. Next a screen appeared explaining that the participant would now hear some information about the animals. A picture of an adult female (this was actually an "average" female face aged mid-20s, supplied by Professor David Perrett's

TABLE 1
Table showing the format of the causal learning task

Counterbalancing order	Predictive task (1st 40 trials)	1st a posteriori judgement		Predictive task (2nd 40 trials)	2nd a posteriori judgement	
		Predictors	Outcomes		Predictors	Outcomes
Positively described animal, congruent trials first	20 × positively described animal	16 × happy face 4 × fearful face	Out of the 20 people who met the [+vely described animal], how many had a bad time?	20 × positively described animal	4 × happy face 16 × fearful face	Out of the last 20 people who met the [+vely described animal], how many had a bad time?
	20 × no information animal	4 × happy face 16 × fearful face	Out of the 20 people who met the [no information animal], how many had a bad time?	20 × no information animal	16 × happy face 4 × fearful face	Out of the last 20 people who met the [no information animal], how many had a bad time?
Positively described animal, incongruent trials first	20 × positively described animal	4 × happy face 16 × fearful face	Out of the 20 people who met the [+vely described animal], how many had a bad time?	20 × positively described animal	16 × happy face 4 × fearful face	Out of the last 20 people who met the [+vely described animal], how many had a bad time?
	20 × no information animal	16 × happy face 4 × fearful face	Out of the 20 people who met the [no information animal], how many had a bad time?	20 × no information animal	4 × happy face 16 × fearful face	Out of the last 20 people who met the [no information animal], how many had a bad time?

(Continued overleaf)

TABLE 1 (Continued)

Counterbalancing order	Predictive task (1st 40 trials)	1st a posteriori judgement		Predictive task (2nd 40 trials)	2nd a posteriori judgement	
		Predictors	Outcomes		Predictors	Outcomes
Negatively described animal, congruent trials first	20 × negatively described animal	16 × fearful face 4 × happy face	Out of the 20 people who met the [+vely described animal], how many had a bad time?	20 × negatively described animal	4 × fearful face 16 × happy face	Out of the last 20 people who met the [-vely described animal], how many had a bad time?
	20 × no information animal	4 × fearful face 16 × happy face	Out of the 20 people who met the [no information animal], how many had a bad time?	20 × no information animal	16 × fearful face 4 × happy face	Out of the last 20 people who met the [no information animal], how many had a bad time?
Negatively described animal, incongruent trials first	20 × negatively described animal	16 × fearful face 4 × happy face	Out of the 20 people who met the [-vely described animal], how many had a bad time?	20 × negatively described animal	4 × fearful face 16 × happy face	Out of the last 20 people who met the [-vely described animal], how many had a bad time?
	20 × no information animal	4 × fearful face 16 × happy face	Out of the 20 people who met the [no information animal], how many had a bad time?	20 × no information animal	16 × fearful face 4 × happy face	Out of the last 20 people who met the [no information animal], how many had a bad time?

laboratory at St Andrews University, UK) appeared on the left side of the screen and a picture of the animal they were talking about appeared on the right side of the screen. Children heard the information through headphones from a pre-recorded MP3 file voiced by a female in her mid 20s. As such, the delivery of the information was completely controlled across children. Which two animals the information referred to was given by the counterbalancing order to which the child had been randomly assigned. As a further counterbalancing measure, within each order, approximately half the children received the threat information first, and the other half received the positive information first. Following the information, children completed the FBQ again and, finally, the causal learning prediction task was used.

RESULTS

Although $p < .05$ is used as a criterion for significance throughout, all results are reported at $p < .001$ unless otherwise stated. Effect sizes are reported as r when interpretable.

Self-reported fear beliefs

The effect of information on fear beliefs was examined in a 2-way ANCOVA, with Time (before and after information) and Information Type (positive, threat and none) as repeated measures and the FSSC-R animal subscale score as covariate. The expected increase in fear beliefs with threat information and decrease with positive information was found, as evidenced by an Information Type × Time interaction, $F(2, 234) = 78.52$. Contrasts showed significant differences between the pre- to post- change in the threat condition compared to the no-information condition, $F(1, 117) = 41.22$, $r = .51$, and between the pre- to post- change in the positive condition compared to the no-information conditions, $F(1, 117) = 35.30$, $r = .48$ (see Figure 1). The FSSC-R subscale did predict fear beliefs overall, $F(1, 117) = 19.37$, $p < .001$, but most important it did not influence the Information Type × Time interaction, $F(2, 234) = 0.28$, $p = .75$.

Causal learning

Given the complexity of the design, and the difficulty of interpreting a 5-way ANOVA, the data were broken down into four groups. The first two groups contained data for the threat-information animal versus the control animal. Group 1 had the congruent block of causal learning trials before the incongruent block, whereas Group 2 had the incongruent block before the congruent block. Groups 3 and 4 contained data for the positive-information animal versus the control animal. Group 3 had the congruent block of

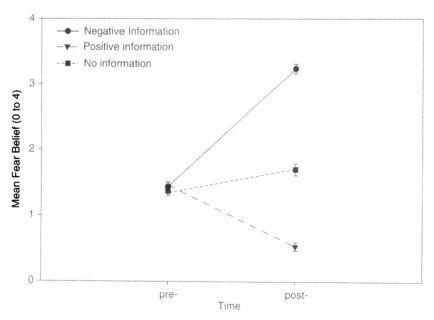

Figure 1. Graph showing the mean (and *SE*) fear-belief scores before and after the presentation of positive, negative, or neutral information.

causal learning trials before the incongruent block, whereas Group 4 had the incongruent block before the congruent block. Figure 2 shows the estimates of associative strength (contingency) in all conditions of the causal learning task. The values are the proportion of trials (out of 10) for which children responded in accordance with the information presented about the valenced animal: for example, in the left panels, these values represent the proportion of occasions on which children predicted a bad outcome in the causal learning trials (but for the right panels it represents the number of times that the children predicted a good outcome). These values are the perceived associative strength between an animal and an outcome (see Collins & Shanks, 2002). Within each panel, the lines represent different groups of children (i.e., the children who experienced a .8 contingency with a bad outcome in the first 40 trials for the threat-information animal were different to those experiencing a .8 contingency with a bad outcome for the no-information animal).

Learning involving the threat-information animal. The left panels of Figure 2 show the contingency estimates (i.e., the perceived associative strength) for threat and no-information animals for two different contingencies: .8 and .2. The top panel shows the data when 40 congruent trials

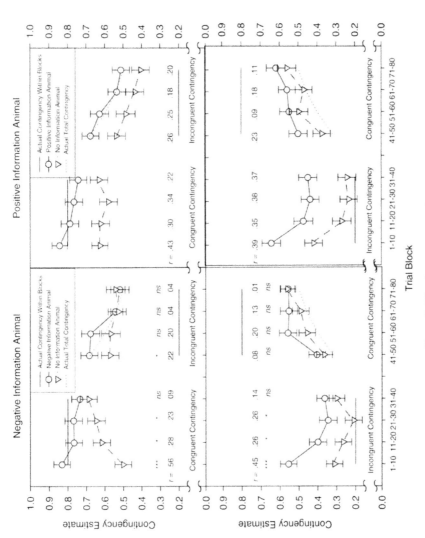

Figure 2. (*Caption on next page*)

were followed by 40 incongruent trials and the bottom panel shows the reverse order of trials. When children experienced congruent trials (i.e., the .8 contingency) first, it is clear that they more accurately predicted the associative strength between an animal and negative outcomes after threat information about an animal than after no information. However, when the contingency switched (there was now a low contingency with negative outcomes) children continued to overestimate the number of negative outcomes for the first 20 trials (the dotted line shows the cumulative contingency as it changes after the contingency switches), but after 20 trials regardless of the information provided children's predictions converged on the actual total contingency (top left panel of Figure 2).

A two-way 8 (Block: 1–10, 11–20, 21–30, 31–40, 41–50, 51–60, 61–70, 71–80) × 2 (Animal Type: threat-information animal vs. no-information animal) mixed ANOVA with repeated measures on block was used to analyse the data.[1] Sphericity was violated for the effect of Block, $W = .42$, $\chi^2 = 49.78$, $p < .01$, and so multivariate test statistics are reported for repeated-measures effects; specifically Pillai's Trace, which is the most robust (see Field, 2005). There were significant main effects of Block, $V = .33$, $F(7, 54) = 3.80$, $p < .01$, and animal type, $F(1, 60) = 8.52$, $p < .01$: overall, estimates of negative outcomes were significantly higher for the animal about which threat information had been given. There was also a significant Block × Animal Type interaction, $V = .25$, $F(7, 54) = 2.53$, $p < .05$, indicating that difference in contingency estimation between the threat-information animal and the no-information animal changed over the course of the causal learning task. To break down this interaction a simple effects analysis was done to look at the difference between the no-information animal and the threat-informa-tion animal for each block of trials: there were significant differences during trials 1–10, 11–20, 21–30, and 41–50: $Fs(1, 60) = 27.47$, 5.24 ($p < .05$), 3.39 ($p < .05$, 1-tailed) and 2.91 ($p < .05$, 1-tailed), respectively. There were no significant differences for trials 31–40, 51–60, 61–70 or 71–80, $Fs(1, 60) = 0.54$, 2.43, 0.08 and 0.11, respectively. Effect sizes for these differences

---

Figure 2 (previous page). Estimates of associative strength between an outcome and a threat information animal (left panels) or a positive information animal (right panels) and a control animal. These outcomes were either congruent or incongruent with the prior information about the animal (see text for further details). The grey lines represent the true contingency within blocks and across all contingencies (dotted).

---

[1] The data were analysed in this way because we wanted to track learning throughout the 80 trials. There is some case for analysing the data as a 4 (block: first 10, second 10, third 10, fourth 10 trials) ×2 (contingency: .8 or .2) ×2 (animal type: negative or no information) mixed ANOVA. However, this is inappropriate because it assumes that each block of 10 trials in the .8 contingency is comparable to the equivalent block for the .2 contingency and this is not the case: in the .2 contingency blocks there has been greater prior experience with the task.

are shown in the top-left panel of Figure 2. These results suggest that for the first 30 trials, the threat information makes children accurately predict the associative strength between the animal and a negative outcome (it is worth noting that children are not performing at ceiling or overestimating the contingency). However, when no information is given children underestimate the associative strength between the animal and negative outcomes. When the contingency switches, threat information makes children predict negative outcomes significantly more for the animal about which they have had threat information compared to an animal about which they have been told nothing. Looking at the contingency across all trials (the dotted line in Figure 2), threat information produces accurate predictions for the first 10 trials after the switch but leads to overestimation of negative outcomes after 20 trials. For the no-information animal children underestimate negative outcomes for the first 10 trials after which their estimates converge on the true total contingency. After 70 trials the perceived associative strength for the threat-information and no-information animals converge on the actual contingency across all trials.

When children experienced incongruent trials (i.e., the .2 contingency) first, it is clear (Figure 2, bottom-left panel) that they overestimate the associative strength between an animal and negative outcomes after threat information compared to no information. However, when the contingency switched the predictions for the no-information animal tracked the change in the total contingency experienced. However, after threat information, predictions led to an overestimation of negative outcomes (notably after 20 trials). A two-way 8 (Block: 1–10, 11–20, 21–30, 31–40, 41–50, 51–60, 61–70, 71–80) × 2 (Animal Type: threat-information animal vs. no-information animal) mixed ANOVA with repeated measures on block was used to analyse the data. Sphericity was again violated for the effect of block, $W = .35$, $\chi^2 = 60.69$, and the same statistics are reported as before. There were again significant main effects of Block, $V = .47$, $F(7, 54) = 6.75$, and animal type, $F(1, 60) = 7.97$, $p < .01$: overall, estimates of negative outcomes were significantly higher for the animal about which threat information had been given. There was also a significant Block × Animal Type interaction, $V = .22$, $F(7, 54) = 2.19$, $p = .05$, indicating that difference in contingency estimation between the threat-information animal and the no-information animal changed over the course of the causal learning task. A simple effects analysis was again conducted as before and there were significant differences during trials 1–10, 11–20, and 21–30: $Fs(1, 60) = 15.53$, 4.44 $(p < .05)$, and 4.21 $(p < .05)$, respectively. There were no significant differences for trials 31–40, 41–50, 51–60, 61–70 or 71–80, $Fs(1, 60) = 1.18$, 0.41, 2.61, 0.99, and 0.01, respectively. Effect sizes for these differences are shown in the bottom-left panel of Figure 2. These results suggest that for the first 30 trials, the threat information made children overestimate the contingency between the animal and a negative outcome. However, when no information is given children quickly estimate the contingency accurately. The data converge after 40 trials. When the contingency switches, the differences between the animals associated with different types of information become nonsignificant, however, the effect sizes show a trend (small to medium effect) for estimates to increase more quickly to a plateau for the threat information animal (20 trials compared to 30). One-sample t-tests also revealed that following threat information, when the contingency switched, children significantly overestimated the number of negative outcomes after the first 10, 20 and 30 trials, $ts(29) = 2.39$, 3.35 and 2.13, $rs = .41$, $.53$, and $.37$, respectively; but not after 40 trials, $t(29) = 1.53$, $r = .27$, although the effect size was medium. For the no-information animal none of the estimates differed significantly from the true cumulative contingency, $ts(31)$ for trials 41–50, 51–60, 61–70 and 71–80 $= 0.92$, 1.30, 0.65 and 1.47, $rs = .16$, $.23$, $.12$, and $.26$, respectively.

Learning involving the positive-information animal. The right panels of Figure 2 show the perceived associative strength for positive- and no-information animals and outcomes. When children experienced congruent trials (i.e., the .8 contingency) first, it is clear that they more accurately predicted the associative strength after positive information about an animal than after no information. This trend continued after the contingency switched: the estimates fall almost exactly on the line showing the true contingency over all trials. Sphericity was again violated $W = .40$, $\chi^2 = 50.60$, $p < .01$. A two-way mixed ANOVA (as described previously) revealed significant main effects of Block, $V = .55$, $F(7, 52) = 9.14$, $p < .01$, and Animal Type, $F(1, 58) = 13.29$, $p < .01$: overall, estimates of positive outcomes were significantly higher for the animal about which positive information had been given. Unlike for threat information, the Block × Animal Type interaction was not significant, $V = .07$, $F(7, 52) = 0.54$, indicating that difference in the perceived associative strength between the threat-information animal and the no-information animal remained similar over the course of the causal learning task; because of this a simple effects analysis was not appropriate, although effect sizes for the differences can still be found in Figure 2 (top right panel).

When children experienced incongruent trials (i.e., the .2 contingency) first, they overestimated the associative strength after positive information about an animal compared to no information (Figure 2, bottom-right panel). Sphericity was again violated, $W = .34$, $\chi^2 = 60.45$. A mixed ANOVA (as described previously) showed significant main effects of Block, $V = .43$, $F(7, 52) = 5.65$, and Animal Type, $F(1, 58) = 19.36$: overall, estimates of positive outcomes were significantly higher for the animal about which positive information had been given. The Block × Animal

Type interaction was not significant, $V = .08$, $F(7, 52) = 0.64$, indicating that differences in perceived associative strength between the positive-information animal and the no-information animal were similar over the course of the causal learning task. As such, a simple effects analysis was unjustified, but effect sizes for the differences can be found in Figure 2 (bottom-right panel). One-sample t-tests also revealed that following positive information, when the contingency switched, children significantly overestimated the number of positive outcomes after trials 41–50, 51–60, 61–70 and 71–80, $ts(28) = 3.83$, 2.86, 2.14 and 2.49, $rs = .41$, .48, .37 and .43, respectively. For the no-information animal none of the estimates differed significantly from the true cumulative contingency apart from after 51–60 trials, $ts(31)$ for trials 41–50, 51–60, 61–70 and 71–80 $= 1.17$, 2.06, 0.24 and 1.18, $rs = .21$, .35, .04, and .21, respectively.

A posteriori covariation judgements

Figure 3 shows the number of encounters out of 20 that children estimated would give rise to a negative (top panel) or positive (bottom panel) experience. The dotted lines show the correct contingency: so, for example, after the first 40 trials of the causal learning task, if the valenced animal had had a negative outcome on 80% of trials (the congruent condition) then the correct response is 16 out of 20. However, in the same condition, after 80 trials the contingency has switched so the correct response would be 20% or 4 out of 20. The graph shows few differences between children's estimates for the animals about which information was given (threat or positive) and the no-information control animals. T-tests revealed only one significant difference: when threat information was followed by congruent causal learning trials children estimated a significantly higher contingency than for the no-information animal, $t(47.02) = 1.81$, $p < .05$ (1-tailed). However, even this significant difference gave rise to only a modest effect size ($r = .26$) and the value estimated equated to a 60% contingency rather than the actual 80% contingency. All other comparisons were nonsignificant and gave rise to small effect sizes (see Figure 3).

DISCUSSION

This experiment replicated the finding that threat information increased self-reported fear beliefs about novel animals in children. However, it also showed that when verbal information is followed by associative learning trials consistent with that information, the perceived associative strength is significantly more accurate and more rapidly acquired than when no information is given. Valenced information does not lead to an over-estimation of contingencies, but an absence of information does lead to a

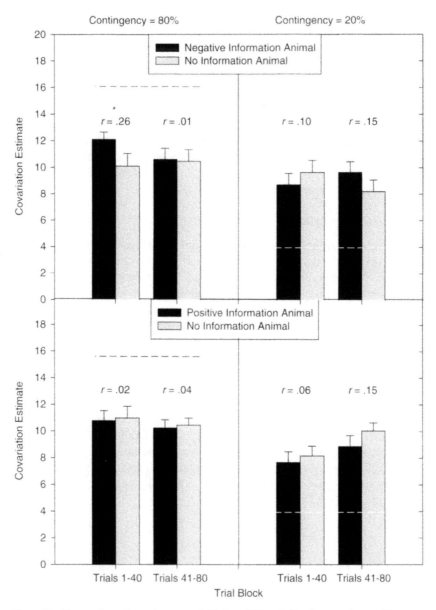

Figure 3. The number of occasions out of 20 that children believed a negative, positive or no information animal would give rise to a negative (top panel) or positive (bottom panel) experience. The dotted lines represent the "correct" contingency.

slower acquisition of the true associative strength. The implication is clear: in the absence of any verbal information it takes a child a great many trials (40) to detect and accurately predict a contingency between an animal and a "bad" outcome. However, threat information makes the acquisition of this contingency quicker (almost immediate). This is true for positive information also. The second finding was that when verbal information is followed by associative learning trials that are inconsistent with that information, children significantly overestimate the associative strength of animals and outcomes consistent with the information they have heard: the acquisition of the true contingency is retarded compared to when no information is given. When no information is given children quickly acquire the correct associative strength.

When the contingency between animals and good and bad outcomes switched there was a difference depending on whether the prior information was positive or threatening and whether the contingency became more congruent with the initial information or more incongruent. For positive information, when the contingency switched from congruent to incongruent, children's predictions accurately tracked the contingency as it changed. In this case, no information led to the contingency being underestimated. When the contingency switched from incongruent to congruent, the positive information led to an overestimation of positive outcomes compared to when no information was given (after which contingency estimation tracked the actual change in contingency). For threat information the picture was slightly more complicated: when the contingency switched from congruent to incongruent, threat information led to accurate contingency prediction for the first 10 trials after the switch, then an overestimation for the second 10 trials, then for the remaining 20 trials estimates accurately tracked the true contingency. In contrast, when no information was given there was an underestimation of the contingency for the first 10 trials after which estimates accurately reflected the true contingency. When the contingency changed from incongruent to congruent children consistently overestimated the number of threat outcomes for the first 30 trials after threat information; however, after no information their estimates did not differ significantly from the true contingency.

Implications for theories of anxiety

Contemporary conditioning theories of phobia acquisition (Davey, 1997; Mineka & Zinbarg, 2006) emphasise that if beliefs about the outcomes of interacting with a particular stimulus (CS) are consistent with the actual outcome (US), the formation of an associative link between that stimulus and the outcome is facilitated (Davey, 1992). In this case, having a strong negative attitude about an animal will facilitate the creation of an association between that animal and a traumatic event (and hence a negative conditioned response, CR, to the animal) should the person experience such a conditioning episode. It should also increase the associative strength between the stimulus and negative outcome. The results of the current study showed that when associative learning was broadly consistent with prior information, the perceived associative strength between an animal and an outcome was very accurate; however, in the absence of information children perceived the associative strength to be less than it actually was. When contingencies switched to be inconsistent, threat information led to relatively short-term overestimations of the associative strength between animals and bad outcomes. Perhaps a more important finding was that when associative learning was broadly inconsistent with prior information, threat and positive information led to overestimations of the associative strength between animals and outcomes congruent with prior information. Several authors (e.g., Field, 2006c; Mineka & Zinbarg, 2006) have noted that the role that associative learning plays in fear acquisition is contingent upon the many known phenomena of this form of learning. One important aspect of associative learning is prior learning: associative strength is typically dependent upon prior learning (as is shown in the current study when no information is given). However, our results showed that verbal information interacts with prior learning such that the associative strength between an animal and outcomes consistent with this information is overestimated (Trials 41–80) when prior associative learning experiences (trials 1–40) have been inconsistent with this information (bottom panels of Figure 2).

These findings strongly support the general thrust of Davey's (1997) conditioning model. However, they also support other theories of anxiety that suggest verbal information or social learning is a vulnerability factor that interacts with future learning such as Mineka and Zinbarg (2006) and Muris and Merckelbach (2001). Finally, in terms of Rachman's original model, the current results offer a clear causal mechanism through which information has an effect on the cognitive and behavioural components of the fear emotion (Lang, 1985): information biases cognition and behaviour directly but also biases future judgements of associative strength of the likely outcomes from encountering an animal.

The results were broadly consistent between positive and threat information, which could be considered problematic for threat information as a pathway to fear. However, none of the models of fear acquisition involving information predict selective effects of threat information. In fact, models of associative learning would have a great deal of difficulty explaining hugely different effects arising from positive information compared to threat (see Field, 2006c). The fact that positive beliefs and overestimations of positive outcomes arose from positive information suggests that prevention should be targeted at using positive information to promote positive fear beliefs about animals. This experiment showed that the knock-on effect of this would be to promote accurate perception of the associative strength between that animal and a positive outcome even in the experience of some negative experiences. Of course, the true protective value of such information is unknown: the overestimation of positive outcomes in the face of negative associative learning lasted 40 trials in the current study, but for ethical reasons these trials consisted of very mild learning episodes, not personally traumatic events. It is also possible that differences in the effect of positive or negative information would differ in trait-anxious children. Field (2006b), for example, has shown that trait anxiety moderates the effect of verbal threat information on avoidance and attentional bias; therefore we might expect it to also affect subsequent learning (although consistent with the current results, Field did not find differential moderation effects for positive and threat information).

One disappointing aspect of the results was that children's post-block contingency judgements appeared to be relatively unaffected by fear information. The only exception was that threat information led to greater estimates of the contingency between an animal and negative outcomes. However, the estimated contingency was still below the true contingency. The likely explanation for these findings is simply that children did not understand the task: the experiments were done in an age group for whom proportions and percentages would not yet have been taught at school, and so estimating a "number of occasions out of 20" would be very difficult. (Anecdotal evidence suggests that many children were confused by this part of the experiment.) Muris, de Jong, Meesters, Waterreus, and van Lubeck (2005) also found that spider-fearful children aged 8 to 13 years did not show a covariation bias and concluded that children of this age may lack the cognitive skills to apply such abstract mental operations. The trial-by-trial contingency estimates are, therefore, likely to be the better reflection of the associative strength perceived by children.

Summary

This experiment showed that a short burst of information about novel animals is sufficient to create beliefs about the affective valence of those animals that impact on future associative learning such that in the face of contradictory learning experiences the associative strength between the animal and outcomes consistent with the initial information are over-estimated.

REFERENCES

Aitken, M. R. F., Larkin, M. J. W., & Dickinson, A. (2000). Super-learning of causal judgments. *Quarterly Journal of Experimental Psychology*, *53B*, 59–81.

Chapman, G. B., & Robbins, S. J. (1990). Cue interaction in human contingency judgment. *Memory and Cognition*, *18*, 537–545.

Collins, D. J., & Shanks, D. R. (2002). Momentary and integrative response strategies in causal judgment. *Memory and Cognition*, *30*, 1138–1147.

Davey, G. C. L. (1992). An expectancy model of laboratory preparedness effects. *Journal of Experimental Psychology: General*, *121*, 24–40.

Davey, G. C. L. (1997). A conditioning model of phobias. In G. C. L. Davey (Ed.), *Phobias: A handbook of theory, research and treatment* (pp. 301–322). Chichester, UK: Wiley.

De Houwer, J., & Beckers, T. (2002). A review of recent developments in research and theories on human contingency learning. *Quarterly Journal of Experimental Psychology*, *55B*, 289–310.

Dickinson, A. (2001). Causal learning: An associative analysis. *Quarterly Journal of Experimental Psychology*, *54B*, 3–25.

Dickinson, A., Shanks, D. R., & Evenden, J. L. (1984). Judgment of act–outcome contingency: The role of selective attribution. *Quarterly Journal of Experimental Psychology*, *36A*, 29–50.

Eley, T. C., Bolton, D., O'Connor, T. G., Perrin, S., Smith, P., & Plomin, R. (2003). A twin study of anxiety-related behaviours in pre-school children. *Journal of Child Psychology and Psychiatry*, *44*, 945–960.

Field, A. P. (2005). *Discovering statistics using SPSS for Windows* (2nd ed.). London: Sage.

Field, A. P. (2006a). Watch out for the beast: Fear information and attentional bias in children. *Journal of Clinical Child and Adolescent Psychology*, *35*(2), 337–345.

Field, A. P. (2006b). The behavioral inhibition system and the verbal information pathway to children's fears. *Journal of Abnormal Psychology*, *115*(4), 742–752.

Field, A. P. (2006c). Is conditioning a useful framework for understanding the development and treatment of phobias? *Clinical Psychology Review*, *26*, 857–875.

Field, A. P., Argyris, N. G., & Knowles, K. A. (2001). Who's afraid of the big bad wolf? A prospective paradigm to test Rachman's indirect pathways in children. *Behavior Research and Therapy*, *39*, 1259–1276.

Field, A. P., Hamilton, S. J., Knowles, K. A., & Plews, E. L. (2003). Fear information and social phobic beliefs in children: A prospective paradigm and preliminary results. *Behavior Research and Therapy*, *41*, 113–123.

Field, A. P., & Lawson, J. (2003). Fear information and the development of fears during childhood: Effects on implicit fear responses and behavioral avoidance. *Behavior Research and Therapy*, *41*, 1277–1293.

Field, A. P., Lawson, J., & Banerjee, R. (in press). The verbal threat information pathway to fear in children: The longitudinal effects on fear cognitions and the immediate effects on avoidance behavior. *Journal of Abnormal Psychology*.

Greenwald, A. G., McGhee, D. E., & Schwartz, J. L. K. (1998). Measuring individual differences in implicit cognition: The implicit association test. *Journal of Personality and Social Psychology*, *74*, 1464–1480.

Jara, E., Vila, J., & Maldonado, A. (2006). Second-order conditioning of human causal learning. *Learning and Motivation*, *37*, 230–246.

Lang, P. J. (1985). The cognitive psychopathology of emotion: Fear and anxiety. In A. H. Tuma & J. D. Maser (Eds.), *Anxiety and the anxiety disorders* (pp. 131–170). Hillsdale, NJ: Lawrence Erlbaum Associates, Inc.

Last, C. G., Francis, G., & Strauss, C. C. (1989). Assessing fears in anxiety-disordered children with the Revised Fear Survey Schedule for Children (FSSC-R). *Journal of Clinical Child Psychology, 18,* 137–141.

Lawson, J., Banerjee, R., & Field, A. P. (2007). The effects of verbal information on children's fear beliefs about social situations. *Behaviour Research and Therapy, 45,* 21–37.

Le Pelley, M. E., & McLaren, I. P. L. (2003). Learned associability and associative change in human causal learning. *Quarterly Journal of Experimental Psychology, 56B,* 68–79.

Lober, K., & Shanks, D. R. (2000). Is causal induction based on causal power? Critique of Cheng (1997). *Psychological Review, 107,* 195–212.

Mackintosh, N. J. (1975). A theory of attention: Variations in the associability of stimuli with reinforcement. *Psychological Review, 82,* 276–298.

Mineka, S., & Zinbarg, R. (2006). A contemporary learning theory perspective on the etiology of anxiety disorders: It's not what you thought it was. *American Psychologist, 61,* 10–26.

Muris, P., Bodden, D., Merckelbach, H., Ollendick, T. H., & King, N. (2003). Fear of the beast: A prospective study on the effects of negative information on childhood fear. *Behavior Research & Therapy, 41,* 195–208.

Muris, P., de Jong, P. J., Meesters, C., Waterreus, B., & van Lubeck, J. (2005). An experimental study of spider-related covariation bias in 8- to 13-year-old children. *Child Psychiatry and Human Development, 35,* 185–201.

Muris, P., & Field, A. P. (2008). Distorted cognition and pathological anxiety in children and adolescents. *Cognition and Emotion, XX,* XXX–XXX.

Muris, P., Huijding, J., Mayer, B., den Breejen, E., & Makkelie, M. (2007). Spider fear and covariation bias in children and adolescents. *Behaviour Research and Therapy, 45,* 2604–2615.

Muris, P., & Merckelbach, H. (2001). The etiology of childhood specific phobia: A multifactorial model. In M. W. Vasey & M. R. Dadds (Eds.), *The developmental psychopathology of anxiety* (pp. 355–385). Oxford, UK: Oxford University Press.

Muris, P., Merckelbach, H., Gadet, B., & Moulaert, V. (2000). Fears, worries, and scary dreams in 4- to 12-year-old children: Their content, developmental pattern, and origins. *Journal of Clinical Child Psychology, 29,* 43–52.

Ollendick, T. H. (1983). Reliability and validity of the revised fear survey schedule for children (FSSC-R). *Behaviour Research and Therapy, 21,* 685–692.

Ollendick, T. H., & King, N. J. (1991). Origins of childhood fears: An evaluation of Rachman's theory of fear acquisition. *Behavior Research and Therapy, 29,* 117–123.

Perales, J. C., & Shanks, D. R. (2003). Normative and descriptive accounts of the influence of power and contingency on causal judgment. *Quarterly Journal of Experimental Psychology, 56A,* 977–1007.

Rachman, S. J. (1977). The conditioning theory of fear acquisition: A critical examination. *Behavior Research and Therapy, 15,* 375–387.

Rescorla, R. A., & Wagner, A. R. (1972). A theory of Pavlovian conditioning: Variations in the effectiveness of reinforcement and non-reinforcement. In A. H. Blake & W. F. Prokasy (Eds.), *Classical conditioning II: Current research and theory* (pp. 64–99). New York: Appleton-Century-Crofts.

Shanks, D. R., Holyoak, K. J., & Medin, D. L. (Eds.). (1996). *The psychology of learning and motivation: Vol. 34. Causal learning.* San Diego, CA: Academic Press.

COGNITION AND EMOTION
2008, 22 (3), 480–496

Experiential avoidance in the parenting of anxious youth: Theory, research, and future directions

Shilpee Tiwari, Jennifer C. Podell, Erin D. Martin,
Matt P. Mychailyszyn, Jami M. Furr, and Philip C. Kendall

Temple University, Philadelphia, PA, USA

Empirical findings support the notion that overprotective and intrusive parenting practices may contribute to the maintenance of anxiety in youth (e.g., Ginsburg & Schlossberg, 2002). It appears that parents of anxious youth are more likely to intervene during anxiety-provoking situations for their child when he/she displays negative emotion or distress (e.g., Hudson, Comer, & Kendall, 2008). It remains unclear, however, why anxious children's displays of negative emotion are difficult for parents to tolerate. One possible explanation is that parents of anxious youth are more likely to engage in experiential avoidance, the inability or unwillingness to tolerate one's own internal distress, which manifests as intrusive behaviour designed to reduce the child's distress, and thereby the parent's own internal distress. This article reviews the theoretical and empirical underpinnings of experiential avoidance, describes its potential role in the parenting of anxious children, and discusses implications for treatment and future directions for research.

Parents, be it through genetics or their socialisation practices, are often viewed in some way as responsible for the actions and reactions of their offspring. Data suggest that factors related to the family (i.e., parental psychopathology, negative interactions) contribute to the development and maintenance of anxiety disorders in youth (e.g., Ginsburg, Siqueland, Masia-Warner, & Hedtke, 2004; Wood, McLeod, Sigman, Hwang, & Chu, 2003). Specifically, the thinking, theorising, and research have focused on particular parenting behaviour that may contribute to the maintenance of distressing anxiety in children (see Ginsburg & Schlossberg, 2002, for a review). For example, several studies have found that parents of anxious

Correspondence should be addressed to: Philip C. Kendall, Temple University, Department of Psychology, Weiss Hall, 1701 N. 13th St., Philadelphia, PA 19122, USA. E-mail: pkendall@temple.edu

Preparation of this manuscript was facilitated by research grant awards from the National Institute of Mental Health to PCK (MH59087; MH63747).

The authors would like to thank Dr Laurie A. Greco for her valuable contributions to the preparation of this manuscript.

DOI: 10.1080/02699930801886599

children are more likely to engage in intrusive, over-protective, and over-controlling behaviour relative to parents of non-anxious children (e.g., Greco & Morris, 2002; Hudson, Comer, & Kendall, 2008; Wood, 2006).

Although differences between parents of anxious and non-anxious youth have been documented, less is known about the mechanisms that may explain these differences. The role of *experiential avoidance* (EA; Hayes & Gifford, 1997), a recent construct borne out of Acceptance and Commitment Therapy (ACT; Hayes, Strosahl, & Wilson, 1999), has been proposed as a potential explanatory mechanism. Specifically, EA refers to an inability or unwillingness to tolerate one's own experience of negative emotion—to *experientially* avoid internal distress. It has been hypothesised that parents of anxious children have an inability (or limited ability) to tolerate seeing their children in distress, and this lack of tolerance may be due to their *own* experience of negative emotion (i.e., fear, anxiety, irritability, anger, frustration, etc.) in situations that are anxiety provoking for their children.

EA is increasingly receiving empirical attention. Learning more about the processes involved in EA may inform us about why child distress during anxiety-provoking situations is so difficult for parents to tolerate—information that has valuable treatment implications. The purpose of the present article is to review the theoretical and empirical underpinnings of the potential role played by EA in the relationship between parenting behaviour and the maintenance of anxiety disorders in youth. To this end, we (a) review relevant findings from the child-anxiety literature that relate to parenting behaviour; (b) further define EA, discuss the cognitive and emotional processes involved, and outline extant research findings related to this construct; (c) discuss how EA may play a role in the parenting of anxious children; (d) describe an instrument designed to measure EA; and (e) suggest future directions for research on EA and its relationship to parenting and child anxiety. To understand how EA may lead to parental anxiety-maintaining behaviour, it is first necessary to examine the research findings examining how different types of parenting behaviour contribute to the maintenance of child anxiety.

PARENTING BEHAVIOUR AND THE MAINTENANCE OF ANXIETY

Studies have found that parents of children with anxiety disorders, compared to parents of children without anxiety disorders, exercise a higher degree of control over their child and are more intrusive in interactions with their child (e.g., Hudson & Rapee, 2001; Siqueland, Kendall, & Steinberg, 1996), tend to be perceived by their child as being overprotective (e.g., Leib et al., 2000), and are more likely to model anxiety or reinforce their child's anxious avoidance (e.g., Barrett, Rapee, Dadds, & Ryan, 1996; Chorpita, Albano, & Barlow, 1996; Dadds, Barrett, Rapee, & Ryan, 1996). Although initial research in this area focused primarily on the relationship between intrusive or over-controlling maternal behaviour and child anxiety (e.g., Whaley, Pinto, & Sigman, 1999), more recent studies have demonstrated that these findings also extend to fathers of anxious children (e.g., Greco & Morris, 2002). A meta-analysis of the association between parenting and childhood anxiety (McLeod, Wood, & Weisz, 2007) found modest support (i.e., parenting accounted for 4% of the variance in child anxiety). The authors noted methodological limitations (e.g., inconsistency of constructs and measurement across studies) that might explain why parenting was found to exercise minimal influence. In fact, when focusing on studies involving observational measures of parenting and removing those using purely self-report measures, the variance accounted for increases to 8%.

Although some data and several theories support a meaningful relationship between the behaviour of parents and the maintenance of unwanted anxiety in children, the direction of effects and the specific processes involved remain in question. Is it a unidirectional causal arrow? Is there particular parenting behaviour that causes or leads to specific child behaviour, or does an anxious child's behaviour trigger identifiable parental reactions? Other researchers have adopted a transactional approach to the study of the relationship between parenting and child anxiety, seeking to identify aspects of the child's behaviour that may elicit protective parental responses. For example, Woodruff-Borden, Morrow, Bourland, and Cambron (2002) found that anxious parents were likely to withdraw from interactions in which their child was experiencing stress, as manifested by, for example, frustration stemming from an inability to complete a task, *until* the child expressed some type of negative emotion (e.g., anxiety, fear), at which point they exerted excessive control. Turner, Beidel, Roberson-Nay, and Tervo (2003) assessed parental behaviour during routine activities and a non-conflictual play task and similarly found that anxious parents were no more likely than non-anxious parents to engage in overly restrictive or intrusive behaviour. Importantly, however, anxious parents reported higher levels of distress when their children were engaged in these activities. This pattern of parental responding suggests that children's expressions of negative emotion are uncomfortable for anxious parents and often lead to parental distress. The inclusion of anxious parents in this line of research provides insight into potential mechanisms of transmission of anxiety from parent to child. It remains unclear, however, whether parental psychopathology moderates the relationship between parenting behaviour and child anxiety.

A more recent study of child behaviour during parent–child interactions (Hudson et al., 2008) found that perhaps it is the child's emotional state that moderates the relationship. The authors examined the behaviour of parent–child dyads during an emotion-discussion task (i.e., five-minute videotaped discussions of a recent situation in which the child felt angry, anxious, or happy). The results indicate that relative to mothers of non-anxious children, mothers of anxious children were more likely to display intrusive involvement (i.e., "taking over" the task) when the child displayed *negative* emotion (i.e., anxiety or anger), but not in situations involving *positive* emotion. These findings are similar to those from previous research indicating that parents of anxious children are often intrusive in interactions with their child (e.g., Siqueland et al., 1996). Taken with the findings from Woodruff-Borden and colleagues, a pattern emerges: observable displays of *negative emotion* may act as a signal that children are experiencing distress, which elicits attempts to control or stop this distress by way of protective parental responses (i.e., either parental withdrawal or intrusiveness, depending on the parent's own level of anxiety). This body of research provides valuable information regarding the transactional relationship between the parent's behaviour and the behaviour of anxious children.

EXPERIENTIAL AVOIDANCE

The clinical application of basic research results could be enhanced as we better understand mechanism(s) underlying protective parental responses to a child's display of negative emotion. Unfortunately, these mechanisms have received less research attention. That said, researchers are beginning to examine the role of EA as a potential explanatory mechanism for parents' inability to tolerate their anxious child's distress. To better understand the notion of EA and its potential relationship to parenting and child anxiety, it is important to understand the nature of avoidance and how it relates to the maintenance of anxiety.

Avoidance remains a key behavioural characteristic of anxiety in adults (Barlow, 2002; Borkovec, Alcaine, & Behar, 2004) and children (Kendall & Suveg, 2006). Avoidance responses are made consistent with the belief that they will prevent a negative/unwanted condition. Escape responses, which often precede avoidance, are responses that "stop" a negative condition from occurring. The avoidance seen in anxiety disorders is the continuation of a response, which is not needed, but which is believed to prevent the negative/unwanted condition. Thus, avoidance persists even in the absence of any functional value. Avoidance can be adaptive when it helps individuals steer clear of situations that have true potential to induce harm. However, avoidance is maladaptive when it is linked to marked distress, such as when a feared situation/stimulus is avoided due to unreasonable or excessive responses to *perceived* as opposed to actual threat, and perhaps most clearly when this avoidance begins to interrupt developmentally appropriate activities (Himle, Fischer, Lee, & Muroff, 2006). For example, imagine a child living in a dangerous neighbourhood in which he/she regularly witnesses or encounters some form of violence or aggression. Over time, this child is likely to have discovered ways to protect him/herself from harm, by avoiding walking home alone from school or leaving his/her house after dark to play outside, and for an older child, by checking the doors and windows of his/her house before going to bed to ensure the safety of his/her family. Given this child's environment, his/her avoidance of particular people or situations, this need to protect him/herself, is adaptive and necessary. If, however, this child lived in a safe neighbourhood where crime was not a concern, similar expressions of avoidance would be excessive and unreasonable and might prevent the child from engaging in developmentally appropriate activities, such as riding his/her bicycle or playing outside with his/her friends. In the latter case, the child's avoidance would be considered maladaptive.

Avoidance is typically manifested in overt and observable behaviour. However, avoidance may also apply when one is trying to cope with internal processes of discomfort and distress. *Experiential* avoidance has been used to refer to a person's unwillingness to remain in contact with particular private experiences (e.g., bodily sensations, emotions, thoughts, memories, behavioural dispositions), specifically those experiences that are linked to negative emotions, such as fear or anxiety, and that induce distress, as well as the subsequent attempts to alter the form or frequency of these events and the contexts in which they occur (Hayes & Wilson, 1993; Hayes, Wilson, Gifford, Follette, & Strosahl, 1996). According to this view, when individuals with agoraphobia avoid public places, they are not avoiding the *places* themselves; rather, they are avoiding their experience of thoughts and the emotion(s) that are associated with the panic elicited when they are in public places. Similarly, as described by Eifert and Forsyth (2005), individuals with obsessive-compulsive disorder may avoid touching a doorknob they feel has germs on it not because they fear being contaminated, but because they are attempting to avoid the negative thoughts (regarding contamination) and emotion that touching the doorknob would produce. In other words, the behavioural avoidance that is characteristic of anxiety disorders (e.g., avoiding public places, public speaking, touching contaminated doorknobs) may be the overt manifestation of EA—avoidance of psychological and emotional experiences. EA stands in contrast to *psychological acceptance*, which is the openness or willingness to experience private events fully and in their entirety, without struggle or defence (Hayes et al., 1999).

EA is purported to stem from the bidirectionality of language and verbal knowledge. In other words, the development of language allows for individuals to become "entangled" with the content of their minds. This entanglement is especially true in the case of human emotions, as they tend to require a verbal label or appraisal as a cognitive component (Lazarus, 1982). Therefore, as described in Hayes et al. (1996), "anxiety" is not just a set of bodily sensations and behavioural dispositions; rather, it is a label that represents an evaluative and descriptive category of integrated experiences, such as memories, thoughts, social comparisons, etc. The evaluative component of emotion labels alters the function of the private experiences of those labels. As it relates to anxiety, for example, individuals may categorise a set of physiological cues and bodily sensations as "anxiety" and evaluate them as "bad" (Hayes et al., 1996; Hayes & Gifford, 1997). As described by Hayes et al. (1996), the bidirectionality of human language can create the illusion that this "badness" is an inherent quality of anxiety as an emotion ("anxiety is a bad emotion", not "anxiety is an emotion, and I am evaluating it as 'bad'"), and the presence of the emotion elicits immediate or automatic attempts to suppress or avoid experiencing the internal distress associated with the negative emotion. Individuals can become unable to distinguish their private experiences (having a thought: "I have a thought that other kids will laugh at me") from reality ("buying into" a thought: "Other kids will laugh at me"). Socialisation practices may further dictate that the experience of any form of negative emotional experience is harmful and should be avoided at all costs (Greco, Blackledge, Coyne, & Ehrenreich, 2005a). Children may often be taught to deliberately regulate their expression of emotion (e.g., "stop crying; that won't help you"). In this way, EA may become a negatively reinforced behaviour.

As with behavioural avoidance, EA can be adaptive or maladaptive. EA has been associated with behavioural effectiveness in some contexts, such as when using distraction techniques with children during routine immunisation procedures (e.g., Cohen, Bernard, Greco, & McClellan, 2002). However, when individuals *routinely* act to avoid, suppress, and escape from negative emotions, associated thoughts, physical sensations, and the circumstances that elicit these feelings, they are likely devoting time, effort, and energy in this struggle. Under these circumstances, EA is maladaptive, and it is this rigid and inflexible application of an otherwise adaptive process that is believed to be involved in various forms of psychopathology. Specifically, research on EA has demonstrated how individuals who are more likely to engage in this process show increased vulnerability to various forms of fear and anxiety (Feldner, Zvolensky, Eifert, & Spira, 2003; Karekla, Forsyth, & Kelly, 2004). Feldner et al. (2003) reported that participants scoring the highest on measures of EA reported higher anxiety and distress associated with a CO_2 challenge task. These results suggest that individuals who displayed a greater tendency to engage in EA rated this aversive experience as "more aversive" than individuals low on EA. It is important to note, however, that the direction of effects between EA and vulnerability to anxiety remains unclear, and these results should be interpreted with caution.

Sloan (2004) found that individuals scoring high on a measure of EA, the Action and Acceptance Questionnaire (AAQ; Hayes et al., 2004), reported greater emotional experiencing of unpleasant and pleasant stimuli (i.e., film clips) compared to individuals scoring low on these measures. Interestingly, however, high-EA individuals exhibited an attenuated psychophysiological response to unpleasant stimuli, as measured by decreased heart rate. The author hypothesised that this attenuated pattern of heart rate may reflect attempts by high EA participants to regulate their heightened internal experiences, implying that, in the short term, engaging in EA during stressful or negative situations may actually *reduce* negative experiences. Sloan (2004) further hypothesised that if the high-EA group was attempting to alter its emotional experience, individuals in this group would actually show *greater* physiological activity at a subsequent time point (i.e., rebound effect; Gross & Muñoz, 1995), consistent with other research on the effects of suppression or elimination of private experience (e.g., Cioffi & Holloway, 1993; Clark, Ball, & Pape, 1991).

Although the Sloan (2004) study did not allow for direct examination of this phenomenon, results from research studying the psychology of pain, and using a different paradigm, provided results consistent with a possible rebound effect. Using a cold-pressor task, which assesses individuals' reactions to and efforts to cope with pain induced by placing their hand in a container filled with ice water, Feldner et al. (2006) found that high-EA individuals showed lower pain endurance and tolerance and also took more time to recover from the aversive event. In other words, high-EA participants were more likely to report higher levels of pain after hand removal than their low-EA counterparts. The results were interpreted to mean that deliberate suppression of pain increases the perception of and the experience of pain in future circumstances. These findings are meaningful since previous research has demonstrated that low tolerance for emotional distress elicited by physical stress is associated with poorer emotional adjustment (Brown, Lejuez, Kahler, & Strong, 2002).

As with behavioural avoidance, individuals are likely to engage in EA because the immediate effects are positive: the avoidance strategy initially results in an apparent decrease in emotional experiencing (Wenzlaff & Wegner, 2000). However, as with behavioural avoidance, active avoidance of the feared stimulus only leads to increased fear and a decreased sense of mastery or competence in future situations involving the stimulus. Specifically, an increase in avoidance of internal events may inadvertently associate private reactions with pathological forms of avoidance, and reduce access to personal data that inhibits informed decision making and blocks useful information about the contexts that occasion such private reactions. Given the hypothesised long-term detrimental effects of EA, it is unsurprising that research has found that this method of coping is associated with poor outcomes across clinical populations (see Greco et al., 2005a). Consistent with this, research indicates that an avoidant attachment style, a construct from the field of developmental psychology, is associated with increased physiological responsiveness and susceptibility to stress and physical and mental illness (Maunder & Hunter, 2001).

EXPERIENTIAL AVOIDANCE IN PARENTS OF ANXIOUS YOUTH

High levels of EA play a role in predicting psychological stress across a broad range of groups (Feldner et al., 2003, 2006; & Sloan, 2004). Accordingly, it could be posited that parents who score highly on measures of EA may be experiencing more stress and increased emotional responsiveness to their child, especially if the child is displaying distress. This notion is consistent with Hudson and colleagues' (2008) finding that parents display intrusive involvement when their children show negative, but not positive emotion. Thus, understanding EA seems particularly important when examining the relationship between parenting and child anxiety, as it may provide one possible explanation of why parents of anxious children are more likely to respond to their child in ways that maintain the child's anxiety. As proposed by Greco and colleagues (2005a), most parents have pre-existing beliefs in the form of verbal rules about their child's experience of anxiety as being an intolerable and horrific experience, as well as about their child's ability to handle or manage their anxiety. Research suggests that parents of children with anxiety disorders are more likely to display negative beliefs or expectations regarding their child's ability to cope under stressful circumstances (Kortlander, Kendall, & Panichelli-Mindel, 1997), implying that parents of anxious children are quick to intervene in an anxiety-provoking situation for the child, given pre-existing beliefs (i.e., rules) that the child is incapable of handling the situation independently (e.g., "It's just too much for him/her"). From the EA standpoint, it is possible that such rules regarding the child's distress or inability to cope elicit the parent's *own* negative emotions, and the need to ameliorate or suppress this mood state then drives parental responses that are seen as overprotective, intrusive, or over-controlling. Interestingly, parents experiencing their own struggle with anxiety display a different behavioural manifestation of EA during anxiety-provoking situations for their child (i.e., withdrawal), perhaps because their experience of negative emotion is so intense and overwhelming that the only way they can cope is by immediately removing or distancing themselves from the distressing situation. The end result, however, is the same: the child is unable to develop a sense of mastery or control over his or her anxiety in the situation, and the child's anxiety is maintained.

As noted previously, EA is an emerging construct, with research examining the impact of parents of anxious children engaging in this method of coping and thereby contributing to the maintenance of anxiety still in its nascent stage. More generally, research examining the potential mediational role of EA in maternal responses to a stressful parenting event (i.e., preterm birth of a child; Greco et al., 2005b) suggests that high levels of EA (i.e., low levels of psychological acceptance) may interfere with healthy adaptation and coping following the event. EA may compromise the ability of a parent to adequately manage a stressful situation.

TREATMENT IMPLICATIONS

Children, invariably, find themselves in situations that can stir emotional reaction—both positive and negative. It simply is not possible for any parent, no matter how Herculean the effort, to prevent a child from experiencing emotional stress and challenge. Nor, one can argue, would it be worthwhile for a parent to make such efforts. A parent's inability to tolerate their anxious child's distress during a stressful situation has significant treatment implications.

When treating anxiety disorders in youth, CBT has been identified as an empirically supported treatment (e.g., Kendall, 1994; Kendall et al., 1997). One of the purported active ingredients in CBT is the inclusion of exposure tasks in which the child in treatment is exposed to the situations that induce the negative emotion (Kendall et al., 2005). These are the very situations that the anxious youth want to avoid. As numerous children who completed treatment have reported years later: "You made me do things I didn't want to do" (Kendall & Southam-Gerow, 1996). Parents are often involved in the structuring of the exposure tasks that are designed for their children—both the exposure tasks that take place in sessions and those that take place between sessions. As described by Greco et al. (2005a), it may be difficult for parents to watch their child experience distress during these intentionally anxiety-provoking situations (i.e., exposure tasks), and this may hold even more true for parents who are struggling with EA and perhaps their own psychopathology. In fact, research involving anxiety-disordered children often implicates both maternal (e.g., Hudson & Rapee, 2001; Whaley et al., 1999) and paternal (Podell & Kendall, 2008) anxiety as factors that serve to maintain the child's anxiety.

During exposure tasks, EA may drive parental efforts to reduce their *own* anxiety or discomfort, which could possibly be detrimental to the child's progress in treatment. Take for example a child who has social phobia, and as a moderately anxiety-provoking "take-home" task is asked to order dinner at a restaurant. As the waiter approaches, the child becomes visibly anxious, and starts to blush, fidget, and looks down at its menu, unable to speak. Although appearing anxious, the child may be trying to calm itself down internally by using relaxation techniques and changing its anxious self-talk into coping self-talk (e.g., "I can do this"), but this experience of silence from the child may be difficult for its parent(s) to witness and tolerate. This experience may also elicit the parents' own verbal rules about their child's ability to endure anxiety ("She/he looks so scared and anxious; this must be so awful for her/him", i.e., expectations regarding their child's ability to perform during anxiety-provoking situations; see Cobham, Dadds, & Spence, 1999). Unable to tolerate their own response to the child's visibly anxious affect, the parent may intervene and order for the child, leaving it to feel as though it is, once more, unable to master the situation. This reduced sense of competence is likely to affect the child's anxiety level in similar situations in the future, as well as its perception of its ability to control or affect the environment (Rapee, 2001), which is detrimental to its progress in treatment. Thus, it appears that addressing parents' negative expectations about their child's ability to cope during anxiety-provoking situations (Cobham et al., 1999), such as exposure tasks, should be an essential component of child anxiety treatment.

To increase the completion of difficult exposure tasks, it may be worthwhile to expand CBT to incorporate additional strategies, such as mindfulness, to foster parents' psychological acceptance, thereby undermining EA. As described by Dumas (2005), mindfulness is a state of mind characterised by careful, compassionate, and considerate attention, that is focused on *being* rather than *doing*, and on experiencing present, immediate experiences as they unfold, rather than on problem solving. Mindfulness-based parenting practices are designed to disrupt the automaticity associated with everyday parent–child interaction that has developed over time, for instance, the parent of the anxious child who quickly (perhaps due to their own emotional distress) jumps in to solve a situation in which their child is distressed. Consistent with traditional learning theory, Dumas hypothesised that with repeated practice under comparable learning conditions, parents and children often develop common patterns of interaction referred to as *automatised transactional procedures* (ATPs). ATPs become over learned to the point that they give access to automated thoughts, feelings, and actions and are often called upon during stressful situations since they provide immediacy and efficiency. As such, the processes involved in ATPs can be viewed as being *mindless*. With regard to parent–child interactions during anxiety-provoking situations, it is possible that the following ATP has developed: the child engages in a particular behaviour that indicates that he/she is distressed; the parent responds with increased control or intrusive involvement to help momentarily decrease the child's distress, thereby reducing his or her own distress (i.e., EA); the child continues to feel as though he/she has no control over the situation or his/her environment; and the child's anxiety is maintained.

Mindfulness-based parent training, along with other CBT efforts to modify parental responding, may help disrupt the automaticity associated with parent–child interactions by encouraging parents to attend to their immediate thoughts and feelings non-judgementally; to help parents distance themselves from over-learned ways of coping and the negative emotional states with which they have become associated; and by helping parents choose effective goals for themselves and their children. As described by Greco and Eifert (2004), mindfulness-based practices may help undermine EA by allowing parents to experience the dynamic and transient nature of private events such as unwanted thoughts, emotions, and bodily sensations.

Mindfulness-based practices vary from CBT approaches that usually encourage parents to manage their own anxiety during anxiety-provoking situations for their children by *changing* what they are thinking or feeling. Mindfulness-based practices place an emphasis on *being present* with an emotion or thought, *without evaluation*, and without requiring that the thought be changed or altered in any way, experiencing, in a sense, as in an exposure task, the unwanted emotion. Eifert and Forsyth (2005) described this approach as helping people relax *with* their anxiety, by *being* and *moving* with it, not trying to relax *away* their anxiety by "pushing away" their unwanted thoughts or feelings. Incorporating mindfulness into existing cognitive-behavioural interventions may enable parents to make room for the painful thoughts and emotions associated with their child's distress during exposure tasks by being present with their thoughts about what they fear their child is experiencing or what may happen to the child. The emphasis here is not on *changing* thoughts, but rather recognising them as just thoughts and not as a representation of reality. This may allow anxious children to experience the necessary level of anxiety required for exposure tasks to be effective without parental intrusion, which is particularly important given parents' contribution to the generalisation and maintenance of treatment gains. Mindfulness-based practices have shown promise when folded into interventions for adults with anxiety and depression (Baer, 2003), and mindfulness training also seems to be beneficial for children with anxiety disorders (Semple, Reid, & Miller, 2005). Research on mindfulness-based parent training, either alone or incorporated into existing CBT interventions, is yet to be conducted.

MEASUREMENT OF EXPERIENTIAL AVOIDANCE

Efforts to test theory and evaluate the role of a psychological construct in the prediction of maladjustment require comparable efforts to develop and evaluate appropriate measurement strategies. To examine the role that EA may play in parenting, researchers have begun to develop measures to assess parental tolerance of their child's distress. For example, the *Parental Acceptance and Action Questionnaire* (PAAQ; Cheron & Ehrenreich, 2008) is a 15-item parent self-report questionnaire that is a modified version of the AAQ (Hayes et al., 2004). The PAAQ was designed to assess the need of parents for emotional and cognitive control of their child's behaviour as well as for avoidance of their child's negative private events and parents' inability to take needed action during these negative private events. It is hypothesised that the PAAQ assesses parents' cognitive entanglement in relation to their children, including negative evaluations of their child's private experiences and their own negative self-references in relation to their child's experiences.

Factor analysis of the PAAQ yielded two separate subscales similar to the AAQ. These two factors were labelled Action and Willingness. High scores on the Action Subscale are hypothesised to indicate parents who are less able to take action when their children have emotional experiences. High scores on the Willingness subscale are hypothesised to indicate parents who are more avoidant of experiencing negative affect associated with their child's emotional experiences. Overall, high scores on the PAAQ Total Scale are hypothesised to indicate parents who display more EA in relation to their child's affective experiences.

Current investigation of the psychometric properties of the PAAQ, by the test developers, resulted in reports of temporal stability (moderate; $r = .68$–$.72$) and internal consistency in the individual subscales and the full scale is also moderate ($\alpha = .64$–$.65$). Initial reports of data that address the validity of the PAAQ seem to be supportive (i.e., correlates well with measures of parent EA (AAQ), parent psychopathology, and measures of control). When ascertaining the PAAQ's unique contribution to variance in child psychopathology in an anxious sample through regression analysis, variations in parent ratings and clinician ratings of child psychopathology were uniquely accounted for by variations in PAAQ scores.

Although this new measure is promising, much work needs to be done to determine the degree to which it is distinct from other related constructs and the degree to which it provides incremental predictive information. Also, research involving the use of the PAAQ or similar measures to examine group differences between parents of anxious versus non-anxious children is yet to be conducted.

FUTURE DIRECTIONS

As the bidirectional role of parent and child behaviour in general merits increased attention, so too do features or styles of parenting that may influence and maintain child psychopathology. Research examining a wide range of parenting styles and behaviour, in response to anxious and non-anxious children, will be informative and valuable. The possible role of EA in the relationship between parenting behaviour and the maintenance of child anxiety has the potential to contribute to the growing body of literature on the relationship between parenting and childhood anxiety. Do parents of anxious children, relative to parents of non-anxious children, endorse higher self-reported EA? If EA is higher, might this help to explain why parents of anxious children are more likely than parents of non-anxious children to engage in overly restrictive and controlling behaviour? Importantly, given that there exist few methodologically sophisticated and controlled laboratory tests of EA, additional basic research is needed. For instance, responses to pleasant and unpleasant emotionally evocative stimuli could be compared between groups of parents of anxious versus non-anxious children. Multi-method assessment could be incorporated into this body of research via the inclusion of measures of physiological reactivity (e.g., respiration, skin conductance, EEG) and cognitive processing (self-statement questionnaires, endorsement methods; Kendall & Hollon, 1981) to tap the "private" experiences that define EA. Multimethod assessment is particularly important when researching EA, given the intensely private processes involved in this method of coping.

A challenge facing psychopathology and psychotherapy is the specificity of this hypothetical explanatory construct. Is it true for anxiety disorders in youth alone, or is it true for parents and youth with other disorders? Studies using multiple groups of youth (with relatively distinct pathologies) are needed to examine whether high levels of parent EA are specific to parents of anxious children or if they are present in parents of children with various forms of psychopathology. In addition, the role of parental psychopathology separate from high levels of EA must also be considered. Parents who are experiencing their own struggle with anxiety may be less able to tolerate the distress associated with their anxious child's inability to adequately cope with a stressful situation.

Another potential area for research is the possible transmission of EA from parent to child. It is possible that parents of anxious children model EA in the same way that they have been demonstrated to model behavioural avoidance (e.g., Barrett et al., 1996; Chorpita et al., 1996), ultimately leading to the maintenance of their child's anxiety. Perhaps children develop their own verbal rules about anxiety being "bad" from observing their parents' attempts to avoid or suppress negative emotional states; therefore EA may become socialised as a coping strategy, compromising the child's ability to develop a complete emotion repertoire. Indeed, research has shown that families of children with an anxiety disorder often exhibit truncated emotional expressivity (Suveg, Zeman, Flannery-Schroeder, & Cassano, 2005). In a similar vein, research has found that infants who are insecurely attached to their caregivers show decreased emotional understanding (Laible & Thompson, 1998), possibly resulting from caregivers' withdrawal in situations where the child displays negative emotion. Insecure attachment may help explain, in part, the Woodruff-Borden et al. (2002) results indicating that anxious parents are initially withdrawn and detached during stressful situations for their child. Examining the relationship between experiential avoidance and attachment style may inform how parenting influences the development and maintenance of child anxiety.

Although progress has been made in the development and evaluation of interventions that can be effective for youth with anxiety disorders (APA Task Force on the Promotion and Dissemination of Psychological Procedures, 1995; Ollendick, King, & Chorpita, 2006), it is not yet clear how best to improve these procedures or to treat those who are deemed "non-responders" to these programs. Researching ways to improve and expand therapeutic interventions for childhood anxiety may benefit from considerations of parent EA as a potential force in child treatment outcome. Although findings regarding the inclusion of parents as "co-clients" in CBT are mixed (see Barmish & Kendall, 2005), there remains the need for study of the mechanisms via which parents may influence treatment results. Might the explicit targeting of parent EA in a child's treatment lead to better management of the child's anxiety outcome? Involving parents as collaborators in CBT treatment, by recruiting their efforts to design and execute between-session exposure tasks, provides not only valuable opportunities for the child to reduce anxiety but also affords opportunities to examine parent EA in response to anxiety-provoking exposure tasks for the child. Much like a child's subjective units of distress (SUDs) are monitored before, during, and after an exposure task, parent EA could be similarly monitored and examined for changes over the course of successful and less-successful treatment. Mindfulness-based parent training could be incorporated into existing CBT interventions to assist parents with tolerating the distress associated with observing their child partake in anxiety-provoking exposure tasks, potentially leading to improved outcome. Parents are involved, to varying degrees, in the psychological treatment of their children. The inclusion of EA and related notions into existing treatments for child anxiety merits attention.

REFERENCES

APA Task Force on Promotion and Dissemination of Psychological Procedures. (1995). Training in and dissemination of empirically validated psychological treatments: Report and recommendations. *The Clinical Psychologist, 48*, 3–24.

Baer, R. A. (2003). Mindfulness training as a clinical intervention: A conceptual and empirical review. *Clinical Psychology: Science and Practice, 10*, 125–143.

Barlow, D. H. (2002). *Anxiety and its disorders: The nature and treatment of anxiety and panic* (2nd ed). New York: Guilford Press.

Barmish, A., & Kendall, P. C. (2005). Should parents be co-clients in cognitive-behavioral therapy for anxious youth? *Journal of Clinical Child and Adolescent Psychology, 34*, 569–581.

Barrett, P. M., Rapee, R. M., Dadds, M. M., & Ryan, S. M. (1996). Family enhancement of cognitive style in anxious and aggressive children. *Journal of Abnormal Child Psychology, 24*(2), 187–203.

Borkovec, T. D., Alcaine, O. M., & Behar, E. (2004). Avoidance theory of worry and generalized anxiety disorder. In R. Heimberg, C. L. Turk, & D. S. Mennin (Eds.), *Generalized anxiety disorder: Advances in research and practice* (pp. 77–108). New York: Guilford Press.

Brown, R. A., Lejuez, C. W., Kahler, C. W., & Strong, D. R. (2002). Distress tolerance and duration of past smoking cessation attempts. *Journal of Abnormal Psychology, 111*, 180–185.

Cheron, D. M., & Ehrenreich, J. T. (2008). *Assessment of parental experiential avoidance in an anxious population: Development of a Parental Acceptance and Action Questionnaire (PAAQ)*. Manuscript in preparation.

Chorpita, B. F., Albano, A. M., & Barlow, D. H. (1996). Cognitive processing in children: Relation to anxiety and family influences. *Journal of Child Clinical Psychology, 25*(2), 170–176.

Cioffi, D., & Holloway, J. (1993). Delayed costs of suppressed pain. *Journal of Personality and Social Psychology, 64*, 274–282.

Clark, D. M., Ball, S., & Pape, D. (1991). An experimental investigation of thought suppression. *Behaviour Research and Therapy, 29*, 253–257.

Cobham, V. E., Dadds, M. R., & Spence, S. H. (1999). Anxious children and their parents: What do they expect? *Journal of Clinical Child Psychology, 28*(2), 220–231.

Cohen, L. L., Bernard, R. S., Greco, L. A., & McClellan, C. (2002). Using a child-focused intervention to manage procedural pain: Are parent and nurse coaches necessary? *Journal of Pediatric Psychology, 27*, 749–757.

Dadds, M. R., Barrett, P. M., Rapee, R. M., & Ryan, S. (1996). Family process and child anxiety and aggression: An observational analysis. *Journal of Abnormal Child Psychology, 24*(6), 715–734.

Dumas, J. E. (2005). Mindfulness-based parent training: Strategies to lessen the grip of automaticity in families with disruptive children. *Journal of Clinical Child and Adolescent Psychology, 34*(4), 779–791.

Eifert, G. H., & Forsyth, J. P. (2005). *Acceptance and commitment therapy for anxiety disorders: A practitioner's treatment guide to using mindfulness, acceptance, and values-based behavior change strategies*. Oakland, CA: New Harbinger.

Feldner, M. T., Hekmat, H., Zvolensky, M. J., Vowles, K. E., Secrist, Z., & Leen-Feldner, E. W. (2006). The role of experiential avoidance in acute pain tolerance: A laboratory test. *Journal of Behavior Therapy and Experimental Psychiatry, 37*, 146–158.

Feldner, M. T., Zvolensky, M. J., Eifert, G. H., & Spira, A. P. (2003). Emotional avoidance: An experimental test of individual differences and response suppression using biological challenge. *Behaviour Research and Therapy, 41*, 403–411.

Ginsburg, G. S., & Schlossberg, M. C. (2002). Family based treatment of childhood anxiety disorders. *International Journal of Psychiatry, 14*, 142–153.

Ginsburg, G. S., Siqueland, L., Masia-Warner, C., & Hedtke, K. A. (2004). Anxiety disorders in children: Family matters. *Cognitive and Behavioral Practice, 11*(1), 28–43.

Greco, L. A., Blackledge, J. T., Coyne, L. W., & Ehrenreich, J. (2005a). Integrating acceptance and mindfulness into treatments for child and adolescent anxiety disorders: Acceptance and commitment therapy as an example. In S. M. Orsillo & L. Roemer (Eds.), *Acceptance and mindfulness-based approaches to anxiety* (pp. 301–322). New York: Springer.

Greco, L. A., & Eifert, G. H. (2004). Treating parent–adolescent conflict: Is acceptance the missing link for an integrative family therapy? *Cognitive and Behavioral Practice, 11*, 305–314.

Greco, L. A., Heffner, M., Poe, S., Ritchie, S., Polak, M., & Lynch, S. K. (2005b). Maternal adjustment following preterm birth: Contributions of experiential avoidance. *Behavior Therapy, 36*, 177–184.

Greco, L. A., & Morris, T. L. (2002). Paternal child-rearing style and child social anxiety: Investigation of child perceptions and actual father behavior. *Journal of Psychopathology and Behavioral Assessment, 24*(4), 259–267.

Gross, J. J., & Muñoz, R. F. (1995). Emotion regulation and mental health. *Clinical Psychology: Science and Practice, 2*, 151–164.

Hayes, S. C., & Gifford, E. V. (1997). The trouble with language: Experiential avoidance, rules, and the nature of verbal events. *Psychological Science, 8*, 170–173.

Hayes, S. C., Strosahl, K. D., & Wilson, K. G. (1999). *Acceptance and commitment therapy: An experiential approach to behavioral change.* New York: Guilford Press.

Hayes, S. C., Strosahl, K. D., Wilson, K. G., Bissett, R. T., Pistorello, J., Toarmino, D., et al. (2004). Measuring experiential avoidance: A preliminary test of a working model. *The Psychological Record, 54*, 553–578.

Hayes, S. C., & Wilson, K. G. (1993). Some applied implications of a contemporary behavior analytic account of verbal behavior. *The Behavior Analyst, 16*, 283–301.

Hayes, S. C., Wilson, K. G., Gifford, E. V., Follette, V. M., & Strosahl, K. (1996). Experiential avoidance and behavioral disorders: A functional dimensional approach to diagnosis and treatment. *Journal of Consulting and Clinical Psychology, 64*(6), 1152–1168.

Himle, J. A., Fischer, D. J., Lee, M. V. E., & Muroff, J. R. (2006). Childhood anxiety disorders. In R. J. Waller (Ed.), *Fostering child & adolescent mental health in the classroom* (pp. 77–98). Thousand Oaks, CA: Sage.

Hudson, J. L., Comer, J. S., & Kendall, P. C. (2008). *Children's emotions and parental anxiety in the parenting of anxious children.* Manuscript submitted for publication.

Hudson, J. L., & Rapee, R. M. (2001). Parent–child interactions and anxiety disorders: An observational study. *Behaviour Research & Therapy, 39*, 1411–1427.

Karekla, M., Forsyth, J. P., & Kelly, M. M. (2004). Emotional avoidance and panicogenic responding to a biological challenge procedure. *Behavior Therapy, 35*(4), 725–746.

Kendall, P. C. (1994). Treating anxiety disorders in children: Results of a randomized clinical trial. *Journal of Consulting and Clinical Psychology, 62*, 100–110.

Kendall, P. C., Flannery-Schroeder, E., Panichelli-Mindel, S. M., Southam-Gerow, M., Henin, A., & Warman, M. (1997). Therapy for youths with anxiety disorders: A second randomized clinical trial. *Journal of Consulting and Clinical Psychology, 65*, 366–380.

Kendall, P. C., & Hollon, S. D. (1981). Assessing self-referent speech: Methods in the measurement of self-statements. In P. C. Kendall & S. D. Hollon (Eds.), *Assessment strategies for cognitive-behavioral interventions* (pp. 85–118). New York: Academic Press.

Kendall, P. C., Robin, J. A., Hedtke, K. A., Gosch, E., Flannery-Schroeder, E., & Suveg, C. (2005). Conducting CBT with anxious youth? Think exposures. *Cognitive and Behavioral Practice, 12*, 136–150.

Kendall, P. C., & Southam-Gerow, M. A. (1996). Long-term follow-up of a cognitive-behavioral therapy for anxiety-disordered youth. *Journal of Consulting and Clinical Psychology, 64*, 724–730.

Kendall, P. C., & Suveg, C. (2006). Treating anxiety disorders in youth. In P. C. Kendall (Ed.), *Child and adolescent therapy: Cognitive-behavioral procedures* (3rd ed., pp. 243–294). New York: Guilford Press.

Kortlander, E., Kendall, P. C., & Panichelli-Mindel, S. M. (1997). Maternal expectations and attributions about coping in anxious children. *Journal of Anxiety Disorders, 11*(3), 297–315.

Laible, D. J., & Thompson, R. A. (1998). Attachment and emotional understanding in preschool children. *Developmental Psychology, 34*(5), 1038–1045.

Lazarus, R. S. (1982). Thoughts on the relations between emotion and cognition. *American Psychologist, 37*, 1019–1024.

Leib, R., Wittchen, H., Hofler, M., Fuetsch, M., Stein, M., & Merikangas, K. R. (2000). Parental psychopathology, parenting styles, and the risk of social phobia in offspring: A prospective, longitudinal community study. *Archives of General Psychiatry, 57*, 859–866.

Maunder, R. G., & Hunter, J. J. (2001). Attachment and psychosomatic medicine: Developmental contributions to stress and disease. *Psychosomatic Medicine, 63*, 556–567.

McLeod, B. D., Wood, J. J., & Weisz, J. R. (2007). Examining the association between parenting and childhood anxiety: A meta-analysis. *Clinical Psychology Review, 27*(2), 155–172.

Ollendick, T., King, N., & Chorpita, B. (2006). Empirically supported treatments for children and adolescents. In P. C. Kendall (Ed.), *Child and adolescent therapy: Cognitive-behavioral procedures* (3rd ed.). New York: Guilford Press.

Podell, J. C., & Kendall, P. C. (2008). *Parents in family cognitive-behavioral therapy for anxious youth: Fathers matter.* Manuscript submitted for publication.

Rapee, R. M. (2001). The development of generalized anxiety. In M. W. Vasey & M. R. Dadds (Eds.), *The developmental psychopathology of anxiety* (pp. 481–503). New York: Oxford University Press.

Semple, R. J., Reid, E. F. G., & Miller, L. (2005). Treating anxiety with mindfulness: An open trial of mindfulness training for anxious children. *Journal of Cognitive Psychotherapy: An International Quarterly, 19*(4), 379–392.

Siqueland, L., Kendall, P. C., & Steinberg, L. (1996). Anxiety in children: Perceived family environments and observed family interaction. *Journal of Clinical Child Psychology, 25*(2), 225–237.

Sloan, D. M. (2004). Emotion regulation in action: Emotional reactivity in experiential avoidance. *Behaviour Research and Therapy, 42*, 1257–1270.

Suveg, C., Zeman, J., Flannery-Schroeder, E., & Cassano, M. (2005). Emotion socialization in families of children with an anxiety disorder. *Journal of Abnormal Child Psychology, 33*(2), 145–155.

Turner, S. M., Beidel, D. C., Roberson-Nay, R., & Tervo, K. (2003). Parenting behaviors in parents with anxiety disorders. *Behaviour Research and Therapy, 41*, 541–554.

Wenzlaff, R. M., & Wegner, D. M. (2000). Thought suppression. *Annual Review of Psychology, 51*, 59–91.

Whaley, S. E., Pinto, A., & Sigman, M. (1999). Characterizing interactions between anxious mothers and their children. *Journal of Consulting and Clinical Psychology, 67*(6), 826–836.

Wood, J. J. (2006). Parental intrusiveness and children's separation anxiety in a clinical sample. *Child Psychiatry and Human Development, 37*, 73–87.

Wood, J. J., McLeod, B. D., Sigman, M., Hwang, W. C., & Chu, B. C. (2003). Parenting and childhood anxiety: Theory, empirical findings, and future directions. *Journal of Child Psychology and Psychiatry, 44*(1), 134–151.

Woodruff-Borden, J., Morrow, C., Bourland, S., & Cambron, S. (2002). The behavior of anxious parents: Examining mechanisms of transmission of anxiety from parent to child. *Journal of Clinical Child and Adolescent Psychology, 31*, 364–374.

COGNITION AND EMOTION
2008, 22 (3), 497–508

Threat interpretation bias in anxious children and their mothers

Sara Gifford, Shirley Reynolds, Sarah Bell, and
Charlotte Wilson

University of East Anglia, Norwich, Norfolk, UK

The role of parents in the development of anxiety disorders in children is of increasing research and clinical interest. This study investigated interpretation biases of anxious children and their mothers using the ambiguous stimuli task developed by Hadwin, Frost, French, and Richards (1997). Three groups of children (aged 7 to 12 years) and their mothers were recruited; 23 non-clinical controls, 18 children with an anxiety disorder and 15 children with an externalising disorder. Following diagnostic assessments of the children, children and their mothers independently completed the homophone task and self-report measures of anxiety. Mothers of anxious children had significantly higher self-reported anxiety than mothers of non-clinical children. As hypothesised, children in the anxious group had higher threat interpretation scores than the non-clinical group. The hypothesis that mothers of anxious children would make more threat interpretations was not supported. Paired correlations showed no significant association between threat interpretations made by children and their mothers. There was a significant positive correlation between maternal threat interpretation and child anxiety. The results suggest that there is a complex association between mother's anxiety and cognitions and those of their children, which requires further examination in controlled observational and experimental studies, including treatment trials.

Understanding and treating anxiety in children requires consideration of developmental and family processes, which are generally given less attention in therapy with adults. Therefore, theories of childhood anxiety, research, and increasingly treatment models, have begun to incorporate these wider considerations. This study builds on recent theoretical and empirical developments and examines the extent to which anxious children and their mothers interpret ambiguous stimuli as threatening.

Correspondence should be addressed to: Shirley Reynolds, School of Medicine, Health Policy and Practice, University of East Anglia, Norwich, Norfolk NR4 7TJ, UK. E-mail: s.reynolds@uea.ac.uk

DOI: 10.1080/02699930801886649

Threat interpretation is a key feature of cognitive models of anxiety. Beck and Emery (1985) proposed that anxious people have a number of information-processing biases that maintain their anxiety. One such bias is the tendency to see threat in ambiguous situations, where non-anxious people are more likely to interpret the situation as benign. Several paradigms have been used to measure adult and child threat interpretation bias in laboratory tasks and naturalistic observations. For example, Butler and Mathews (1983) gave participants ambiguous stories such as: "You wake suddenly in the night, thinking you heard a noise but all is quiet" and asked them to choose between a neutral and a threatening interpretation. Anxious adults chose the threatening interpretation more frequently.

A number of studies have capitalised on the inherent ambiguity of the English language, including the existence of ambiguous homophones (words with both threatening and non-threatening meanings, which each have a distinctive spelling (e.g., die/dye, bury/berry). Eysenck, MacLeod, and Mathews (1987) presented ambiguous homophones and filler words over headphones and asked adult participants to write down the word that they heard. Adults with high trait anxiety were more likely to spell the word associated with threat, e.g., die not dye, thus choosing the threatening interpretation of the ambiguous homophone. Mathews, Richards, and Eysenck (1989) repeated this with a clinical population and found that clinically anxious participants produced the threatening spellings significantly more often than the non-anxious controls.

Eysenck, Mogg, May, Richards, and Mathews (1991) found a similar interpretation bias in clinically anxious adults using ambiguous homographs (words which look and sound the same but have different meanings, e.g., "They discussed the priest's convictions", where "convictions" could mean strong beliefs or criminal record). In a subsequent recognition test, clinically anxious adults were significantly more likely to remember seeing the threatening meaning than controls or recovered anxious participants.

Similar paradigms have been used to investigate interpretation biases and anxiety in children but these require adaptations to overcome the challenge of children's developing reading and writing skills. Hadwin, Frost, French, and Richards (1997) presented ambiguous homophones and homographs aurally along with pictures of both interpretations (e.g., bark–dog, bark–tree) to non-clinical children. Pictures were used to reduce the possible confounding effect created by individual differences in children's reading and writing abilities. The number of threat interpretations made (shown by which picture they chose) was positively correlated with trait anxiety scores. Muris and colleagues (e.g., Muris, Luermans, Merckelbach, & Mayer, 2000; Muris, Merckelbach, Schepers, & Meesters, 2003) used ambiguous stories and found that children high in trait anxiety and those with anxiety symptoms made more biased interpretations of threat than non-anxious children.

Interpretation biases have also been found in children from clinical populations. Taghavi, Moradi, Neshat-Doost, Yule, and Dalgleish (2000) asked clinically anxious children and adolescents and a non-clinical control group to construct a sentence using an ambiguous homograph (e.g., arms). As expected, anxious participants constructed sentences using the threatening interpretation more often than the controls. Bögels and Zigterman (2000) found that children with clinical levels of anxiety interpreted ambiguous stories as threatening more often than clinical controls (diagnosed with oppositional defiant disorder, attention deficit hyperactivity disorder, or conduct disorder) and non-clinical controls.

Thus, the available evidence has consistently shown that children with anxiety make biased interpretations in the same way as adults with anxiety. Of additional interest in the aetiology of anxiety in children is the role of parental behaviours and cognitions in the development and maintenance of children's fears. Ginsburg and Schlossberg (2002) suggested that parental anxiety interferes with the parent's ability to cope with difficulty, leading to behaviours, such as modelling, reinforcing the child's avoidance, catastrophising and being over protective. They proposed that these behaviours increase their child's vulnerability to anxiety as the child learns that anxious behaviours, such as avoidance, are functional in temporarily reducing anxiety. Hudson and Rapee (2004) included parental cognitions in their model of the development and maintenance of childhood generalised anxiety. In cognitive behavioural terms, parental cognitions about their child's vulnerability or the dangerousness of the world, may "drive" parental behaviour, such as over protectiveness (Kortlander, Kendall, & Panichelli-Mindel, 1997). This over protectiveness may in turn reinforce avoidance of situations that parents perceive to be threatening, and verbal information may be given to the child about possible threats.

Two main paradigms have been used to examine the association between cognitive biases in children and a parent. Hypothetical ambiguous situations where the child and their parent are individually presented with a scenario and asked how the child would respond have been used most often (e.g., Barrett, Rapee, Dadds, & Ryan, 1996; Bögels, van Dongen, & Muris, 2003; Chorpita, Albano,, & Barlow, 1996; Creswell, Schniering, & Rapee, 2005; Shortt, Barrett, Dadds, & Fox, 2001). Two studies exposed children to mildly stressful situations and asked children and their parent to anticipate the child's response (Cobham, Dadds, & Spence, 1999, Kortlander et al., 1997). Results from both methods of investigation showed that anxious children and their parents (usually their mothers) demonstrated interpretation biases. Chorpita et al. (1996) found that children with higher trait anxiety interpreted threat more frequently and, after a family discussion, chose more avoidant plans. Barrett et al. (1996) included a clinical control group and found children with oppositional defiant disorder (ODD) and their parents made the most threat interpretations, followed by children with an anxiety disorder and their parents. While cognitive biases were common to both diagnostic groups, there were marked differences in the subsequent plans that children made. Anxious children were avoidant while children with ODD were aggressive. After family discussion, anxious children were even more likely to choose avoidant coping plans. Shortt et al. (2001) also found that anxious and externalising children and their mothers made more threatening interpretations than non-clinical children and that anxious children made more avoidant plans than the externalising children.

These data suggest that biased interpretations are demonstrated by anxious children and by their parents. However, it is unclear whether parents of anxious children have a general and internal threat interpretation bias or if, being aware that they have sensitive children with a history of fear, they accurately predict their children's behaviours. Bögels et al. (2003) attempted to overcome this problem by asking parents "What would *a* child think?" (rather than, "What would *your* child think?"). Children's negative interpretations were related to the negative interpretations parents attributed to children in general and thus suggested that parents had general interpretation biases. Creswell et al. (2005) used adapted (adult relevant) stories for parents. Anxious children and their mothers chose more threat interpretations than non-clinical children and their mothers. In addition the number of threat interpretations made by mothers and their children were positively correlated and this correlation was larger than the correlation between self-reported anxiety symptoms of children and their mothers. Kortlander et al. (1997) and Cobham et al. (1999) found that only mothers who were themselves anxious, predicted that their child would show more anxiety and avoidance when exposed to a mildly threatening experience.

The aim of the current study was to extend Creswell et al. (2005) by including a clinical control group (children with externalising problems and their mothers), which would allow the specificity of threat interpretation in anxiety disorders to be considered in comparison to other clinical diagnoses. In addition we used a measure of interpretation bias, which was relatively context free, and thus reduced potential confounding variables such as the impact of the shared social experiences of the child and their mother. Our hypotheses were that:

1. There would be significant group differences in interpretation bias among children and their mothers; specifically children with anxiety would choose threatening interpretations more often than children with externalising problems and non-clinical control children, and mothers of children with an anxiety disorder would choose threatening interpretations more often than mothers of children with an externalising disorder and mothers of non-clinical children.

2. Anxiety and threat interpretation bias would be significantly correlated within the group of children and also within the mothers.
3. Children's anxiety and threat interpretation bias would be significantly correlated with their mothers' anxiety and threat interpretation bias.

METHOD

Design

The current study used a between-groups design with three groups of child–mother dyads; these were anxious children and their mothers, children with an externalising disorder and their mothers, and non-clinical children and their mothers.

Participants

Children were aged 7 to 12 years. Children from the clinical groups were recruited from Child and Adolescent Mental Health Services (CAMHS) in Norfolk and Cambridgeshire, UK. Children in the anxious group met criteria for a primary diagnosis of anxiety (determined by a clinician score above 4 on the Anxiety Diagnostic Interview Schedule for Children-IV; child and parent versions (ADIS-IV C/P; Silverman & Albano, 1996) and if they scored above 60 on the Spence Children's Anxiety Scale (SCAS; Spence, 1998). They were excluded if they had a comorbid externalising disorder. Children were included in the externalising group if they met the criteria for an externalising disorder on the Child Behaviour Checklist (CBCL; Achenbach & Rescorla, 2001). They were excluded if they met criteria for a comorbid anxiety disorder (determined by the ADIS). Children in the non-clinical control group were recruited from local primary schools and had no mental health problems as assessed by the CBCL and the ADIS. In all groups, children and their mothers were excluded if they were not fluent in English, had severe physical disabilities, sensory impairments or intellectual difficulties (determined as a score of less than 70 on the Wechsler Abbreviated Scale of Intelligence 2-scale (WASI; Wechsler, 1999).

There were 18 children with anxiety (6 boys and 12 girls), 15 children with externalising problems (7 boys and 8 girls), and 23 non-clinical children (11 boys and 12 girls).

Measures

ADIS-IV (Silverman & Albano, 1996).   The ADIS interview schedules are based on criteria from the fourth edition of the *Diagnostic and Statistical Manual of Mental Disorders* (DSM-IV; American Psychiatric Association,

1994) and allow diagnoses of anxiety disorders to be made, and also allow the clinician to rule out alternative diagnoses, such as mood and externalising disorders. The ADIS-IV is considered to be a widely used, "gold standard" method of establishing diagnoses. Silverman, Lissette, and Armando (2001) reported good levels of reliability.

Spence Children's Anxiety Scale (SCAS; Spence, 1998).   The SCAS is a simple self-report measure assessing specific anxiety symptoms in children, relating to six different diagnoses of anxiety (social phobia, separation anxiety, panic attack/agoraphobia, obsessive-compulsive disorder, generalised anxiety and physical injury fears). Psychometric data reported by Spence (1998) suggests the SCAS is a reliable and valid measure.

State-Trait Anxiety Inventory-Trait (STAI-T; Spielberger, 1983).   The STAI-T is a well-established 20-item self-report measure of anxiety. Spielberger (1983) reported good test–retest correlations and internal consistency coefficients.

Wechsler Abbreviated Scale of Intelligence (WASI; Wechsler, 1999).   The WASI is a brief, well-standardised assessment of intellectual abilities for 6- to 89-year-olds. Two subtests (Vocabulary and Matrix Reasoning) were used to provide a full-scale intelligence quotient (FSIQ) score. Internal consistency of the two-scale FSIQ is high and test–retest and interrater reliability is also satisfactory. Convergent validity is satisfactory as the WASI FSIQ correlates with the Wechsler Adult Intelligence Scale-III (WAIS; a more comprehensive and well-known measure) at $r = .81$.

Child Behaviour Checklist (CBCL; Achenbach & Rescorla, 2001).   The CBCL is a 118 item questionnaire completed by parents. The first section asks parents about their child's activities, relationships and academic performance. The second section is based on DSM criteria and considers affective problems, anxiety problems, somatic problems, attention deficit/hyperactivity problems, oppositional defiance problems and conduct problems. The scales have been normed on 1753 children aged 6 to 18, without mental-health difficulties or special educational needs. Achenbach and Rescorla (2001) reported good psychometric properties.

Interpretation bias: Homophone paradigm.   The homophone paradigm was based on Hadwin et al. (1997). It uses homophones (words which sound the same but are spelt differently, e.g., berry and bury) and homographs (words which sound the same and are spelt the same, e.g., sink–kitchen and sink–boat). Here we refer to the stimuli as homophones although both types of stimuli were used. Forty pairs of colour Clip Art pictures (Microsoft

Office®, retrieved 2005) were presented in a random order on a computer screen using E-Prime software (Psychology Software Tools, Pittsburgh, PA). Fourteen pairs of pictures made up the experimental stimuli of homophones/homographs. These showed both possible interpretations, e.g., bury/berry. Twenty-six filler items were also presented, to reduce the aim of the experimental paradigm being obvious to participants. Five picture pairs were used as practice stimuli. In each pair of pictures, the words were matched for length. Responses were recorded using a dual-key button-press device attached to the computer.

For each pair of pictures a pre-recorded word (either a homophone or filler) was presented aurally, and the pair of pictures was shown on the computer screen for 5000 milliseconds or until the participant responded. To measure threat interpretation, participants received a score of 1 when they chose the threatening interpretation, and a score of 0 when they chose the neutral interpretation, giving a maximum score of 14.

Procedure

Ethical approval for the study was given by the NHS Peterborough and Fenland Research Ethics Committee, following approval from the clinical sites at which participants were recruited. Children in the clinical groups were recruited from clinic waiting lists and non-clinical children were recruited via information packs distributed by class teachers. Parents received detailed information about the study and gave signed consent. Children were given adapted information sheets and gave assent to take part. At the first appointment diagnosis was confirmed by clinical interviews with the child and parent (the ADIS-C and P), self-report questionnaires (the SCAS, CBCL, the STAI-T) and the WASI were completed The child and mother completed the homophone paradigm at a second appointment, which was scheduled within two weeks.

RESULTS

As expected there was significant group difference in children's self-reported anxiety, $F(2, 57) = 12.99$, $p < .0001$; Table 1 shows that the anxious children had the highest mean score. Post hoc Bonferroni tests showed that this was due to significant differences between anxious children and the non-clinical children; there was no significant difference between children with anxiety and children with externalising problems.

There was also a significant group difference in maternal anxiety, $F(2, 53) = 5.53$, $p < .01$. As shown in Table 1, mothers of children with anxiety and children with externalising problems had had higher anxiety scores than mothers of non-clinical children. Post hoc Bonferroni tests identified that

TABLE 1
Mean threat scores, self-reported anxiety, IQ and age by group for children and mothers

	N	Homophones		Anxiety[a]		IQ		Age in months	
		Mean	SD	Mean	SD	Mean	SD	Mean	SD
Children									
Anxious	18	8.6	1.5	46.1	12.9	104	13.2	119	15.1
Externalising	15	7.9	2.4	32.2	16.5	99	9.2	134	20.5
Non-clinical	23	7.0	1.6	22.6	14.3	108	11.6	110	11.4
Mothers									
Anxious	18	8.2	2.2	45.6	12.1	103	10.7	480	75.6
Externalising	15	6.9	2.4	42.1	9.4	102	6.2	444	45.6
Non-clinical	23	6.8	1.8	35.0	9.3	110	8.0	468	46.8

Notes: Mean threat score for children (homophones) is adjusted for child age, gender and self-reported anxiety. [a]Self-reported anxiety: for children, Spence Children's Anxiety Scale; for mothers, State-Trait Anxiety Scale.

mothers of anxious children were significantly more anxious than mothers of non-clinical children but did not differ from mothers of children with externalising problems.

Hypothesis testing

We hypothesised that anxious children would make more threatening interpretations than children with an externalising disorder and non-clinical control children. Groups were not matched for child age, gender or IQ so we controlled for these variables in the analysis. There was a significant group difference in interpretation bias, $F(2, 50) = 3.53$, $p < .05$. Adjusted mean values of children's interpretation bias are shown in Table 1. After a Bonferroni correction for multiple comparisons, anxious children made significantly more biased interpretations than non-clinical children, $p < .05$. There was no significant difference in interpretation bias between the externalising and non-clinical children or between the externalising and anxious children. Gender and IQ were associated with threat interpretation; gender, $F(1, 50) = 4.42$, $p < .05$; IQ, $F(1, 50) = 5.96$, $p < .05$. Beta values showed that girls and children with higher IQ scores made fewer interpretation biases. Children's age was not significantly associated with interpretation bias.

We also hypothesised that mothers of anxious children would have increased threat perception compared with mothers of children with an externalising disorder and mothers of non-clinical control children. Table 1 shows that mothers of anxious children made more threat interpretations than the other two groups of mothers. However, this difference was not significant, $F(2, 53) = 2.46$, $p < .10$.

Our second hypothesis was that anxiety and threat interpretation bias would be significantly correlated within the group of children and within the group of mothers ($N = 56$). Anxiety and threat interpretation scores were normally distributed for both mothers and children. Children's anxiety and threat interpretations were significantly correlated ($r = .31$, $p < .05$). However, mothers' anxiety symptoms were not associated with the number of threat interpretations they made ($r = .04$, ns).

The third hypothesis was that mother's anxiety and interpretation bias would be significantly correlated with those of their child. As expected there was a significant association between anxiety symptoms in mothers and anxiety symptoms in their children ($r = .34$, $p < .05$). However, there was no significant association between children's interpretation biases and those of their mothers ($r = .07$, $p < .50$). Interestingly, mothers' interpretation bias was significantly positively correlated with child anxiety ($r = .32$, $p > .02$) and child interpretation bias was significantly associated with maternal anxiety ($r = .26$, $p < .05$).

DISCUSSION

The current study investigated whether anxious children and their mothers shared a threat interpretation bias. In addition, relationships between maternal and child anxiety and maternal threat interpretation and child anxiety were examined. Mothers and their children completed the same context-free threat interpretation task (based on Hadwin et al., 1997). This task, which required participants to interpret single words rather than short stories, allowed direct and independent comparison of interpretation bias in mothers and their children as they did exactly the same task, rather than adapted versions of the same task. In addition the possible confounding effect of their shared social environment was reduced. The inclusion of a clinical control group allowed the specificity of threat interpretation biases to be examined.

As hypothesised, anxious children chose the threatening interpretation significantly more often than the children without a clinical diagnosis. However, anxious children did not significantly differ from children with externalising disorders. In previous research, externalising children and their parents made more threat interpretations than anxious children (Barrett et al., 1996). However, that task involved interpretation of, and response to, ambiguous stimuli and so was not a direct test of interpretation bias. The data from the present study place externalising children in an intermediate position between non-clinical and anxious children. It appears, however, that the tendency to interpret ambiguous stimuli as threatening is not a process that is unique to anxiety disorders.

The current study also measured maternal anxiety and threat interpretation. Mothers of the anxious children were more anxious than mothers of non-clinical children and maternal and child anxiety symptoms were significantly correlated. Our hypothesis that mothers of children with anxiety would chose threatening interpretation more often than the mothers of children in the non-clinical group was not supported. In addition, we found no association between mothers' trait anxiety and their threat interpretations. This conflicts with other studies of adults and may reflect the use of an alternative method of threat interpretation, which was developed specifically for children and relied on visual and aural processing rather than on written information.

Current cognitive behavioural models of child anxiety emphasise the role of parental cognitions and behaviours in the development and maintenance of childhood anxiety. Based on these, and on the data reported by Creswell et al. (2005), we hypothesised that within dyads, the child's and mother's threat interpretation scores would be correlated. The absence of any within-dyad correlation between threat interpretations was surprising, especially given that there were significant associations between maternal and child self-reported anxiety symptoms. We found that children who were more anxious had mothers who made more threat interpretations and that mothers who were more anxious had children who made more threat interpretations. Thus, mother's threat interpretations were related not to their own anxiety but to the level of anxiety expressed by their child suggesting that there are subtle dyadic influences between information processing and anxiety.

Generally, the data point to a complex set of interactions between information processing biases and anxiety symptoms within mother–child dyads. This cross-sectional, correlational study is limited in that it cannot elucidate these relationships further but its strength is that the associations between participants cannot easily be dismissed. The clinical participants in this study were drawn from a clinical population and meet diagnostic criteria for either an anxiety or an externalising disorder (but not both). The data suggest that children's anxiety, the interpretation biases they make, and their mother's cognitions and anxiety symptoms are not independent. The data also imply that individuals (in this case, mothers) can have interpretive biases but may not feel anxious. Therefore children may be exposed to anxiety-enhancing environments within their family even if their parents do not experience symptoms of anxiety themselves. This finding enhances cognitive behavioural theories of child anxiety by highlighting that even in the absence of elevated parental anxiety, parental cognitions around threat-related stimuli may be potent.

We, like most previous researchers, have focused on mothers and their children. The rationale is that mothers still tend to be the primary caretakers of children, and therefore we infer that their behaviours and cognitions will be the primary influence on children's emotional development. However, there is increasing interest in fathers and their role in the development and maintenance of anxiety in their children and this is to be welcomed.

From a clinical perspective these data add tentative support to theories that include parental cognitions as a key element in the child's environment. The role of parents and their own beliefs, affect and behaviours should be included in clinical formulations and influence the delivery of treatment. It may not be possible to infer parental cognitions from their affect and behaviours so this area may require specific assessment. Creswell et al. (2005) showed that CBT for children with anxiety led to reduced interpretation bias in the children and their mothers. Additional studies that focus on the mechanisms of change could add to our knowledge base. There are some families for whom CBT for their child's anxiety is not effective (Bögels & Siqueland, 2006) and further research is needed to identify whether there is an association between CBT effectiveness and reduction in parental biased cognitions.

REFERENCES

Achenbach, T. M., & Rescorla, L. A. (2001). *Manual for the ASEBA School-Age Forms and Profiles.* Burlington, VT: University of Vermont, Research Center for Children, Youth, and Families.

American Psychiatric Association. (1994). *Diagnostic and Statistical Manual of Mental Disorders: DSM-IV* (4th ed.). Washington, DC: American Psychiatric Association.

Beck, A. T., & Emery, G. (1985). *Anxiety disorders and phobias: A cognitive perspective.* New York: Basic Books.

Bögels, S. M., & Siqueland, L. (2006). Family cognitive behavioural therapy for children and adolescents with clinical anxiety disorders. *Journal of the American Academy of Child and Adolescent Psychiatry, 45,* 134–141.

Bögels, S. M., van Dongen, L., & Muris, P. (2003). Family influences on dysfunctional thinking in anxious children. *Infant and Child Development, 12,* 243–252.

Bögels, S. M., van Oosten, A., Muris, P., & Smulders, D. (2001). Familial correlates of social anxiety in children and adolescents. *Behaviour Research and Therapy, 39,* 273–287.

Bögels, S. M., & Zigterman, D. (2000). Dysfunctional cognitions in children with social phobia, separation anxiety and generalised anxiety disorder. *Journal of Abnormal Child Psychology, 28,* 205–211.

Butler, G., & Mathews, A. (1983). Cognitive processes in anxiety. *Advances in Behaviour Research and Therapy, 5,* 51–62.

Chorpita, B. F., Albano, A. M., & Barlow, D. H. (1996). Cognitive processing in children: Relationship to anxiety and family influences. *Journal of Clinical Child Psychology, 25,* 170–176.

Cobham, V. E., Dadds, M. R., & Spence, S. H. (1999). Anxious children and their parents: What do they expect? *Journal of Clinical Child Psychology, 28,* 220–231.

Creswell, C., Schniering, C. A., & Rapee, R. M. (2005). Threat interpretation in anxious children and their mothers: Comparison with non-clinical children and the effects of treatment. *Behaviour Research and Therapy, 43*, 1375–1381.

Eysenck, M. W., MacLeod, C., & Mathews, A. (1987). Cognitive functioning and anxiety. *Psychological Bulletin, 49*, 189–195.

Eysenck, M. W., Mogg, K., May, J., Richards, A., & Mathews, A. (1991). Bias in interpretation of ambiguous sentences related to threat in anxiety. *Journal of Abnormal Psychology, 2*, 144–150.

Ginsburg, G. S., & Schlossberg, M. C. (2002). Family based treatment of childhood anxiety disorders. *International Review of Psychiatry, 14*, 143–154.

Hadwin, J., Frost, S., French, C. C., & Richards, A. (1997). Cognitive processing and trait anxiety in typically developing children: Evidence for interpretation bias. *Journal of Abnormal Psychology, 106*, 486–490.

Hudson, J. L., & Rapee, R. M. (2004). From anxious temperament to disorder: An etiological model of generalized anxiety disorder. In R. G. Heimberg, C. L. Turk, & D. S. Mennin (Eds.), *Generalized anxiety disorder: Advances in research and practice* (pp. 51–74). New York: Guilford Press.

Kortlander, E., Kendall, P. C., & Panichelli-Mindel, S. M. (1997). Maternal expectations and attributions about coping in anxious children. *Journal of Anxiety Disorders, 11*, 297–315.

Mathews, A., Richards, A., & Eysenck, M. W. (1989). The interpretation of homophones related to threat in anxiety states. *Journal of Abnormal Psychology, 98*, 31–34.

Muris, P., Luermans, J., Merckelbach, H., & Mayer, B. (2000). "Danger is lurking everywhere": The relationship between anxiety and threat perception abnormalities in normal children. *Journal of Behavior Therapy and Experimental Psychiatry, 31*, 123–136.

Muris, P., Merckelbach, H., Schepers, S., & Meesters, C. (2003). Anxiety, threat perception abnormalities, and emotional reasoning in nonclinical Dutch children. *Journal of Clinical Child and Adolescent Psychiatry, 32*, 453–459.

Shortt, A. L., Barrett, P. M., Dadds, M. R., & Fox, T. L. (2001). The influence of family and experimental context on cognition in anxious children. *Journal of Abnormal Child Psychology, 29*, 585–596.

Silverman, W. K., & Albano, A. M. (1996). *The Anxiety Disorders Interview Schedule for Children for DSM-IV: Child and Parent Versions.* San Antonio, TX: Psychological Corporation.

Silverman, W. K., Lissette, M. S., & Armando, A. P. (2001). Test–retest reliability of anxiety symptoms and diagnoses with the Anxiety Disorders Interview Schedule for DSM-IV: Child and Parent Version. *Journal of American Academy of Child and Adolescent Psychiatry, 40*, 937–944.

Spence, S. H. (1998). A measure of anxiety symptoms among children. *Behaviour Research and Therapy, 36*, 545–566.

Spielberger, C. D. (1983). *Manual for the State-Trait Anxiety Inventory.* Palo Alto, CA: Consulting Psychologists Press.

Taghavi, R., Moradi, A., Neshat-Doost, H., Yule, W., & Dalgleish, T. (2000). The interpretation of ambiguous emotional information in clinically anxious children and adolescents. *Cognition and Emotion, 14*, 809–822.

Wechsler, D. (1999). *Manual for the Wechsler Abbreviated Scale of Intelligence.* San Antonio, TX: Psychological Corporation.

COGNITION AND EMOTION
2008, 22 (3), 509–521

Do anxiety-related attentional biases mediate the link between maternal over involvement and separation anxiety in children?

Gisela Perez-Olivas, Jim Stevenson, and Julie A. Hadwin

University of Southampton, Southampton, UK

This study explored attentional mechanisms via which maternal over involvement could contribute to a child's separation anxious symptomatology across development. Consistent with developmental theories of cognition and childhood anxiety age was found to moderate the relationship between attentional biases towards threatening (angry) faces and separation anxiety. In addition, the results highlighted that maternal over involvement enhanced a child's separation anxiety via an attentional bias to angry faces. The results suggest that vigilance for threat partially mediates the association between maternal over involvement and symptoms of childhood separation anxiety. The implications and limitations of these findings are discussed.

Anxiety is an increasingly common phenomenon in childhood, with separation anxiety being one of the most prevalent disorders; especially in children below 12 years of age (Cartwright-Hatton, McNicol, & Doubleday, 2006). Theoretical models have highlighted the role of cognitive and family factors in the development of childhood anxiety (e.g., Hudson & Rapee, 2004; Rapee, 2001). The need to investigate these cognitive factors within a development framework has been emphasised (Kindt & van den Hout, 2001). The aim of the current study was to look at the relationships between parenting, cognition and symptoms of separation anxiety in children. Specifically, it explored possible cognitive pathways via which mothers might enhance a child's separation anxiety and whether consideration of these pathways changes across development.

Correspondence should be addressed to: Julie A. Hadwin, Developmental Brain-Behaviour Unit, School of Psychology, University of Southampton, Southampton SO17 1BJ, UK. E-mail: jah7@soton.ac.uk

This research was supported with an ESRC studentship (PTA-030-00206) and funding from the School of Psychology, University of Southampton, awarded to the first author.

We are very grateful to all the families who took part in this research project and to local schools for their invaluable help with recruitment.

Cognitive models of adult anxiety have suggested that anxious individuals will selectively attend to (e.g., Eysenck, 1997) or demonstrate vigilance–avoidance of threatening information (Mogg & Bradley, 1998). Recent research in separation anxiety has shown some support for these models. For example, Stirling, Eley, and Clark (2006) investigated attentional biases to threat in children using facial expressions of emotion. They found an attentional bias away from angry and fearful faces depicting threat in typically developing children with elevated self-report social anxiety and found a trend in their data suggestive of a similar effect in children with self-report separation anxiety. Although these findings need to be replicated in future studies due to small effect sizes, the authors suggested that cognitive biases in separation anxiety may be similar to those seen in social anxiety.

Recent research has considered the role of development in understanding attentional processes in childhood anxiety (Kindt & van den Hout, 2001; Lonigan, Vasey, Phillips, & Hazen, 2004; see Hadwin, Garner, & Perez-Olivas, 2006, for a review). The theoretical framework proposed by Kindt and van den Hout (2001) suggests that a failure to acquire inhibitory control across development places anxious children at risk of developing anxiety-related attentional biases. This proposition was based on empirical research, which found that children under 10 years of age showed a general attentional bias towards threat and not an anxiety-related attentional bias (Kindt, Brosschot, & Everaerd, 1997). Early research exploring the development of inhibitory control across childhood and into adolescence supports this proposition. Using a stop-signal task Williams and colleagues, for example, found improved inhibitory control skills in children from age 10 and above compared with younger children (Williams, Ponesse, Schachar, Logan, & Tannock, 1999).

Further empirical work has explored links between parental behaviours and separation anxiety. Maternal over protection, for example, has been associated with enhanced levels of childhood separation anxiety (Wood, 2006). In his model of the development of anxiety Rapee (2001) proposed that parental over protection could augment a child's vulnerability to anxiety by increasing their tendency to perceive threat (see also Hudson & Rapee, 2004). A number of pathways have been suggested through which cognitive biases might stem from the relationship between parenting characteristics and childhood anxiety and include, modelling or observational learning (Rachman, 1991) and verbal information (Field, 2006).

The present study used a developmental approach to extend previous research on attentional biases in anxiety in order to understand more clearly links between maternal over protection and separation anxiety. In this paper expressed emotion was used as a measure of parental over involvement (a subdimension of parental over protection). Expressed emotion represents an index of a caregiver's attitudes and feelings towards the offspring, which has been found to have good reliability and validity (e.g., Beck, Daley, Hastings, & Stevenson, 2004). This measure has recently been used to examine parental over involvement or parental criticism exhibited towards the child as enhancers of a child's internalising problems, such as anxiety (McCarty & Weisz, 2002). Based on previous theory and research it was hypothesised that a developmental course in the emergence of attentional biases to threatening (angry) faces would be observed. Furthermore, following Rapee's (2001) model it was expected that maternal over involvement would contribute to a child's separation anxiety via an enhanced vigilance for threat.

METHOD

Participants and procedures

The sample consisted of 129 non-referred children and their mothers. The age range of the children was 6.3–14.58 years ($M = 9.9$ years; $SD = 26.12$ months; 67 females). A total of 69 children were aged 10 years or under ($M = 8.45$; $SD = 12.76$ months) and 60 children were aged over 10 years ($M = 12.23$; $SD = 13.26$ months). Participants were recruited through primary and secondary schools in Southampton, UK. Families were sent an information letter about the study via schools. When informed consent was obtained a package with the questionnaires to be completed by the mother was sent to their homes. In addition, following Beck et al. (2004) the child's mother was given a five-minute interview over the phone to measure their expressed emotion. The child's assessment took place individually in a quiet environment after informed consent from the child and the mother was obtained. At the end of the assessment mother and child were debriefed.

Child measures

Childhood anxiety. The Revised Child Anxiety and Depression Scales–Child Version (RCADS; Chorpita, Yim, Moffitt, Umemoto, & Francis, 2000) is a 47-item self-report measure that assesses symptoms of DSM IV-defined anxiety disorders and depression. The RCADS consists of six scales, tapping into separation anxiety disorder, generalised anxiety disorder, panic disorder, social phobia, obsessive-compulsive disorder and depression. The scales have been found to have adequate internal consistency $\alpha = .70–.80$ and test–retest stability $r = .65–.80$ (Chorpita et al., 2000). This study focused on individual differences in separation anxiety.

Visual search task.   Attentional biases to angry faces were assessed with a visual search task (see Hadwin et al., 2003). Facial stimuli were configured using a set of black and white schematic faces 40 mm in diameter. The target faces were formed with three sets of features (eyebrows, eyes and mouth) to represent angry, neutral and happy faces. Distractor items were formed by inverting the features from the target faces. Each child saw 72 randomly presented computer trials in total, comprising three blocks related to searches for angry, happy and neutral faces. Before each block children were shown hard copies of the target face and told: "Press the 'Yes' button if the face is there and the 'No' button if it is not there". The presentation of the blocks was counterbalanced. Within each block, the target face was present in half of the trials and absent in the other half. Target-present trials consisted of one target face and one, three or five distractors to make set sizes of two, four and six, respectively. Target-absent trials consisted of two, four, or six distractors. In each block, 24 trials of each set size, 12 with target-present trials and 12 with target-absent trials were presented. Trials remained on screen until children responded. After children had responded a blank screen appeared for 500 ms before the next trial screen was displayed.

To assess the reliability of the visual search task separate functions for target-absent and target-present trials were computed. Previous research employing this paradigm with children has found larger effects of target with greater set sizes showing that reaction times increased on absent compared with present trials in a ratio of approximately 2.5:1 (see Hadwin et al., 2003). Using presentation trials with different set sizes allows a calculation of a slope gradient that reflects the extent to which reaction times change across different set sizes. In addition, if a target is presented across different set sizes and the gradient of the slope is shallow, the time taken to find the target is relatively independent of the number of distractors and is proposed to be automatic (Wolfe, Cave, & Franzel, 1989). In the current paper, the examination of anxiety-related attentional biases was based on the gradient of the slope in the target-present trials, where present trials are argued to depict attentional deployment (Rinck, Becker, Kellermann, & Roth, 2003).

Maternal measures

Maternal over involvement.   The Five Minute Speech Sample (FMSS; Magana et al., 1986) was employed to assess expressed emotion. The mother was asked to express feelings and attitudes about the offspring for five minutes over the phone. One category in the FMSS is Emotional Over Involvement (EOI). A high EOI rating is given in the presence of: self-sacrificing/over-protective behaviours; emotional display (e.g., caregiver cries while being interviewed) and any two of the following: excess detail about the offspring's past; one or more statements of attitude (e.g., caregiver expresses very strong feelings of love); or five or more positive comments. A borderline EOI rating is given when there is no evidence for self-sacrificing/over-protective behaviours or emotional display and there is evidence for: one or more statements of attitude; excess detail about the past; or five or more positive comments. In total 110 samples were coded by a fully trained rater blind to the offspring's levels of separation anxiety. To assess interrater reliability 10 of these samples were recoded by another fully trained rater also blind to the offspring's anxious symptomatology. The Cohen's kappa for a borderline rating was 1.0; indicating total interrater agreement.

Parent rating of childhood anxiety. The Revised Child Anxiety and Depression Scales–Parent Version (RCADS-P; Chorpita et al., 2000) was used. The only difference between the RCADS and the RCADS-P is that the wording in every item of the latter is changed from "I" to "My child" and is completed by the parent.

RESULTS

Descriptive statistics

Visual search task. Any reaction time above or below 2.5 standard deviations from condition means were excluded from the analysis. To explore reactions times a 3 (Emotion Condition: angry, happy, neutral) $\times$ 2 (Target: present, absent) $\times$ 3 (Set Size: 2, 4, 6) repeated measures ANOVA was carried out. This highlighted significant main effects of Emotion Condition, $F(2, 128) = 21.28$, $p < .01$, Target, $F(1, 128) = 228.67$, $p < .01$, and Set Size, $F(2, 128) = 604.21$, $p < .01$. These indicated that children were slower to search for neutral ($M = 1707.51$ ms, $SE = 46.71$) compared with happy ($M = 1577.66$ ms, $SE = 39.36$) and angry ($M = 1575.33$ ms, $SE = 43.61$) faces; were faster in target-present ($M = 1454.27$ ms, $SE = 36.26$) compared with target-absent ($M = 1786.06$ ms, $SE = 48.19$) trials; and searched faster in set size two ($M = 1274.96$ ms, $SE = 33.41$) compared with set sizes four ($M = 1614.74$ ms, $SE = 42.11$) and six ($M = 1970.78$ ms, $SE = 51.05$). There were also significant interactions between Emotion Condition and Set Size, $F(4, 128) = 6.43$, $p < .01$, and between Target and Set Size, $F(2, 252) = 117.08$, $p < .01$; indicating that slower reactions times for neutral compared to happy and angry faces were more evident in set sizes four and eight compared with set size two and that reactions times to find target faces increased with set size at a ratio of 2.5:1. Consistent with previous research (e.g., Öhman, Lundqvist, & Esteves, 2001), a Target and Emotion interaction effect was not found.

The gradient of slope for each target face was calculated. In all cases these exceeded 20 ms/item; which indicates attentive and not automatic processing (Wolfe et al., 1989). A linear trend analysis was carried out for each target face to examine whether the gradient of the slope for each target face linearly increased with set size. For all target faces the amount of variance accounted for by a linear component was significant (in all cases $R^2 > .92$).

Separation anxiety.   Based on the normative data of the RCADS for separation anxiety, the levels reported by the child ($M = 4.86$, $SD = 4.06$) or the mother ($M = 4.25$, $SD = 2.96$) fell within the normal range.

Maternal over involvement.   The variability in the FMSS rating scores was very low. No mothers were rated as showing high EOI; none were rated with self-sacrificing/over-protective behaviours or emotional display. Fifty-one mothers were rated with a borderline EOI, because they expressed five or more positive comments about their offspring, see Table 1.

Visual search and age

A linear regression analysis highlighted a trend in the data to support a negative association between angry slopes and self-report separation anxiety ($\beta = -.18$, $p = .06$), indicating that as anxiety increased the relative increase in reaction times with increased set size was lower. Further analyses examined whether chronological age (CA) could be moderating the relationship between angry slopes and separation anxiety in the child. The values in the CA and angry slopes variables were centred and the CA × angry slopes interaction term computed. A regression analysis showed that the CA × angry slopes interaction term approached significance ($\beta = -.19$, $p = .06$) when predicting self-reported separation anxiety in the child; highlighting that attentional biases to angry faces are subject to age-related effects.

TABLE 1
Frequencies and percentages of the five-minute speech sample ($N = 110$) emotional over involvement (EOI) category

EE Variables	Frequency (%)
Self-sacrificing/over-protective behaviour	Absent
Emotional display	Absent
Excessive detail about the past	Absent
Statements of attitude	Absent
Positive comments:	
Four or less	59 (53.6%)
Five or more	51 (46.4%)

Following the theoretical framework of Kindt and van den Hout (2001) attentional biases to angry faces were therefore examined separately in two age groups (children aged over 10 years and children aged 10 years or below). A t-test showed no differences in the levels of maternal or self-reported separation anxiety for either age group. When the predictive value of angry slopes was examined for children aged over 10 years, angry slopes were found to significantly predict the levels of self-reported separation anxiety in the child ($\beta = -.27$, $p < .05$); the negative sign of the beta value indicates that children who reported having high levels of separation anxiety took less time to detect the presence of an angry face When the predictive value of angry slopes was examined for children aged 10 years and below, angry slopes did not significantly predict the levels of self-reported separation anxiety ($\beta = -.002$, $p = .98$). Further analyses indicated that search for angry faces was not associated with maternal reports of separation anxiety in either the older or the younger age groups (the beta and p-values were $\beta = -.06$, $p = .67$ and $\beta = -.09$, $p = .54$, respectively). Only child-report separation anxiety was, therefore, tested in the mediation model.

Maternal over involvement and child separation anxiety

A t-test did not show significant mean differences in the child's separation anxiety for groups with borderline EOI and low EOI using child, $t(105) = -0.08$, $p = .93$, or maternal reports, $t(104) = -0.00$, $p = .99$, of child separation anxiety.

Evidence for a cognitively mediated pathway

Data were analysed using structural equation modelling (SEM) with AMOS 6.0. Prior to conducting SEM, linear regression analyses were conducted to test for the statistical significance of the pathways in the mediation model. Following Shrout and Bolger's (2002) recommendations the statistical significance of the pathways linking maternal borderline EOI (independent variable) with an attentional bias towards angry faces (mediator) and the pathway linking an attentional bias towards angry faces and a child's separation anxiety (dependent variable) were tested. The authors argued that the association between an independent and a dependent variable could be distal and non-significant in cases in which the expected effect size of the association is small. Based on the review by McLeod, Wood, and Weisz (2007) the expected effect size of the association between EOI and separation anxiety in the current study was small. Bootstrapping was applied in the SEM analyses. Bootstrapping is a method used to determine the significance of an indirect effect, which is useful in relatively small samples. In contrast to Sobel's test it does not assume that the sampling distribution of the indirect effect is normal

(MacKinnon, Lockwood, Hoffman, West, & Sheets, 2002). One thousand bootstrap samples were created with the bias-corrected method.

The previous analyses on attentional biases towards angry faces had already given support for the feasibility of a pathway linking this bias with self-report separation anxiety in older children. Thus, the pathway in which maternal EOI could be enhancing a child's threat-related attentional bias was explored. A linear regression analysis showed that the predictive value of maternal borderline EOI for angry slopes approached significance ($\beta = -.25$, $p = .05$). Because this pathway approached significance the mediation model was tested with SEM. In order to interpret the data, the p-value of the standard estimates for pathways 2 and 3 in Figure 1 and for the indirect pathway (pathway $2 \times$ pathway 3) were taken into consideration. The bootstrap confidence interval of the indirect pathway was employed to determine the significance of the indirect effect, see Figure 1 where the standard estimates and standard errors are displayed. The significant pathways are given in bold.

Figure 1 shows that maternal borderline EOI was associated with flatter angry slopes (indicating increased vigilance to threat). Vigilance for threat was associated with higher levels of self-reported separation anxiety in the child. As expected the direct pathway linking maternal borderline EOI with the child's separation anxiety was not significant ($\beta = -.11$, $p = .39$). When the mediator was introduced in the analysis the strength of the relationship between maternal EOI and separation anxiety changed, although it remained non-significant ($\beta = -.19$, $p = .11$). The indirect effect between maternal EOI and separation anxiety via the mediator was significant as indicated by the p-value of pathway $2 \times$ pathway 3 ($\beta = .07$, $p < .05$). In addition the bootstrap confidence interval of the indirect effect did not include zero (0.007, 0.20); confirming the significance of the effect. The effect size of the indirect effect was the product of pathway 2 ($\beta = -.31$) $\times$ pathway 3 ($\beta = -.25$), this is ($\beta = .07$). The small effect size of the indirect effect is expected based on the small effect sizes obtained in the association between maternal EOI and separation anxiety in the child. The goodness-of-fit index (GFI) of the SEM model was above .90. No values for chi-square index were obtained for the model as it was just-identified. These results indicate that maternal EOI was increasing the levels of a child's separation anxiety via an indirect effect involving vigilance for threat.

DISCUSSION

The findings in this study demonstrated age-related effects in the emergence of attentional biases towards threat. Consistent with recent theoretical

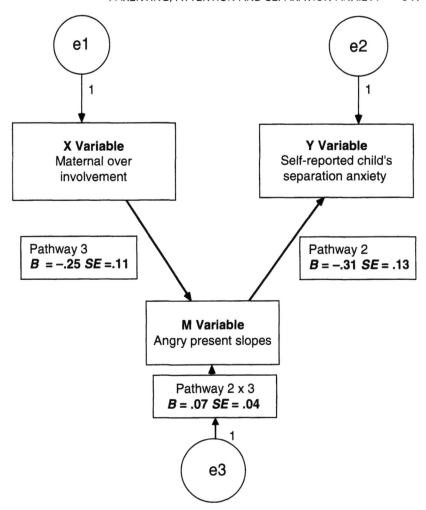

Figure 1. Path model showing partial mediation of attentional biases towards angry faces from maternal over involvement to children's self-reported separation anxiety.

models (Kindt & van den Hout, 2001) children with elevated self-report separation anxiety symptoms over 10 years of age showed an attentional bias towards angry faces. This bias was not evident in younger children. The results of the present study contrast with those of Stirling et al.'s (2006) study, which provided some evidence to suggest that children with separation anxiety would show an attentional bias away from threat (angry and fearful) faces. The difference in findings between the present study and that of Stirling et al. (2006) may be a function of the different paradigms used. Chen and colleagues, for example, hypothesised that if the experimental task constrains the individual's attention towards the threatening stimulus, then the individual can show vigilance for threat (Chen, Ehlers, Clark, & Mansell 2002).

The relationship between anxiety and attention to threat was not evident when considering maternal-report symptoms of separation anxiety. Previous research has also found a relationship between child self-report anxiety and behavioural measures in the absence of a similar relationship between parent- and teacher-report anxiety and behaviour (DiBartolo & Grills, 2005). Together with the current study, this pattern of findings highlights the importance of self-report in understanding symptoms of anxiety and behavioural correlates in children.

The present study did not reveal anxiety-related attentional biases in a group of children younger than 10 years of age. This finding is in line with Kindt et al.'s (1997) work and it suggests that the maturation of attentional cognitive skills may protect the child from attending to threat. It is also consistent with Williams et al.'s (1999) work, which found that inhibitory control skills for younger children (mean age 7.5 years) were not as developed as they were in older children (mean age 11.1 years). Interestingly, Rueda, Posner, and Rothbart (2004) highlighted that some attentional maturational processes occur from 10 years through to adulthood that involve a decrease in sensitivity to incoming stimuli.

No significant link between maternal EOI and a child's separation anxiety was observed in the present study. Although this result does not corroborate Wood's (2006) findings, it is in line with McLeod et al.'s (2007) review, which highlighted small effect sizes in the relationship between parental over protection and childhood anxiety. The present paper did, however, show some support for a developmental pathway to explain how maternal over-protective attitudes might impinge on a child's separation anxiety. In this pathway maternal borderline EOI contributed to a child's vigilance for angry faces (pathway 3). This vigilance for angry faces in turn augmented a child's levels of separation anxiety (pathway 2). Indeed, when the mediator (vigilance for angry faces) was introduced in the analysis linking maternal EOI with separation anxiety, pathway 2 × pathway 3 was significant and the bootstrap confidence intervals support this finding. (It should be noted that despite the beta-value of the maternal EOI–separation anxiety relationship augmented when the mediator was introduced in the model, there is no evidence for true suppression because the p-value was not significant.) Thus the results suggest that vigilance for threat could be partially mediating a distal association between maternal EOI and separation anxiety in child-hood. In the partial mediation model this distal association could be explained by several mediators that taken together completely mediate this relationship (Shrout & Bolger, 2002). Thus mediators other than vigilance for threat could account for the association between maternal EOI and separation anxiety. This would explain the small effect size of the indirect effect.

One possible mediator to account for the maternal EOI–child's anxiety linkage is neuroticism. Neuroticism has been identified as a highly heritable personality trait that could be maintained in the child due to parental reactions to a child's behaviour (Rapee 2001). In addition, neuroticism has been outlined as a temperamental dimension that can increase the risk for anxiety (Lonigan et al., 2004). This risk would be partially mediated by neuroticism's association with an automatic threat-related processing bias. Interestingly, inhibitory control processes could moderate the extent to which this automatic bias prevails in situations in which inhibitory control skills would allow the individual to stop attending to threat. Lonigan et al.'s (2004) model fits well with the moderating role that age was found to have in the emergence of anxiety-related attentional biases. It could be hypothesised that older children have acquired inhibitory control skills that allowed them to stop attending to threat. A further examination of the moderating role of inhibitory control skills in the appearance of anxiety-related attentional biases throughout childhood is merited.

The partial model found in the present study is consistent with Rapee's (2001) and Hudson and Rapee's (2004) models where no direct link between parental over-protective reactions and a child's anxiety is outlined. According to these models parental over protection would increase the child's tendency to perceive threat and this increased perception of threat contributes to the development of anxiety in the child. Thus, further exploration of the indirect effect of maternal EOI with a child's separation anxiety through the mediator (vigilance for threat) is of theoretical interest.

In summary, the findings in the present study support the proposition that borderline maternal EOI may contribute to separation anxiety in the child via an enhanced vigilance for threat. The relevance of these findings stem from identifying mechanisms of transmission of anxiety from the mother to the child. The findings also suggest that anxiety-related attentional biases most clearly emerge in children aged over 10. While these results are consistent with previous empirical work (e.g., Kindt et al., 1997) they should be treated with caution. Smaller age bands with increased sample sizes are needed to fully explore the development of maturational processes such as inhibitory control skills and their influence on the emergence of anxiety-related attentional biases in childhood. Further limitations to the study should be noted. Only reports from the mother and the child were available, thus future research would benefit from incorporating reports from other informants (Bögels & Brechman-Toussaint, 2006; De Los Reyes & Kazdin, 2005). In addition, only anxious symptoms and not clinical diagnoses were examined, which restricts the application of the findings to clinical samples. Furthermore, the study was cross-sectional in nature, therefore no conclusions about the directionality of the relationships found can be made. Longitudinal or intervention studies are needed to address these issues.

REFERENCES

Beck, A., Daley, D., Hastings, R. P., & Stevenson, J. (2004). Mother's expressed emotion towards children with and without intellectual disabilities. *Journal of Intellectual Disability Research, 48,* 628–638.

Bögels, S. M., & Brechman-Toussaint, M. L. (2006). Family issues in child anxiety: Attachment, family functioning, parental rearing and beliefs. *Clinical Psychology Review, 26,* 834–856.

Cartwright-Hatton, S., McNicol, K., & Doubleday, E. (2006). Anxiety in a neglected population: Prevalence of anxiety disorders in pre-adolescent children. *Clinical Psychology Review, 26,* 817–833.

Chen, Y. P., Ehlers, A., Clark, D. M., & Mansell, W. (2002). Patients with generalized social phobia direct their attention away from faces. *Behaviour Research and Therapy, 40,* 677–687.

Chorpita, B. F., Yim, L., Moffitt, C., Umemoto, L. A., & Francis, S. E. (2000). Assessment of symptoms of DSM-IV anxiety and depression in children: A revised Child Anxiety and Depression Scale. *Behaviour Research and Therapy, 38,* 835–855.

De Los Reyes, A., & Kazdin, A. E. (2005). Informant discrepancies in the assessment of childhood psychopathology: A critical review, theoretical framework, and recommendations for further study. *Psychological Bulletin, 131,* 483–509.

DiBartolo, P. M., & Grills, A. E. (2005). Who is best at predicting children's anxiety in response to a social evaluative task? A comparison of child, parent and teacher reports. *Journal of Anxiety Disorders, 20,* 630–645.

Eysenck, M. (1997). *Anxiety and cognition.* Hove, UK: Psychology Press.

Field, A. P. (2006). Watch out for the beast: Fear information and attentional bias in children. *Journal of Clinical Child and Adolescent Psychology, 35,* 431–439.

Hadwin, J. A., Donnelly, N., French, C., Richards, A., Watts, A., & Daley, D. (2003). The influence of children's self-report anxiety and depression on visual search for emotional faces. *Journal of Child Psychology and Psychiatry, 44,* 432–444.

Hadwin, J. A., Garner, M., & Perez-Olivas, G. (2006). The development of information processing biases in childhood anxiety: An exploration of its origins in parenting. *Clinical Psychology Review, 26,* 876–894.

Hudson, J. L., & Rapee, R. M. (2004). From anxious temperament to disorder: An etiological model of generalized anxiety disorder. In R. G. Heimberg, C. L. Turk, & D. S. Mennin (Eds.), *Generalized anxiety disorder: Advances in research and practice* (pp. 51–74). New York: Guilford Press.

Kindt, M., Brosschot, J. F., & Everaerd, W. (1997). Cognitive processing bias of children in a real life stress situation and a neutral situation. *Journal of Experimental Child Psychology, 64,* 79–97.

Kindt, M., & van den Hout, M. (2001). Selective attention and anxiety: A perspective on developmental issues and the causal status. *Journal of Psychopathology and Behavioral Assessment, 23,* 193–202.

Lonigan, C. J., Vasey, M. W., Phillips, B. M., & Hazen, R. A. (2004). Temperament, anxiety, and the processing of threat-relevant stimuli. *Journal of Clinical Child and Adolescent Psychology, 33,* 8–20.

MacKinnon, D. P., Lockwood, C. M., Hoffman, J. M., West, S. G., & Sheets, V. (2002). A comparison of methods to test mediation and other intervening variable effects. *Psychological Methods, 7,* 83–104.

Magana, A. B., Goldstein, M. J., Karno, M., Miklowitz, D. J., Jenkins, J., & Falloon, I. R. H. (1986). A brief method for assessing expressed emotion in relatives of psychiatric patients. *Psychiatry Research, 17,* 203–212.

McCarty, C. A., & Weisz, J. R. (2002). Correlates of expressed emotion in mothers of clinically referred youth: An examination of the five-minute speech sample. *Journal of Child Psychology and Psychiatry and Allied Disciplines, 43,* 759–768.

McLeod, B. D., Wood, J. J., & Weisz, J. R. (2007). Examining the association between parenting and childhood anxiety: A meta-analysis. *Clinical Psychology Review, 27,* 155–172.

Mogg, K., & Bradley, B. P. (1998). A cognitive-motivational analysis of anxiety. *Behaviour Research and Therapy, 36,* 809–848.

Öhman, A., Lundqvist, D., & Esteves, F. (2001). The face in the crowd revisited: A threat advantage with schematic stimuli. *Journal of Personality and Social Psyhcology, 80,* 381–396.

Rachman, S. (1991). Neo-conditioning and the classical theory of fear acquisition. *Clinical Psychology Review, 11,* 155–173.

Rapee, R. M. (2001). The development of generalized anxiety disorder. In M. W. Vasey & M. R. Dadds (Eds.), *The developmental psychopathology of anxiety* (pp. 481–504). New York: Oxford University Press.

Rinck, M., Becker, E. S., Kellermann, J., & Roth, W. T. (2003). Selective attention in anxiety: Distraction and enhancement in visual search. *Depression and Anxiety, 18,* 18–28.

Rueda, M. R., Posner, M. I., & Rothbart, M. K. (2004). Attentional control and self-regulation. In R. F. Baumeister & K. D. Vohs (Eds.), *Handbook of self-regulation. Research, theory, and applications* (pp. 283–300). New York: Guilford Press.

Shrout, P. E., & Bolger, N. (2002). Mediation in experimental and nonexperimental studies: New procedures and recommendations. *Psychological Methods, 7,* 422–445.

Stirling, L. J., Eley, T. C., & Clark, D. M. (2006). Preliminary evidence for an association between social anxiety symptoms and avoidance of negative faces in school-age children. *Journal of Clinical Child and Adolescent Psychology, 35,* 440–445.

Williams, B. R., Ponesse, J. S., Schachar, R. J., Logan, G. D., & Tannock, R. (1999). Development of inhibitory control across the life span. *Developmental Psychology, 35,* 205–213.

Wolfe, J. M., Cave, K. R., & Franzel, S. L. (1989). Guided search: An alternative to the feature integration model for visual search. *Journal of Experimental Psychology, Human Perception and Performance, 15,* 419–433.

Wood, J. J. (2006). Parental intrusiveness and children's separation anxiety in a clinical sample. *Child Psychiatry and Human Development, 37,* 73–87.

COGNITION AND EMOTION
2008, 22 (3), 522–538

Parental rearing as a function of parent's own, partner's, and child's anxiety status: Fathers make the difference

Susan M. Bögels

University of Amsterdam, Amsterdam, The Netherlands

Lotte Bamelis

University of Maastricht, Maastricht, The Netherlands

Corine van der Bruggen

University of Amsterdam, Amsterdam, The Netherlands

Parents of children with anxiety disorders are found to be over controlling and more rejecting in parent–child interactions than parents of control children. However, most studies included mothers, and the rearing behaviour of fathers of anxious children is largely unknown. Also, it remains unclear whether parents' control and rejection is a response to child's anxiety, or (also) results from parents' own anxiety. Participants were 121 children referred with anxiety disorders and 38 control children, and their parents. The diagnostic status of all parents was assessed. Each child conducted discussions around issues of disagreement, with father, with mother, and with both parents. Compared to parents of control children, fathers and mothers of clinically anxious children displayed more control to their child, but not more rejection, and fathers supported their partner less. Effect sizes, however, were small. In families of fathers with anxiety disorders, fathers were borderline more controlling and rejecting and mothers more rejecting towards their anxious child than in families of fathers without anxiety disorders. Fathers with anxiety disorders dominated the conversation relative to mothers, which was associated with greater controlling of the child. Effect sizes were medium. Mothers' anxiety status was not associated with different rearing behaviours in both parents. It is concluded that fathers' anxiety status seems to make the difference in raising an anxious child.

Correspondence should be addressed to: Susan M. Bögels, University of Amsterdam, Amsterdam, The Netherlands. E-mail: S.M.Bogels@UVA.NL

Data were collected while the first author worked at Maastricht University. This study was supported by ZonMWgrant number 9450–20–52 and NWO-VIDI grant number 4520–53–45 to the first author.

We are grateful to the families who trusted us to study their interactions, the research assistants who gathered the data, the co-ordinators of the participating clinical sites, and Denise Bodden and Sarah de Schutter.

DOI: 10.1080/02699930801886706

INTRODUCTION

There is a strong interest in the role of parental over control and negativity in childhood anxiety disorders. Parental over control has been conceptualised as a pattern of behaviour involving excessive regulation of children's activities and/or routines, high levels of vigilance and intrusion, and the discouragement of independent problem solving. Parental negativity is conceptualised as the absence of warmth and acceptance and the presence of parental criticism and rejection (see Bögels & Brechman-Toussaint, 2006).

A meta-analysis by McLeod, Wood, and Weisz (2007) revealed a medium to strong relationship between parental over control and negativity and child anxiety, but the association of control with child anxiety was stronger than negativity (resp. $d = 0.52$ and 0.41). The direction of the relationship between child anxiety and parental rearing is, however, unclear. That is, do anxiety-disordered children simply encourage their parents to behave in more controlling and negative ways, or does controlling and negative parenting instil anxiety and avoidance in children? If the latter is the case, the question of what contributes towards such parental practices arises. Parents' own anxiety is a likely candidate (e.g., Cobham, Dadds, & Spence, 1998). That is, parents who are anxious themselves may over control and reject the child. There might be several reasons for such behaviour. First, by discouraging children's autonomy, parents prevent exposure to perceived danger, thereby reducing their own fear that something might happen to their child. Second, parental stress might get in the way of inhibiting their first impulses to control or criticise. Third, as fear leads to a flight or fight reaction, responding aggressively can be regarded as parents' fight reaction, and control as a flight reaction.

Few studies have investigated the role of parental anxiety in parental control and rejection. A recent meta-analysis by van der Bruggen, Stams, and Bögels (in press) identified 11 studies, and found no significant association between parental anxiety and over control. Note, however, that mothers were over represented in the included studies. Whether parent gender influenced the relation between parental anxiety and rearing could not be established as there were too few studies including fathers.

Hudson and Rapee (2002) examined both parents' control behaviour in two separate parent–child interactions. They found that mothers, but not fathers, of anxiety-disordered children were more controlling than parents of non-anxious children. However, Greco and Morris (2002) studied father–child interactions (but not mothers) and found that fathers of socially anxious children exhibited more control than fathers of non-anxious children. In a review of research on fathers' role in child anxiety, Bögels and Phares (in press) suggest that fathers' role is important. For example, fathers' closeness to and support of adolescents was a strong predictor of less anxiety in adolescence and young adulthood in several longitudinal studies. In addition fathers may have an indirect role in child anxiety through their support of mothers and the positive effect this may have on mother's rearing (e.g., Cummings & O'Reilly, 1997).

The way parents interact with each other in the presence of the child may also maintain child anxiety. Co-parenting refers to the ways in which partners support one another in their joint role in leading the family. Parents who put each other down in the presence of the child rather than support each other, are found to maintain child anxiety over time (Katz & Low, 2004; McHale & Rasmussen, 1998). Interestingly, when the topic of inter-adult conflict is child related, children respond with even more fear (Grych, Seid, & Fincham, 1991, cited in Gable, Belsky, & Crnic, 1992). Co-parenting may not only directly influence child anxiety, it may also influence the quality of the partner's rearing, and actual partner support has been found to enhance the quality of the mother–child relationship (see Bögels & Brechman-Toussaint, 2006). Therefore, it is important to include partner support in assessments of parent–child interactions, in order to enhance our understanding of the role of rearing in child (and parent) anxiety.

Parents' own anxiety may also influence the other parents' rearing. For instance, one parent's anxiety may make the other parent more controlling of the child. Based on different roles that fathers and mothers may have in rearing their child (fathers being more explorative and challenging and mothers being more protective; see Bögels & Phares, in press), it can be hypothesised that fathers' anxiety may make mothers more controlling and negative towards their child. Little is known about whether and how parental anxiety disorder influences the other parents' rearing behaviour related to child anxiety.

In sum, observational studies on parental rearing in the context of child and parental anxiety have the following limitations. First, the majority of studies have not assessed both parental and child anxiety disorders, making it difficult to determine whether parental control results from child or (also) parental anxiety. Second, most studies did not include fathers, and no research yet exists concerning the effect of paternal anxiety disorder on paternal rearing. Third, the impact of both parents' anxiety disorders on *their partners'* rearing is unknown. Fourth, little is known about the way parents interact with each other in relation to child and parental anxiety disorder. Taking into account limitations of previous research, this study examined parental rearing behaviour in a larger sample of clinic-referred children with anxiety disorders ($n = 121$) and non-referred control children ($n = 38$), during four parent–child conversations, one with father, one with mother, and two with both parents. Anxiety disorders of parents were assessed. The hypotheses were that: (I) rearing behaviour of parents of clinically anxious children would be characterised by control and rejection, compared to that of control children; (II) rearing of anxiety-disordered parents would be characterised by control and rejection; (III) parents of anxiety-disordered children and anxiety-disordered parents would be less supportive towards each other; (IV) the anxious parent would dominate the interaction; and (V) fathers' anxiety disorders would negatively influence mothers' rearing.

METHOD

Participants

Medical-ethical approval was obtained, and families signed informed consent. The clinical group consisted of 121 children from 8 to 18 years referred to one of 8 community mental health centres in the Netherlands because of a primary anxiety disorder. The control group consisted of 38 children recruited through advertisements in journals and magazines distributed to various SES areas. Control families received a €50 fee. Control families were selected for participation based on age, gender and school type of the child, in order to make the control and clinical group comparable on personal characteristics. Every effort was put in having both mother and father participate. Where a biological and a step-parent were available, we invited the biological parent if that parent had regular contact with the child. In Table 1, personal characteristics of both groups are listed.

Assessments

Diagnoses. Children's diagnostic status was assessed using the Anxiety Disorder Interview Schedule (ADIS; Silverman & Nelles, 1998) interviewing separately the child (ADIS-C) and both parents together about their child (ADIS-P). We found it important to conduct the ADIS-P interview, in order to include fathers' and mothers' perspective on the anxiety disorders of their child in the final diagnostic formulation. The ADIS allows for a correction of children's and parents' answers using the clinical impression of the interviewer, before the final diagnostic formulation is made. Interviewers were trained psychology research assistants or clinical psychologists, who had clinical experience in diagnosing anxiety disorders. Interviewers were extensively trained in using the ADIS, and training included the rating of "golden standard" videos of ADIS interviews of Temple University. Interrater reliabilities were high; total interrater agreement (kappa) for all ADIS diagnosis was .89 for child report, and .83 for combined parent report. According to the ADIS instructions, child- and parent-reports were combined to determine diagnosis.

TABLE 1
Characteristics of families of anxiety disordered (n = 121) and control (n = 38) children

	Anxious children	Control children
Number (%) of boys	49 (40%)	15 (39%)
Age child	12.4 (2.7)	12.3 (2.5)
Child position in family (1st to 6th)	2.6 (1.0)	2.5 (1.3)
Number (%) of divorced families	17 (14%)	12 (32%)*
Participation with both parents	105 (87%)	28 (74%)
Participation of step- or adoption father	4 (3%)	1 (4%)
Parental age		
Father	44.9 (5.0)	44.9 (4.9)
Mother	42.0 (5.0)	43.3 (5.0)
Parental educational level[1]		
Father	5.7 (2.0)	6.8 (1.9)*
Mother	5.0 (1.9)	6.6 (1.4)***
Parental professional level[2]		
Father	4.6 (2.0)	5.0 (2.1)
Mother	3.9 (2.1)	4.3 (1.9)
Primary diagnosis child		
Social phobia	44 (36%)	1 (3%)
Generalised anxiety disorder	24 (20%)	
Separation anxiety disorder	29 (24%)	
Simple phobia	17 (14%)	5 (13%)
Agoraphobia and/or panic disorder	7 (6%)	
Primary anxiety diagnosis mother		
Social phobia	13 (11%)	2 (5%)
Generalised anxiety disorder	9 (8%)	2 (5%)
Simple phobia	14 (12%)	
Agoraphobia and/or panic disorder	2 (2%)	
Obsessive-compulsive disorder	2 (2%)	
Posttraumatic stress disorder	2 (2%)	
Primary anxiety disorder father		
Social phobia	7 (39%)	
Generalised anxiety disorder	4 (22%)	
Simple phobia	6 (33%)	
Agoraphobia and/or panic disorder	1 (6%)	
SCARED-Child		
Child self-report	112 (23)	93 (15)***
Father child-report	115 (21)	84 (18)***
Mother child-report	120 (22)	85 (12)***
SCARED-Adult		
Father	88 (16)	85 (11)
Mother	98 (18)	94 (13)
Number of diagnoses		
Child	2.9 (1.3)	0.13 (0.34)***
Father	0.31 (0.83)	0.00 (0.00)*
Mother	0.66 (1.0)	0.24 (0.68)*

Notes: [1]On a scale from 1 (no education) to 9 (university). [2]On a scale from 1 (labour for which no education is required) to 7 (university degree required). *$p < .05$; ***$p < .001$.

Parents' own diagnostic status was assessed with the adult ADIS (DiNardo, Brown, & Barlow, 1994), by the same interviewers. Interrater reliability was high, .94.

Anxiety symptoms.   Children filled in the SCARED-71 (Bodden, Bögels, & Muris, 2008), a reliable and valid self-report questionnaire assessing anxiety symptoms of all DSM-IV anxiety disorders. Both parents filled in the parent version of the SCARED-71 about the anxiety of their child and the adult SCARED (Bögels & van Melick, 2004) concerning their own anxiety symptoms. The adult SCARED also measures adult anxiety on all DSM-IV anxiety disorders. The adult SCARED possesses good homogeneity (Bögels & van Melick, 2004). This study provides first evidence for the discriminative validity of the adult SCARED, as highly significant differences between parents with and without anxiety disorders were obtained (see Table 3).

Family interaction task.   The family interaction task consisted of four 5-minute interactions, one child–mother, one child–father (in random order), and then two child–mother–father interactions, which were videotaped. The first three interactions considered a conversation about a "hot issue" (see Siqueland, Kendall, & Steinberg, 1996). To that end, child, father and mother filled in the Issue Checklist (Robin & Weiss, 1980). This checklist asks respondents to indicate whether and how often 44 issues such as "cleaning up the bedroom" were discussed during the last two weeks within the family, and how calm or angry the discussion was. The fourth interaction concerned a discussion about a severe fear issue. This issue was selected from a list of five situations the child feared and avoided most, which the research assistant formulated with the family. The child and both parents rated the five situations on fear (0–8) and avoidance (0–8). The situation with the highest total fear and avoidance level, averaged across father, mother, and child, became the "fear issue". Since children in the control group did not suffer from anxiety disorders, and therefore were not expected to have "hot issues" around fear, control families only conducted the first three discussions.

Rating.   Two clinical psychologists (the second and third authors), both experts in observation of family interactions, rated the videos. They were blind to the diagnostic status of child and parents. A rating scale (see Appendix) was developed based on Hudson and Rapee (2001, 2002), Siqueland et al. (1996), and Ginsburg, Grover, and Ialongo (2005). Every minute, using 4-point Likert scales, raters judged the level of: (1) non-verbal rejection versus warmth; (2) verbal rejection versus warmth; (3) non-verbal control versus autonomy encouragement; and (4) verbal control versus autonomy encouragement. For the sake of brevity, the warmth versus rejection dimension is called "rejection" and the autonomy encouragement versus control dimension is called "control". Co-parenting was assessed during the two conversations in which parents together interacted with the child, by the level of rejection versus warmth of mother to father and father to mother. Further, raters evaluated conversation dominance, i.e., which of the parents was talking most. A random 38% of the videotapes was rated by both raters. Interrater agreement was satisfactory: intra-class correlations were .91 and .95 for paternal rejection and control, and .86 and .88 for maternal rejection and control. Interrater reliability was .91 for conversation dominance, .76 for fathers' support of mother, and .85 for mothers' support of father.

Data analytic approach

For the comparison between the clinical and control group only three 5-minute interactions could be used, with ratings every minute. For the comparisons within the clinical group, four 5-minute interactions were used (including the mother–father–child "fear issue" discussion). Data were normally distributed.

ANOVAs comparing groups were interpreted one-tailed in case results were in line with the formulated hypotheses. Alpha was set at .95, but borderline significant findings (ps between .05 and .01) are mentioned since for some comparisons power was limited, running the risk of not detecting meaningful differences. Cohen's effect sizes of group differences were interpreted as follows: $< .40$ is small, between .40 and .60 is medium, $> .60$ is large.

Control families had a higher parental educational level and more divorced families (see Table 1) so we checked whether these demographic variables were related to rearing. Note, however, that the number of divorced families in the control group (32%) is representative for the Dutch population. Higher maternal (but not paternal) education was correlated with less control by mother and by father, for both $r = .19$, $p < .05$. Therefore, all analyses were repeated with ANCOVA controlling for both parents' educational level where appropriate. In the clinical group 2 fathers and 14 mothers participated alone in the family discussion task, in the control group 10 mothers participated alone. Mothers who participated alone were more rejecting, $p < .01$, and borderline more controlling, $p < .1$. Divorced mothers were borderline more rejecting, $p < .1$. To control for the possible effects of split-up families (e.g., divorce, lack of partner support, step-parents) on maternal rearing we re-ran the analyses including only families in which both parents participated. In the control group, 5 (13%) children met diagnostic criteria for an anxiety disorder (see Table 1). We kept these children in the control group because: (i) 13% represents a normal percentage of anxiety disorders in Dutch community studies (e.g., Verhulst, Van der Ende, Ferdinand, & Kasius, 1997); (ii) the mean number of control children's diagnoses was substantially lower than that of clinical children; and (iii) control children suffered mostly from simple phobias.

RESULTS

Correlations between interaction measures

Control and rejection were significantly related within parents, Pearson's $r = .51$, $p < .001$ for fathers, $.50$, $p < .001$ for mothers. Rejection of father and mother towards the child were related, $.53$, $p < .001$, as was control of father and mother towards the child, $.43$, $p < .001$. Fathers' and mothers' partner support was highly correlated, $.62$, $p < .001$. Conversation dominance of father was associated with more paternal control, $.32$, $p < .001$, and conversation dominance of mother with somewhat more maternal control, $.19$, $p < .05$.

Parent–child and parent–parent interactions in families of anxious and control children

Descriptive data of the clinical and control children are shown in Table 2, together with Cohen's d effect sizes of difference. Fathers of clinical children displayed borderline more control, $F(1, 134) = 2.3$, $p < .1$, but not more rejection and they supported their partner less, $F(1, 128) = 2.9$, $p < .05$. After controlling for parental education, only paternal partner support remained

TABLE 2
Parent–child and parent–parent interactions in families of anxiety disordered ($n = 121$) and control ($n = 38$) children

	Anxious children	Control children	d
Parent–child interactions			
Paternal control	1.73 (0.38)	1.85 (0.42)	0.30[#]
Paternal rejection	1.99 (0.25)	2.04 (0.21)	0.22
Maternal control	1.72 (0.32)	1.80 (0.36)	0.23
Maternal rejection	2.05 (0.25)	2.03 (0.28)	0.08
Parent–parent interactions			
Partner dominance	2.01 (0.78)	1.89 (0.58)	0.17
Paternal co-parenting	2.13 (0.37)	2.24 (0.25)	0.35*
Maternal co-parenting	2.13 (0.37)	2.20 (0.25)	0.22

Notes: A higher score on control and rejection indicates less control and rejection, or more autonomy encouragement and acceptance. A higher score on dominance indicates that father dominates the conversation, a lower score indicates that mother dominates. A higher score on co-parenting indicates more support, a lower score indicates more rejection of the partner. Effect size differences between groups: *$p < .05$; [#]$p < .1$.

TABLE 3
Characteristics of families with anxious children with anxious fathers ($n=18$) and
non-anxious fathers ($n=97$) and with anxious mothers ($n=42$) and non-anxious
mothers ($n=79$)

	Fathers		Mothers	
	Non-anxious	Anxious	Non-anxious	Anxious
Number (%) of boys	35 (36%)	9 (50%)	34 (43%)	15 (36%)
Age child	12.5 (2.7)	12.4 (2.1)	12.5 (2.6)	12.4 (2.8)
Number (%) of divorced families	8 (8%)	4 (18%)	10 (13%)	7 (17%)
Parental age				
Father	45.0 (4.9)	44.8 (5.9)	45.2 (5.2)	44.4 (4.7)
Mother	42.3 (4.8)	40.9 (5.2)	42.4 (4.9)	41.1 (4.8)
Parental educational level[1]				
Father	5.9 (2.0)	4.5 (1.8)**	5.7 (2.0)	5.7 (2.1)
Mother	5.1 (1.9)	3.9 (1.3)*	5.2 (1.9)	4.5 (1.7)
Parental professional level[2]				
Father	4.9 (1.9)	3.7 (2.1)*	4.6 (2.1)	4.5 (1.8)
Mother	4.0 (2.0)	2.9 (2.2)*	4.1 (2.2)	3.5 (2.0)
SCARED-Child				
Child self-report	119 (22)	123 (26)	120 (24)	120 (21)
Father child-report	114 (21)	123 (21)	116 (22)	113 (18)
Mother child-report	118 (20)	131 (25)*	118 (20)	125 (25)
SCARED-Adult				
Father	85 (11)	110 (25)***	90 (18)	85 (13)
Mother	97 (17)	103 (20)	97 (12)	110 (21)***
Number of diagnoses				
Child	2.7 (1.6)	3.6 (2.3)	2.8 (1.7)	3.1 (1.8)
Father	0.02 (0.14)	1.9 (5.2)***	0.24 (0.67)	0.45 (1.1)
Mother	0.55 (0.85)	1.2 (1.5)*	0.08 (0.27)	1.8 (0.98)***

Notes: [1]On a scale from 1 (no education) to 9 (university). [2]On a scale from 1 (labour for which no education is required) to 7 (university degree required). *$p<.05$; **$p<.01$; ***$p<.001$.

borderline significant ($p<.1$). There was no difference between clinical and control children in maternal control, maternal rejection and maternal partner support. Analyses were repeated including only those families in which both father and mother participated, in order to control for divorce and parental separation. For fathers results were the same, mothers of anxious children now exerted more control than mothers of the control children, $F(1, 132) = 3.3, p<.05, d=0.36$.

Parental anxiety disorders

In the clinical group, 42 (35%) mothers and 18 (16%) fathers had anxiety disorder(s). Table 3 depicts personal characteristics and symptoms of clinical-group families according to paternal and maternal anxiety disorders. Table 4 shows means, standard deviations and effect sizes of rearing behaviours in anxious and non-anxious mothers and fathers.

Fathers who had an anxiety disorder exerted borderline more control, $F(1, 106) = 2.2$, $p < .1$, and more rejection, $F(1, 106) = 2.6$, $p = .05$, towards their children. In these families mothers exerted more rejection, $F(1, 112) = 3.4$, $p < .05$. Fathers who were anxious were borderline more dominant in the conversation, but did not differ from fathers who were not anxious in the support given to their spouses.

As differences in parental rearing and interactions between parents as a function of parental anxiety might be most pronounced when the subject of conversation concerns the child's anxiety problem, results were re-analysed for the "fear issue" interaction only. Fathers with anxiety disorders were more controlling, $F(1, 106) = 3.6$, $p < .05$, $d = 0.56$, and borderline more rejecting, $F(1, 106) = 1.7$, $p < .1$, $d = 0.33$, towards the child, mothers in these families were borderline more rejecting towards the child, $F(1, 112) = 1.7$, $p < .1$, $d = 0.28$. Fathers with anxiety disorders dominated the conversation about the fear issue relative to mothers, $F(1, 102) = 4.9$, $p < .05$, $d = 0.55$. Paternal domination of the fear issue conversation was correlated with paternal control of the child, $r = .44$, $p < .001$. No differences in co-parenting

TABLE 4

Parent–child and parent–parent interactions in families with anxious children; comparison of families with ($n = 18$) and without ($n = 97$) an anxiety disordered father, and families with ($n = 42$) and without ($n = 79$) an anxiety disordered mother

	Fathers		Mothers		Effect size d	
	Non-anxious	Anxious	Non-anxious	Anxious	Fathers	Mothers
Parent–child						
Paternal control	1.84 (0.36)	1.68 (0.42)	1.82 (0.33)	1.82 (0.44)	0.41[#]	0.00
Paternal rejection	2.00 (0.19)	1.92 (0.18)	2.01 (0.16)	1.95 (0.24)	0.43[#]	0.29
Maternal control	1.82 (0.30)	1.72 (0.38)	1.78 (0.29)	1.84 (0.34)	0.29	−0.19
Maternal rejection	2.07 (0.16)	1.98 (0.25)	2.05 (0.14)	2.06 (0.26)	0.43*	0.05
Parent–parent						
Partner dominance	1.87 (0.70)	2.18 (0.91)	1.87 (0.72)	2.00 (0.78)	0.38[#]	0.17
Paternal co-parenting	2.07 (0.26)	2.11 (0.16)	2.10 (0.23)	2.10 (0.30)	−0.19	0.00
Maternal co-parenting	2.08 (0.30)	2.16 (0.23)	2.06 (0.29)	2.16 (0.29)	−0.30	−0.34

Notes: A higher score on control and rejection indicates less control and rejection, or more autonomy encouragement and acceptance. A higher score on dominance indicates that father dominates the conversation, a lower score indicates that mother dominates. A higher score on co-parenting indicates more support, a lower score indicates more rejection of the partner. Effect size differences between groups: *$p < .05$; [#]$p < .1$.

occurred. After correction for differences in parents' educational and professional level (see Table 3), these effects remained.

Families where mothers had an anxiety disorder did not differ from families where the mother did not have an anxiety disorder in rearing behaviour, conversation dominance, and co-parenting.

DISCUSSION

Parental rearing behaviour was studied in the context of child and parental anxiety disorders. The main result are: (I) fathers and mothers of anxiety-disordered children are more controlling or less autonomy encouraging of their child than parents of control children—but this effect was found only in mothers who participated with a partner; (II) fathers of anxiety-disordered children are less supportive towards their partner; (III) in families of fathers with anxiety disorders, *both* parents' rearing is negatively affected (i.e., more controlling and rejecting father–child interaction and more rejecting mother–child interaction, both of medium effect size); and (IV) fathers with anxiety disorders dominate the conversation relative to their partners if the subject of conversation is their child's fear. Anxious fathers' conversational domination was associated with more paternal child control.

Parents of clinically anxious children were more controlling than parents of the control children but effect sizes were small. For mothers, group differences were only found when mothers who participated with a partner were compared and single mothers were excluded. After controlling for differences in parental education, there was no difference in paternal control of anxious and control children. The clinical and control groups did not differ in maternal or paternal rejection of their child. One could therefore conclude that parents of clinically anxious children do not communicate very differently with their anxious child than parents of control children. This does not necessarily mean that parental control and rejection do not play a role in maintaining child anxiety. According to the differential susceptibility theory of rearing (Belsky, 1997) children with a positive or confident nature will hardly be affected by negative or controlling parenting, whereas children with a negative or anxious temperament will be more sensitive to parental influence, for better or worse. Therefore, even if parents of anxious children do not exhibit *more* control and rejection than mothers of control children, the control they do exhibit might still negatively affect an anxious child but would not affect a non-anxious child. Hudson and Rapee (2002) found that mothers of anxious children were more controlling of the anxious child *and* of the anxious child's sibling; however, the children may differ in their susceptibility such that the non-anxious temperament of the sibling makes them less sensitive to the anxiogenic effect of their mother's control.

The finding that mothers in control families who participated alone (mostly because of divorce) were more controlling than mothers in control families who participated with the father is interesting. Divorce may influence the rearing behaviour of the mother, making her more controlling of her child than if she shared the rearing task with the father. This is in line with research in non-divorced families showing that mothers who are or feel supported by their partner, display higher quality mother–child interaction (see Bögels & Brechman-Toussaint, 2006; Bögels & Phares, in press, for reviews). The causal relation between divorce and maternal control is, however, not clear, it might also be that mothers who are controlling tend to divorce more often. In any case, divorce and single-handed parenting is a factor that has to be taken into account in studying parent–child interactions.

Fathers of anxiety-disordered children supported their partner less during the family discussion than fathers of control children, but this effect was not found for mothers' support of their partner. Lack of partner support has been found to be a strong predictor of child anxiety in young children (McHale & Rasmussen, 1998), but, so far, no research existed on partner support associated with anxiety in older children and adolescents. As mothers are in general more engaged with their children (at least in quantity of time) fathers' support of mother, while she is interacting with the child, might be a more important factor in parents coping with child's anxiety than mothers' support of father. The finding that fathers of control children supported their partner more during the family interaction compared to fathers of anxiety-disordered children is in line with the presumed indirect role of the father in child anxiety, described by Bögels and Phares (in press).

Fathers' anxiety disorder appeared to play an important role in parent–child interactions related to child anxiety. The results are in accordance with Bögels and Phares (in press) model, which suggests that fathers have a specific role in encouraging their child to explore the external world and thereby help their child overcome anxiety. We propose that fathers who are anxious themselves will be less effective in their role of autonomy encouragement, which may result in child anxiety. The finding of the present study that anxiety-disordered fathers but not anxiety-disordered mothers are less autonomy encouraging is in line with this idea. Furthermore, the models state that paternal anxiety indirectly affects the child through its effect on mothers' rearing. Consistent with this, mothers were more negative to their anxious child when the father had an anxiety disorder. A possible explanation for the effects of paternal anxiety on maternal rearing behaviour is that paternal anxiety makes mothers of anxious children insecure and less effective as parents. Why fathers have these effects on mothers and not vice versa might result from evolutionary and social-cultural differences in the role of men and women in the family (e.g., Bögels & Phares, in press; Lamb, 1980; Paquette, 2004). Fathers' comparative orientation towards exploring the external world may not only give them an advantage in helping children overcome anxiety of the external world, but also in helping mothers overcome their anxieties about what might happen to their children in the external world.

To our knowledge, this is the first time that conversation dominance among partners has been assessed in the context of parental and child anxiety. No a priori hypothesis was evaluated. That is, anxious parents may retreat from family discussions around "fear issues" of their child, in order to diminish their influence and let the non-anxious partner deal with it (and as such compensate their anxious role). In line with this idea, Suveg, Zeman, Flannery-Schroeder, and Cassano (2005) found that mothers of anxious children spoke less frequently than their child. On the other hand, anxious parents may dominate the conversation in order to make sure that their warnings come across. The clinical impression exists that socially phobic men tend to dominate conversations, for example with their therapist (David Clark, personal communication, 3 May 2006). In line with the latter, fathers with anxiety disorders were more dominant in the fear-related family discussion than their partners and their conversational dominance was associated with more paternal control of the child. The risk is of course that fathers who tend to retreat rather than dominate do not show up on research appointments like the present family discussion task. However, that is unlikely to explain the father partner dominance effect in this study, as only 10% of the fathers of clinical children did not participate.

Men with anxiety disorders were married to women of lower SES than non-anxious men. There was no difference between anxious and non-anxious women. An explanation is that anxiety makes men, but not women, less attractive mating partners and less effective in dating (Caspi, Elder, & Bem, 1988). As lower maternal (but not paternal) SES was somewhat related to more control by both parents, paternal anxiety appears to influence child rearing in indirect ways, through partner selection.

Many directions for future research on the roles of father and mother in child anxiety can be identified on the basis of the present study's results. Most importantly, father's role has been investigated according to the same rearing dimensions as mother's. Fathers may have a different role to play than mothers with respect to a child's coping with anxiety. For example, fathers' role might be to challenge, compete with, and even occasionally scare the child (e.g., "rough-and-tumble" play), and paternal anxiety might get in the way of such behaviour. In line, Turner, Beidel, Roberson-Nay, and Tervo (2003) found that anxiety-disordered parents were less likely to join their child in physical play than non-anxious parents. Therefore, future research on fathers' role should include non-verbal, physical interactions, and measure fathers' (and mothers') behaviour on dimensions such as play and challenge. Another direction for future research is to experimentally investigate the causal relationship between paternal anxiety and maternal rearing behaviour, for example by manipulating paternal anxiety and examining the effects on maternal rearing behaviour, and vice versa. Finally, more research is needed on selective mating processes in men and women with anxiety disorders, in order to deepen our understanding of initial differences in couples of genetically at risk children, and how these determine the balance between rearing behaviours of father and mother.

The clinical implications of the present results are numerous. Interventions directed at prevention or treatment of childhood anxiety disorders, if parents are involved, should focus more on the role of the father and his anxiety. As treatment of parental anxiety disorders seems the most direct approach to prevent childhood anxiety disorders, one way to prevent child anxiety disorders might even be to simply treat anxiety disorders in fathers. In treatments that involve parents, both parents should be involved and the father's role in relation to their child explicitly discussed. Also, one could experiment with father training rather than, or in addition to, mother training. That would be a significant alteration to current clinical practice, which is that in parent training groups mothers often participate alone and few fathers participate without their partner (e.g., Phares, Lopez, Fields, Kamboukos, & Duhig, 2005). Fathers might be better motivated to attend if they were the primary focus of the parent training, and if other fathers participated as well. The finding that anxiety-disordered fathers are dominant in a family discussion relative to their partner, could well be addressed in family interventions, in which the anxious father is encouraged to listen. Another focus of intervention could be, in the light of the finding that fathers of anxiety-disordered children support their partner less in family discussions, to teach fathers in families of anxious children to support their partner when she is interacting with the child about "hot issues".

REFERENCES

Belsky, J. (1997). Variation in susceptibility to environmental influence: An evolutionary argument. *Psychological Inquiry, 8*, 182–186.

Bodden, D. H. M., Bögels, S. M., & Muris, P. (2008). *The diagnostic utility of the Screen for Child Anxiety Related Emotional Disorders-71 (SCARED-71)*. Manuscript submitted.

Bögels, S. M., & Brechman-Toussaint, M. L. (2006). Family issues in child anxiety: Attachment, parental rearing, family functioning, and beliefs. *Clinical Psychology Review, 26*, 834–856.

Bögels, S. M., & Phares, V. (in press). The role of the father in the aetiology, prevention and treatment of childhood anxiety: A review and new model. *Clinical Psychology Review.*

Bögels, S. M., & van Melick, M. (2004). The relationship between child-report, parent self-report, and partner report of perceived parental rearing behaviors and attitudes and anxiety in children and parents. *Personality and Individual Differences, 37*, 1583–1596.

Caspi, A., Elder, G. G. H., & Bem, D. D. J. (1988). Moving away from the world: Life-course patterns of shy children. *Developmental Psychology, 24,* 824–831.

Cobham, V. E., Dadds, M. R., & Spence, S. H. (1998). The role of parental anxiety in the treatment of childhood anxiety. *Journal of Consulting and Clinical Psychology, 66,* 893–905.

DiNardo, P. A., Brown, T. A., & Barlow, D. H. (1994). *Anxiety Disorders Interview Schedule for DSM-IV: Lifetime version (ADIS-IV-L).* San Antonio, TX: Psychological Corporation.

Gable, S., Belsky, J., & Crnic, K. (1992). Marriage, parenting and child development: Progress and prospects. *Journal of Family Psychology, 5,* 276–294.

Ginsburg, G. S., Grover, R. L., & Ialongo, N. (2005). Parenting behaviors among anxious non-anxious mothers: Relation with concurrent and long-term child outcomes. *Child & Family Behavior Therapy, 26*(4), 23–41.

Greco, L. L. A., & Morris, T. T. L. (2002). Paternal child-rearing style and child social anxiety: Investigation of child perceptions and actual father behavior. *Journal of Psychopathology and Behavioral Assessment, 24,* 259–267.

Hudson, J. L., & Rapee, R. M. (2001). Parent–child interactions and anxiety disorders: An observational study. *Behaviour Research and Therapy, 39,* 1411–1427.

Hudson, J. L., & Rapee, R. M. (2002). Parent–child interactions in clinically anxious children and their siblings. *Journal of Clinical Child and Adolescent Psychology, 31,* 548–555.

Katz, L. F., & Low, S. M. (2004). Marital violence, co-parenting, and family level processes in relation to children's adjustment. *Journal of Family Psychology, 18,* 372–382.

Lamb, M. E. (1980). The father's role in the facilitation of infant mental health. *Infant Mental Health Journal, 1,* 140–149.

McHale, J. P., & Rasmussen, J. L. (1998). Coparental and group-level dynamics during infancy: Early family precursors of child and family functioning during preschool. *Development and Psychopathology, 10,* 39–59.

McLeod, B. D., Wood, J. J., & Weisz, J. R. (2007). Examining the association between parenting and childhood anxiety: A meta-analysis. *Clinical Psychology Review, 27,* 155–172.

Paquette, D. (2004). Theorizing the father–child relationship: Mechanisms and developmental outcomes. *Human Development, 47,* 193–219.

Phares, V., Lopez, E., Fields, S., Kamboukos, D., & Duhig, A. M. (2005). Are fathers involved in pediatric psychology research and treatment? *Journal of Pediatric Psychology, 30,* 631–643.

Robin, A. L., & Weiss, J. G. (1980). Criterion-related validity of behavior and self-report measures of problem-solving communication skills in distressed and non-distressed parent–adolescent dyads. *Behavioral Assessment, 2,* 339–352.

Silverman, W. K., & Nelles, W. B. (1998). The Anxiety Disorders Interview Schedule for children. *Journal of the American Academy of Child and Adolescent Psychiatry, 27,* 772–778.

Siqueland, L., Kendall, P. C., & Steinberg, L. (1996). Anxiety in children: Perceived family environments and observed family interaction. *Journal of Clinical Child Psychology, 25,* 225–237.

Suveg, C., Zeman, J., Flannery-Schroeder, E., & Cassano, M. (2005). Emotion regulation in families of children with an anxiety disorder. *Journal of Abnormal Child Psychology, 33,* 145–155.

Turner, S. M., Beidel, D. C., Roberson-Nay, R., & Tervo, K. (2003). Parenting behaviors in parents with anxiety disorders. *Behavior Research and Therapy, 41,* 541–554.

van der Bruggen, C., Stams, G., & Bögels, S. M. (in press). The relationship between parent and child anxiety and parental control parental and child anxiety: A meta-analytic review. *Clinical Child Psychology and Psychiatry.*

Verhulst, F. C., van der Ende, J., Ferdinand, R. F., & Kasius, M. C. (1997). The prevalence of DSM-III-R diagnoses in a national sample of Dutch adolescents. *Archives of General Psychiatry, 54,* 329–336.

APPENDIX A
Behavioural rating of the family interaction task

Behavioural assessment	Definitions and examples
Parent to child	Rated on 0–3 scales: 0 represents the most inadequate outcome, 1 an inadequate outcome, 2 a somewhat adequate outcome, and 3 the most adequate outcome.
Rejection versus warmth	Criticism, hostility, frustration, and indifference versus warmth and support.
Non-verbal	Examples: sarcastic tone of voice and looking away versus smiling and patting on the back.
Verbal	Examples: humiliating the child and cursing versus showing affection.
Control versus autonomy granting	Intrusiveness, constraining verbal expression, guilt induction, invalidating feelings, love withdrawal versus encouragement of and accepting thoughts and emotions.
Non-verbal	Examples: interrupting and hovering over the child versus nodding and following the child's lead.
Verbal	Examples: speaking for the child and discounting expressed feelings versus asking about child's feelings.

(continued on next page)

APPENDIX (*Continued*)

Behavioural assessment	Definitions and examples
Parent to parent	Rated on 0–4 scales: 0 represents the most inadequate outcome, and 4 the most adequate outcome.
Co-parenting	Criticism, hostility, frustration, and indifference versus warmth and support.
Non-verbal	Examples: sarcastic tone of voice and looking away versus smiling and nodding when the partner talks.
Verbal	Examples: humiliating the partner versus expressing support for the partner's point of view.
Conversation dominance	Quantity of talking of each parent: 0 represents a dominant mother (mother talked >80% and father <20%), 1 a somewhat dominant mother (>60%), 2 equal contribution (50/50), 3 a somewhat dominant father (>60%), and 4 a dominant father (>80%).

COGNITION AND EMOTION
2008, 22 (3), 539–551

Cognitive and emotional facets of test anxiety in African American school children

Rona Carter, Sandra Williams, and Wendy K. Silverman

Florida International University, Miami, FL, USA

This study used confirmatory factor analysis (CFA) to investigate whether test anxiety (TA) can be conceptualised as a bidimensional construct consisting of cognitive and emotional facets in 152 African American school children, ages 8 to 13 years, $M = 9.98$ years ($SD = 1.13$ years); 54% girls. A two-factor model was determined a priori by classifying items from the *Test Anxiety Scale for Children* (TASC; Sarason, Davidson, Lighthall, Waite, & Ruebush, 1960) as either "Cognitive" or "Emotional" as determined by independent raters. Results demonstrated distinct cognitive and emotional facets of TA can be meaningfully captured in African American school children. Results also demonstrated African American girls had higher mean scores than African American boys on both the Cognitive and Emotional factors specified by the TASC in the CFA model. Theoretical and practical implications of the results are discussed with respect to the nature of TA in African American school children.

Test anxiety (TA), characterised by worrisome thoughts, increased heart rate, and/or emotional outbursts before, during, or after an examination, has long been recognised as a significant and challenging educational problem in school children, particularly third through fifth grade students (e.g., Ergene, 2003). In the USA, 34–41% of third through fifth grade students experience TA (Ergene, 2003). The relatively high prevalence of TA is of concern as test-anxious children are more likely to receive poor grades, repeat a grade, and perform poorly under evaluative situations than non-test-anxious children (e.g., Warren, Ollendick, & King, 1996). Due to the widespread and growing use of high-stakes standardised tests to track students' academic progress

Correspondence should be addressed to: Wendy K. Silverman, Florida International University, University Park Campus, Department of Psychology, Miami, FL 33199, USA. E-mail: silverw@fiu.edu

This research was supported by a Mid-career Development Award (K24 MH073696) from the National Institute of Mental Health to WKS and a Minority Mental Health Research Fellowship from the American Psychological Association to RC.

We gratefully acknowledge the co-operation and contributions of the school children who participated in the research.

DOI: 10.1080/02699930801886722

and to determine student promotion (or not) to the next grade level in most states (Amrein & Berliner, 2002), the importance of advancing understanding about the nature of TA is even more underscored than in past years.

A further reason for advancing understanding of TA stems from past research indicating that children with elevated TA may suffer from other, pervasive anxiety problems (e.g., Beidel & Turner, 1988). Beidel and Turner (1988), for example, found that 60% of European American children ($N = 83$; grades 3–6) with high TA, assessed using the Test Anxiety Scale for Children (TASC; Sarason, Davidson, Lighthall, Waite, & Ruebush, 1960), manifested pervasive anxiety conditions, including DSM-III anxiety disorders (*Diagnostic and Statistical Manual of Mental Disorders–3rd ed.*; American Psychiatric Association, 1980). Thus, it appears that test-anxious children experience clinically significant psychological distress, suggesting that the presence of TA in school children may serve as an indicator of more pervasive anxiety problems.

For this reason, children with elevated TA who do not seek or receive help may be particularly vulnerable to negative outcomes associated with TA. Given that African American children are underrepresented in mental heath care settings, especially when it comes to seeking and receiving help for anxiety and its disorders (Neal & Ward-Brown, 1994), African American children with elevated TA may be a particularly vulnerable group of children. Indeed, Turner, Beidel, Hughes, and Turner (1993) examined the prevalence of TA in an elementary school sample of African American children ($N = 168$; grades 3–6) and found TA was highly prevalent. It therefore is of public health significance to develop new approaches to identifying African American children who may be exhibiting and suffering from anxiety. Although there are different paths one might take to identify these African American children, one promising path is to assess these children's levels of TA.

Test anxiety in African American school children

Meta-analytic results reveal that African American school children in second to fourth grade, on average, report significantly higher TA scores than their European American counterparts (Hembree, 1988). Relevant to the present investigation was the study cited above by Turner et al. (1993), which found that as many as 41% in their African American school sample reported high TA on the TASC. Moreover, these children with high TA reported significantly more non-test-related fears and significantly lower academic achievement scores than the African American children without TA. Other research also has found that African American children with high TA report more functional impairment than African American children without TA (Hembree, 1988).

The reasons why TA is associated with more functional impairment and/ or results in higher TA scores in African American school children relative to European American school children are not clear. It has been suggested that perhaps it is related to African American children's encounters with distinctive developmental experiences in school and in communities such as negative racial/ethnic stereotypes concerning academic abilities, which in turn may serve to increase the children's fears of evaluative situations (Steele, 1997). Understanding the reasons for the greater impairment associated with TA in African American school children represents a critical and under-studied area for future research. Before such research can move forward, however, it is essential to first have improved understanding about the nature of the TA construct within this population.

The nature of the TA construct in school children

Whereas initial theorising about TA viewed the construct as unidimensional (Sarason, 1961), theorising shifted in the 1960s to viewing TA as bidimensional (e.g., Liebert & Morris, 1967; Spielberger, 1972). Specifically, TA was viewed as a construct comprised primarily of cognitive (e.g., worry, irrelevant thinking) and emotional (e.g., tension, bodily reactions, perceived arousal) facets. Each facet was construed as representing a distinct, but interrelated response channel through which TA may be expressed. This shift to a bidimensional theory of TA also has practical importance. Interventions to reduce TA, for example, typically focus on either its cognitive or emotional facets (Zeidner, 1998). Accordingly, individuals who manifest TA via the cognitive domain may benefit from training in coping with worry and task-irrelevant thinking; individuals who manifest TA via the emotional domain may benefit from training in alleviating negative emotional affect (Zeidner, 1998).

Given that TA was viewed as bidimensional, researchers turned their attention to developing theoretically informed measures of TA (e.g., Liebert & Morris, 1967; Spielberger, 1980). Using factor analytic procedures and college student samples, evidence accumulated documenting the aforementioned cognitive-emotional, bidimensional view of TA (e.g., Morris, Davis, & Hutchings, 1981; Schwarzer, 1984). Research evidence documenting the cognitive-emotional, bidimensional view of TA in samples of school children is scant. Findings from the majority of exploratory factor analytic studies (EFAs) have found that the TASC is comprised of at least four factors (e.g., Dunn, 1964, 1965; Guida & Ludlow, 1989; Ludlow & Guida, 1991; Rhine & Spaner, 1973). Dunn (1964, 1965), for example, identified four factors: (1) Test Anxiety; (2) Recitation Anxiety; (3) Physiological Arousal; and (4) School Anxiety. Overall, these early TASC EFAs provided preliminary evidence for the varied content through which TA in school children may be expressed (e.g., Recitation Anxiety). It remains unknown, however, whether the cognitive-emotional, bidimensional view of TA would be found with African American school children using the TASC.[1]

The present study

The purpose of this study was to investigate whether TA can be conceptualised as a bidimensional construct consisting of cognitive and emotional facets in a sample of African American school children, as found in past research using college students. This study went beyond past research on TA in school children in that it used confirmatory factor analytic procedures (CFA) to investigate the TA construct. CFA was chosen as the data analysis method of choice because it is a theory-driven approach to data analysis that is appropriate for use when the investigator has some theoretical or empirical knowledge about the construct of interest (Brown, 2006).

In this study, a two-factor CFA model was determined a priori by classifying TASC items into Cognitive and Emotional groups as determined by independent raters. Perfect agreement occurred on 29 of the 30 items, with disagreement emerging regarding the classification of only one item, Item 12. After a brief discussion among the judges, Item 12 was rated by all judges as Cognitive. Figure 1 depicts the complete specifications of the two-factor model. Given past research has found significant sex/gender differences on total scores of the TASC (Zeidner 1998), sex/gender was entered as a covariate in the two-factor model.

METHOD

Participants

Third, fourth, and fifth ($N = 467$) grade school children enrolled in an urban elementary school in the Southeast section of the USA were sent home with letters to parents requesting their child's participation in a study on expressions of anxiety in minority school children. Parents were asked to sign an informed consent form if they gave permission for their child's participation, or to indicate if they were declining. Children also were asked to sign the form to provide their assent. Thirty-eight percent ($n = 178$) of the total sample ($N = 467$) of parents agreed to allow their child to participate in the study. Seventeen percent ($n = 78$) of the parents declined to allow their

---

[1] Although there have been a couple of recent studies that have examined the factor structure of TA in school children; neither study used the TASC (Lowe et al., 2007; Wren & Benson, 2004).

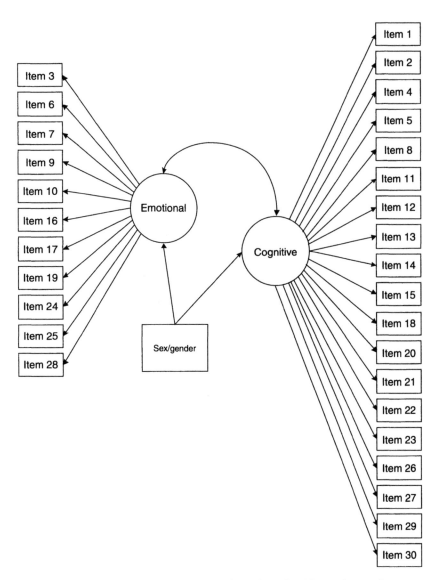

Figure 1. Two-factor CFA model of cognitive and emotional facets of test anxiety.

child to participate and 45% ($n = 211$) did not return the consent forms. Chi-square and analysis of variance results indicated no significant differences on sociodemographic characteristics (i.e., age and free or reduced lunch status) among children with consent/assent, children without consent/assent, and children who did not respond. Because it was of interest in this study to investigate TA in African American school children, only the data of the African American families were included in the analyses; thus, the data of 26 families of non-African Americans were excluded. The final participant sample pool consisted of 152 African American school children—ages 8 to 13 years, $M = 9.98$ years ($SD = 1.13$) years; 54% girls. Thirty-two percent ($n = 49$) were in 3rd grade, 27% ($n = 41$) in 4th grade, and 41% ($n = 62$) in 5th grade; $M = 4.09$ ($SD = 0.86$). According to school records, approximately 74% ($n = 112$) of the participants received free or reduced lunch.

Measures

Test Anxiety Scale for Children (TASC; Sarason et al., 1960). The TASC is a 30-item *true–false* self-rating scale of children's fears surrounding tests and other evaluative situations such as reading in front of the class. Each item is scored either zero (false) or one (true) to yield a total score (ranging from 0 to 30). Previous studies (Ludlow & Guida, 1991; Sarason et al., 1960) have reported high internal consistency (.89) as well as satisfactory test–retest reliability (2-month interval; $r = .75$). In the present sample, the coefficient alpha for the total score was .87. A score was also obtained for TASC items classified as cognitive and emotional facets by adding up items 1, 2, 4, 5, 8, 11, 12, 13, 14, 15, 18, 20, 21, 22, 23, 26, 27, 29, and 30 for the cognitive facet and items 3, 6, 7, 9, 10, 16, 17, 19, 24, 25, and 28 for the emotional facet. The coefficient alphas for the cognitive and emotional facets for the current sample were .79 and .74, respectively.

Procedure

As noted, as part of a larger study on the expressions of anxiety in minority school children, students with signed parent consent and child assent forms were administered several questionnaires on the child's emotional functioning, which included the TASC. The questionnaires were completed during school hours in a small group setting containing 5 to 8 students per group. Each questionnaire was read aloud by two African American female researchers while the children followed along, marking their responses on a separate answer sheet. Total administration time of the questionnaire battery was approximately thirty-minutes. The data were collected over a 3-week period.

TABLE 1
Means and standard deviations for TASC total, cognitive, and emotional facet scores
for the total sample and for girls and boys

Measure	Total (N = 152)		Girls (n = 82)		Boys (n = 70)	
	M	SD	M	SD	M	SD
TASC–total	12.61	6.42	14.37*	6.35	10.54	5.91
TASC–cognitive facet	8.33	4.08	9.44*	3.66	7.03	3.66
TASC–emotional facet	4.28	2.81	4.93*	2.80	3.51	2.64

Notes: *$p <.05$; TASC = Test Anxiety Scale for Children.

RESULTS

Descriptive statistics

Table 1 presents means and standard deviations for the TASC total, cognitive, and emotional facet scores by sex/gender and for the total sample. Statistically significant sex/gender differences were found for the TASC total, cognitive, and emotional facet scores. Girls reported significantly higher scores on the TASC-Total, $F(1, 151) = 14.59$, $p < .001$, Cognitive Facet, $F(1, 151) = 14.31$, $p < .001$, and Emotional Facet, $F(1, 151) = 10.12$, $p < .002$, than boys.

Factor structure of the TASC

A two-factor CFA model was specified a priori in which TASC items classified as cognitive loaded onto the latent factor of Cognitive and items classified as emotional loaded onto the latent factor of Emotional. Item 14 and 25 were used as marker indicators for the Cognitive factor and Emotional factor, respectively. Sex/gender (1 = females; 0 = males) was added to the model as a covariate to examine its direct effect on the latent factors. Correlated errors for the items were permitted within a latent factor but not across latent factors.

Prior to CFA analysis, the data were evaluated for univariate and multivariate outliers by examining leverage indices for each individual. An outlier was defined as a leverage score that was four times greater than the sample mean leverage. No univariate or multivariate outliers were detected. There were small amounts of missing data, occurring sporadically and never exceeding more than 1% of the cases for any given variable. There was no coherent pattern to the missing data. Only 6% of the total number of cases provided at least one missing data point. For those individuals with missing data, values were imputed using the Expectation-Maximisation approach using the computer program AMELIA (Honaker, Joseph, King, Scheve, & Singh, 2003).

Confirmatory factor analysis

The fit of the two-factor model was evaluated with M*plus* (Muthen & Muthen, 1998) using a robust weighted least squares (WLSMV) solution. The WLSMV estimator is the best option for CFA modelling with binary data (Muthen & Muthen, 1998) and has been found to perform well in samples as small as 100 (Flora & Curran, 2004). The fit of the data was evaluated using multiple indicators of model fit: chi-square, the Tucker–Lewis Index (TLI), and the root mean squared error of approximation (RMSEA). Hu and Bentler (1999) suggest TLI values close to 0.95 or greater and RMSEA values close to 0.06 or below represent acceptable model fit.

The overall fit of the two-factor model was acceptable. The chi-square for model fit was non-significant ($\chi^2 = 109.63$, $df = 88$, $p < .06$) and all the traditional indices of overall fit were satisfactory (TLI = 0.96; RMSEA = < 0.04). In addition, more focused fit tests (examination of modification indices, offending estimates, and evaluations of theoretical coherence) all suggested acceptable model fit. Completely standardised factor loadings are presented in Table 2. All freely estimated completely standardised factor loadings were statistically significant (*p*s < .05), except for Item 2 on the Cognitive factor. Inspection of the factor loadings revealed the specified TASC items represent reasonable indicators of the expected Cognitive (range of R^2s = .10–.56) and Emotional (range of R^2s = .24–.70) facets of TA.[2] Moreover, the estimated correlation between the two latent factors was moderate ($r = .42$).

Further, the paths linking Sex/gender to the two latent factors were statistically significant. The mean score of girls was 0.53 units higher than the mean score of boys on the Emotional factor. Sex/gender accounted for 9% of the variance in the Emotional factor. The mean score of girls was 0.36 units higher than the mean score of boys on the Cognitive factor. Sex/gender accounted for 10% of the variance in the Cognitive factor. Inspection of the standardised estimates (*std*) of the paths linking Sex/gender to the two latent factors revealed the magnitude of the Sex/gender difference for both factors is medium, *std* = 0.61 and 0.62 respectively. Brown (2006) suggests a *std* can be interpreted akin to Cohen's *d* by following Cohen's guidelines on how to

---

[2] Given Item 2 did not significantly load onto the cognitive factor; the two-factor model was re-specified so that Item 2 was excluded from the cognitive factor. We compared the re-specified two-factor model to the original two-factor model (in which Item 2 was included in the cognitive factor). The fit of the data was not appreciably altered with the exclusion of Item 2; therefore Item 2 remained in the cognitive factor.

TABLE 2

Completely standardised factor loadings of the two-factor CFA model of cognitive and emotional facets of test anxiety

Item		COG	EMO
1	Worries when teacher says she/he is going to ask questions to find out how much know	0.59	—
2	Worry about being promoted, that is passing from the ... to the ... grade at the end of the year	0.21	—
3	Teacher ask me get up in front of the class and read aloud, afraid going to make some bad mistakes	—	0.61
4	Teacher says, going to call on students in class to do math problems, hope call someone else, not me	0.40	—
5	Sometimes dream at night that I'm in school and cannot answer the teacher's questions	0.54	—
6	Teacher says she/he is going to find out how much have learned, heart begin to beat fast	—	0.55
7	Teacher is teaching about math, feel the other children in the class understand her/him better than me	—	0.53
8	In bed at night, sometimes worry about how going to do in the class the next day	0.60	—
9	Teacher ask me to write on board in front of the class, hand write with sometimes shake a little	—	0.48
10	Teacher is teaching about reading, feel other children in class understand her/him better than me	—	0.49
11	Worry more about school than other children	0.32	—
12	At home, thinking about math lesson for next day, afraid get answers wrong when teacher calls on me	0.75	—
13	Sick and miss school, worry will do more poorly in school-work than others when return to school	0.57	—
14	Sometimes dream at night other boys and girls in the class can do things I cannot do	0.56	—
15	At home and thinking about reading lesson for the next day, worry will do poorly on the lesson	0.49	—
16	Teacher says she/he is going to find out how much I've learned, I get a funny feeling in my stomach	—	0.60
17	Did very poorly when teacher called, probably feel like crying even though would try not to cry	—	0.58
18	Sometimes dream at night that the teacher is angry because I do not know lesson	0.55	—
19	Afraid of school tests	—	0.55
20	Worry a lot before taking a test	0.68	—
21	Worry a lot while taking a test	0.58	—
22	After taking a test worry about how well did on the test	0.55	—
23	Sometimes dream at night that did poorly on a test had in school that day	0.65	—
24	Taking a test, hand writes with shake a little	—	0.43
25	Teacher says she/he is going to give the class a test, afraid will do poorly	—	0.84

TABLE 2 *(Continued)*

Item		COG	EMO
26	When taking a hard test, forget some things knew very well before started taking a test	0.40	—
27	Wish a lot of times that didn't worry so much about test	0.46	—
28	Teacher says she/he is going to give the class a test, get nervous or have a funny feeling	—	0.79
29	While taking a test usually think doing poorly	0.62	—
30	While on way to school, sometimes worry teacher may give the class a test	0.52	—

Notes: COG = Cognitive; EMO = Emotional.

interpret effect size (0.2 is indicative of a small effect, 0.5 a medium and 0.8 a large effect size; Cohen, 1992).

DISCUSSION

The present study's findings provide support for the bidimensional view of TA advanced by Liebert and Morris (1967). All items performed as predicted, with the exception of Item 2, which did not load significantly on the Cognitive factor. Moreover, the two-factor CFA model demonstrated cognitive and emotional facets of TA can be meaningfully captured in African American school children by specifying latent factors of these facets using items from the TASC. Overall, the results are consistent with past research using college students (e.g., Morris et al., 1981; Schwarzer, 1984). Thus, conceptualising and operationalising TA as a bidimensional construct appears appropriate in this sample of African American school children.

In addition, the significant correlation ($r = .42$) between the two latent factors indicates a moderate relationship between Cognitive and Emotional facets of TA. That is, the two latent factors share a modest amount of variance not captured in the CFA model. Indeed, cognitive and emotional facets of TA are theorised to be aroused and maintained by common factors related to the test situation, which in turn influences students' subjective interpretation of the test situation (Liebert & Morris, 1967). Accordingly, further research is needed to specify more clearly the shared and differential impact of the two facets on maladjustment in school children, particularly African American children.

Inspection of the residuals for each TASC item (range of R^2s = .10–.70) further suggests that there is unique information about TA in African American school children not fully captured by the two latent factors. Future research on additional factors that account for the unexplained variance would be important to conduct. One such factor may be stereotype threat (Steele, 1997), which is the fear of confirming a negative stereotype relating to one's group membership. For African Americans, the fear of confirming the negative stereotypes concerning academic abilities is hypothesised to elicit an anxiety response that, in turn, produces cognitive interference that undermines test performance (Steele, 1997).

Consistent with past studies using college students (Benson & Tippets, 1990; Everson, Millsap, & Rodriguez, 1991), the present study also found that the latent factor mean on both factors differed significantly by sex/gender. Specifically, African American girls had a higher mean than African American boys on both factors. Thus, the bidimensional view of TA may be an accurate description of boys' TA responses whereas the emotional and cognitive facets of TA may consolidate into a single unidimensional facet in girls. Due to the small sample size of the present study, tests for invariance of the two-factor model across sex/gender were not performed. Thus, here too further research investigating the factor structure of the TASC as a function of sex/gender in African American school children is needed.

Several limitations to the study should be noted. First, the present study was cross-sectional. Further research is needed to determine the continuity and discontinuity of cognitive and emotional facets of TA over time for African American school children. Second, these findings may not be applicable to school children from other racial/ethnic groups and socio-economic status. The generalisability of the findings may be further limited even among African American school children, given that (1) 73% of the school children in this sample were receiving free or reduced lunch and (2) the response rate for child participation was 55%. However, regarding the second point, analyses indicated no significant differences with respect to age and free or reduced lunch status among children with consent/assent, children without consent/assent, and children who did not respond. More-over, response rates of African Americans willing to participate in scientific research remain relatively low across most behavioural science research (see Graham, 1992, for a review), and thus, the 55% response rate is not unusual for this population. Certainly, improved efforts to increase minority populations' participation in research are needed.

Finally, because Item 2 did not load significantly on the Cognitive factor, replication of the study findings is needed to verify the validity of this item as an indicator of cognitive expressions of TA. For example, perhaps the TASC may be meaningfully improved by removing Item 2 (and possibly other items) and/or by refining existing items in ways that map onto existing theoretical conceptualisations of TA. Such analyses would greatly improve the specificity of the dimensionality of TA in school children.

Limitations notwithstanding, this study highlights the value of examining cognitive and emotional facets of TA in African American school children using the TASC. It is important for future research to examine specific cognitive and emotional facets of TA. For example, cognitive expressions of TA as indicated on the TASC are comprised largely of items representing cognitive preoccupations with failure, lack of confidence in evaluative situations, and negative performance expectations. Cognitive expressions, such as dysfunctional thinking patterns or intrusive thoughts during exams, are not indicated on the TASC. Extending these possible cognitive expressions may advance understanding about the manifestation of TA in school children in general, and African American children in particular. Similar extensions of emotional expressions of TA also may prove useful.

REFERENCES

American Psychiatric Association. (1980). *Diagnostic and statistical manual of mental disorders* (3rd ed.). Washington, DC: American Psychiatric Press.

Amrein, A. L., & Berliner, D. C. (2002). *An analysis of some unintended and negative consequences of high-stakes testing*. East Lansing, MI: The Great Lakes Center for Education Research & Practice.

Beidel, D. C., & Turner, S. M. (1988). Comorbidity of test anxiety and other anxiety disorders in children. *Journal of Abnormal Child Psychology, 16,* 275–287.

Benson, J., & Tippets, E. (1990). A confirmatory factor analysis of the Test Anxiety Inventory. In C. D. Spielberger & J. Diaz-Guerrero (Eds.), *Cross-cultural anxiety* (pp. 149–156). Washington, DC: Hemisphere.

Brown, T. A. (2006). *Confirmatory factor analysis for applied research*. New York: Guilford Press.

Cohen, J. (1992). A power primer. *Psychological Bulletin, 112,* 155–159.

Dunn, J. A. (1964). Factor structure of the Test Anxiety Scale for Children. *Journal of Consulting Psychology, 28,* 92.

Dunn, J. A. (1965). Stability of the factor structure of the Test Anxiety Scale for Children across age and sex groups. *Journal of Consulting Psychology, 29,* 187.

Ergene, T. (2003). Effective interventions on test anxiety reduction: Meta-analysis. *School Psychology International, 24,* 313–328.

Everson, H. T., Millsap, R. E., & Rodriguez, C. M. (1991). Isolating gender differences in test anxiety: A confirmatory factor analysis of the Test Anxiety Inventory. *Educational and Psychological Measurement, 51,* 243–251.

Flora, D. B., & Curran, P. J. (2004). An empirical evaluation of alternative methods of estimation for confirmatory factor analysis with ordinal data. *Psychological Methods, 9,* 466–491.

Graham, S. (1992). "Most of the subjects were white and middle class": Trends in published research on African Americans in selected APA journals, 1970–1989. *American Psychologist, 47,* 629–639.

Guida, F. V., & Ludlow, L. H. (1989). A cross-cultural study of test anxiety. *Journal of Cross-Cultural Psychology, 20,* 178–190.

Hembree, R. (1988). Correlates, causes, effects, and treatment of test anxiety. *Review of Educational Research, 58,* 47–77.

Honaker, J., Joseph, A., King, G., Scheve, K., & Singh, N. (2003). *AMELIA: A program for missing data,* (Windows Version 2.1 ed.). Cambridge, MA: Harvard University.

Hu, L., & Bentler, P. M. (1999). Cutoff criteria for fit indexes in covariance structure analysis: Conventional criteria versus new alternatives. *Structural Equation Modeling, 6,* 1–55.

Liebert, R. M., & Morris, W. (1967). Cognitive and emotional components of test anxiety: A distinction and some initial data. *Psychological Reports, 20*, 975–978.

Lowe, P. A., Lee, S. W., Witteborg, K. M., Prichard, K. W., Luhr, M. E., Cullinan, C. M., et al. (2007). The Test Anxiety Inventory for Children and Adolescents (TAICA): Examination of the psychometric properties of a new multidimensional measure of test anxiety among elementary and secondary school students. *Journal of Psychoeducational Assessment.* Epub ahead of print, DOI: 10.1177/0734282907303773.

Ludlow, L. H., & Guida, F. V. (1991). The Test Anxiety Scale for Children as a generalized measure of academic anxiety. *Educational and Psychological Measurement, 51*, 1013–1021.

Morris, L. W., Davis, M. A., & Hutchings, C. H. (1981). Cognitive and emotional components of anxiety: Literature review and a revised worry-emotionality scale. *Journal of Educational Psychology, 73*, 541–555.

Muthen, L. K., & Muthen, B. O. (1998). *Mplus user's guide.* Los Angeles: Muthen & Muthen.

Neal, A. M., & Ward-Brown, B. (1994). Fears and anxiety disorders in African American children. In S. Friedman (Ed.), *Anxiety disorders in African Americans* (pp. 65–75). New York: Springer.

Rhine, W. R., & Spaner, S. D. (1973). A comparison of the factor structure of the Test Anxiety Scale for Children among lower- and middle-class children. *Developmental Psychology, 9*, 421–423.

Sarason, I. G. (1961). A note on anxiety, instructions, and word association performance. *Journal of Abnormal and Social Psychology, 62*, 153–154.

Sarason, S., Davidson, K. S., Lighthall, F. F., Waite, R. R., & Ruebush, B. K. (1960). *Anxiety in elementary school children.* New York: Wiley.

Schwarzer, R. (1984). Worry and emotionality as separate components in test anxiety. *International Review of Applied Psychology, 33*, 205–220.

Speilberger, C. D. (1972). *Anxiety: Current trends in theory and research.* New York: Academic Press.

Spielberger, C. D. (1980). *Test Anxiety Inventory.* Palo Alto, CA: Consulting Psychologists Press.

Steele, C. M. (1997). A threat in the air: How stereotypes shape intellectual identity and performance. *American Psychologist, 52*, 613–629.

Turner, B., Beidel, D. C., Hughes, S., & Turner, M. W. (1993). Text anxiety in African American school children. *School Psychology Quarterly, 8*, 140–152.

Warren, M. K., Ollendick, T. H., & King, N. J. (1996). Test anxiety in girls and boys: A clinical-developmental analysis. *Behaviour Change, 13*, 157–170.

Wren, D. G., & Benson, J. (2004). Measuring test anxiety in children: Scale development and internal construct validation. *Anxiety, Stress, and Coping, 17*, 227–240.

Zeidner, M. (1998). *Test anxiety: The state of the art.* New York: Plenum Press.

Subject index